**John Francis Hopkins** (Jack) was born in Dublin where he attended Primary and Secondary school.

In 1972 he moved to Australia, on assisted passage, for fun and adventure. There he received a Bachelor of Arts degree (Economics/Philosophy) from the University of Sydney and later completed post graduate Marketing qualifications at Charles Sturt University NSW where he graduated Valedictorian.

He worked in the Pharmaceutical Industry for over 35 years commencing as a Medical Representative eventually progressing to Senior Management (director level).

In addition, he has lectured in Marketing and Senior Sales Management and for leisure plays a five string banjo and button accordion. He currently lives back in Dublin with his wife Christina.

# Brilliantbranes

# Brilliantbranes

JOHN HOPKINS

# Dedication

For Christina

***Acknowledgements:* My thanks to Rita Cott, John Jessup, Robert McDonnell and Alan Nankervis for their comments and suggestions on reading the first draft of this work.**

# Table of Contents

Dedication....7
Preamble....11
Introduction....13
The Universe....25
Evolution....40
The Classical World....53
The Quantum World....64
Quantum Interpretations....79
Information....87
Human beings....101
Consciousness....110
Behaviour....136
Technology....152
Business....161
Finance....171
Economics....182
E-Capitalism 1....197
Conclusion....215
Appendix....221
Post Summary....223
References....249
Measurements....255
Index....259

# Preamble

The *Brilliantbranes* title of this book was chosen to convey two important messages to the reader: Firstly, it is meant to show a gratitude to the 'brilliant brains', I have called upon within, to develop and formulate my theoretical proposition. Secondly, the *branes* part of the title is derived from *brane cosmology* being part of the scientific 'string theory' which postulates that all the particles in the universe are the vibrations of extremely tiny strings. *Branes* themselves, from the word membrane, are areas consisting of different numbers of dimensions. The book title therefore then also refers to the many *brilliant* dimensional processes that have contributed to our human growth and development. It is my contention that one such *brilliant* dimensional process is 'market capitalism' itself, together with its own dimensional workings. Unfortunately, some of these dimensional workings have become dangerously threatening to the system and require a progressive dimensional metamorphosis.

'*Brilliantbranes'* is work for the general reader/consumer presenting an in-depth, and what sometimes may appear to be a science fiction, explanation for what I believe are existing natural defects within capitalism. The book itself however, is actually based on contemporary scientific facts and current scientific propositions/ postulations. In addition, the reader will be presented with a simple but broad methodology to assist in the neutralisation of these capitalist defects for the benefit of themselves, their children and future generations.

According to Professor of mathematics Jordan Ellenberg, writing in *The Wall Street Journal* July 3, 2014[1] two of the books I have referenced in *Brilliantbranes* might just be the most unread but purchased books of all time. These bestselling books namely, *A Brief History of* Time by Stephen Hawking and *Capital in the*

---

1 http://www.wsj.com/articles/the-summers-most-unread-book-is-1404417569 (Retrieved 11/5/15)

*Twenty-First Century* by Thomas Piketty have topped the list as the least read but purchased. Hawking's readers only completing 6.6% while Piketty's only completing 2.4%. The claim is based, Ellenberg advises, on a simple index drawn from e-books based on popular highlights. "Disclaimer: This is not remotely scientific and is for entertainment purposes only". (Ellenberg, 2014). In addition to this entertaining possibility, contemporary readers require almost instant understanding/gratification from their reading material. According to Leon Watson writing in The Telegraph 16/5/15 "A Microsoft study highlights the deteriorating attention span of humans, saying it has fallen from 12 seconds in 2000 to eight seconds."[2]

With all of this in mind, I urge readers to persevere from Chapter 1 to the concluding chapter as I believe this journey will, for our children and future generations' sake, help to inform and enlighten on processes of reality we tend ignore. A future of enterprise, peace and equality is simply achievable rather than, the narcissism, confusion, chaos and hate that abounds.

2 http://www.telegraph.co.uk/news/science/science-news/11607315/Humans-have-shorter-attention-span-than-goldfish-thanks-to-smartphones.html (Retrieved 19/5/15)

# CHAPTER 1
# Introduction

## The Book:

It is my intention to make the reading of this book comfortable, entertaining, and informative. In addition, once read, I hope your recollections and reflections will influence and perhaps spur you on to implement a new approach in your business dealings, be they as, Investor, Employer, Employee, or Customer.

Market economic capitalism has served business as its modus operandi up to the present time. However, few would disagree that it carries considerable self-destructing baggage, and indeed such baggage can account for the global financial crisis of 2008. With this in mind I propose a new/updated version of Market Economic Capitalism which I will designate as E-capitalism 1. My theoretical proposition will use science in its development, however it is intended that the process should be understood by the general reader. Therefore, I can assure all those who make the journey through, *'Brilliantbranes'*, that the narrative will be as simple as possible and explanations will be given where and when appropriate.

My background is in business with a little science, philosophy, and economics and it is a combination of these disciplines that will bring us to our journey's end. Science however, plays a vital role in preparing business and all its players for the challenges ahead. With this said, I should initially state that the scientific 'String theory' will later play a part in my proposal. This theory postulates that the smallest pieces of matter are made up of strings that vibrate like those strings of a violin or guitar, a different vibration representing a different particle. Apart from the 'strings' in this theory there are also areas known as 'branes' (from the word membrane[3]), associated with numbers of dimensions. Astrophysicist John Gribbin explains, "We perceive the world as occupying four dimensions - three of space plus one of time. But in every variation on the string theme, the equations only work if the strings occupy a world with many more dimensions, at least 11 in all - ten of space plus one of time." (Gribbin J., 2009, p. 149) So, we know that we occupy a brane/world of three space and one of time dimensions. But there are other branes with different numbers of dimensions. Indeed, our brane may be beside one of these or even inside another brane that has e.g. six dimensions.

This notion of *branes* of course as mentioned in the 'Preamble' is where I got the idea for the book's title, *Brilliantbranes*. The *branes* themselves, being areas of different numbers of dimensions within market economies. These however, are not simply the classical dimensions/activities such as investment, risk, entrepreneurship, business planning, manufacturing, marketing, financials etc. but also deeper, more fundamental human layers that are pervasive in the system, yet for the most part are ignored. In light of this it is my contention that capitalist market economies, as we know them today, need to change dramatically in the coming years. One might say then, that there has to be a major paradigm shift in the way business within is conducted. Those, I believe, who prepare and implement specific strategies for this shift, will reap the benefits, while those who don't, may well struggle to survive.

One of the first questions we learn to ask when just a toddler is 'Why?' Why is his face white, when mine is black? Why is that woman so fat? Why has that man got no hair? Why is that other man fat, small, got no hair, and only one leg? Embarrassing, to be sure, when asked to a parent in public. Then it's why do I have to go to school? Why can I not stay out late? Why can I not smoke dope? Etc. etc. Then in adulthood it is why did she get the job over me? Why does she not like me? Why can't I afford that new dress? Why are some people healthy and some unhealthy? Why are some people smart and some not so smart? Why are some rich and some poor? Why are some cruel and some kind? Then there are questions on the environment. Why is the sea so blue? Why is the grass so green? Why are the flowers so pretty? Why is it all so beautiful? Or, why is there polluting graffiti on city walls? Why are rivers, seas, and territories and the life within all damaged through exploitation? Why can't everyone sort out their differences and live in peace and harmony for the benefit of all and future generations?

So, without doubt this general question of why, it seems, is extremely important to us as human beings. To be sure on occasions most of us will do somethings in

---

[3] The word "membranes" motivated the choice of the word "brane" because membranes, like branes, are layers that either surround or run through a substance.' (Randall, 2006, pp. 50-51)

blind faith but in general we do it because we know the reason why, or perhaps think we know the reason why we are doing it! In addition we may not always have the latest facts/information/reasons for doing something and perhaps if we had more information we would change. Two points to make then are, firstly, we act in a certain way for specific reasons, and really need to understand that these reasons are sound in their truth as far as possible, and secondly, we only change the way we act for a different reason provided we are sure it is sound in its truth.

With this in mind, I will examine the 'whys' of our existing behavioural activities, together with their legitimacy/truth, and if found wanting, then present a different proposition for consideration hopefully demonstrating its legitimacy/truth. I will proceed with this task from the beginnings of the universe, through its development up to the processes of market capitalism, and hopefully some of the answers to the 'whys?' will emerge. Certainly, many of the 'whys?' will not be answered. However, if a small footstep is gained in our quest it may be all that is needed for many competent minds to take up the task for significant or even revolutionary positive change for all.

It should be noted that because an examination of the origins of the universe and life itself is necessary to prepare for a new form of capitalism, I will use scientific facts and propositions in my deliberations from the beginning. I do realise nonetheless, that many readers may have a religious leaning and/or belief in a god, and while such is absent from the world I present, please feel free to insert a deity where-so-ever you please. Personally, I am inclined to emulate the great mathematician John Von Neumann and lean in the direction of Pascal's wager[4].

For a complete and/or a fundamental understanding of scientific facts and propositions, the physics community advises that a sound knowledge of mathematical equations and calculations would be nice. However, in the scheme of mathematical propositions we must never forget the work of a personal friend of Albert Einstein, one Kurt Godel[5], "a mathematician (probably one of the best of all time) and logician most famous for his proof of the undecidability of mathematical

[4] Blaise Pascal (1623-1662) offers a pragmatic reason for believing in God: even under the assumption that God's existence is unlikely, the potential benefits of believing are so vast as to make betting on theism rational. The super-dominance form of the argument conveys the basic Pascalian idea, the expectations argument refines it, and the dominating expectations argument gives a more sophisticated version still. "Pascal's Wager About God" by Paul Saka, *The Internet Encyclopedia of Philosophy,* ISSN 2161-0002, http://www.iep.utm.edu/ (Retrieved 25/01/2016)

[5] Kurt Friedrich Gödel in 1931, using modern logic in his 'Incompleteness Theorem', "showed there will always be some mathematical statements that cannot be proven either true or false. You will never be able to reduce mathematics to the application of fixed rules; there will always be truths that will elude proof." (Sattary, 2008)

propositions." (Wheeler & Ford, 2000, p. 311) But like music, one does not have to understand musical notation or be an accomplished musician to grasp the emotional sense and appreciation of it. Indeed, something as mundane as driving a car may be enjoyed without understanding the workings of the internal combustion engine. So, I will not be using math equations and calculations throughout with the exception of the Einstein's famous $E=Mc^2$, and of this I propose to give you a reasonably simple understanding. Nonetheless, it is fair to say that the more information we have on anything the better we might understand it. For this reason therefore it is necessary for me to bring you through the basics of some science in order understand how we have arrived in the place and time we are now at. Indeed, only then, will you firstly be in a position to play your part in the change for 'E-capitalism 1', and secondly, have good reason for the change.

Throughout the book I will treat 'Information' as the most fundamental entity in the universe.[6] For this reason Fig: 1-1 below is attempting to convey that everything within the model is made up of 'bits' of information. Everything in the universe, that is, matter/energy from sub-atomic particles and their fields, to people, planets, stars, galaxies and space-time is made up of 'bits'(binary digits 1 and 0) of information. Information then is the universe's most fundamental ingredient and therefore will also be a key to the door of E-capitalism 1.

---

6 In 2003 physicist Jacob Beckenstein advised us that, "a century of developments in physics has taught us that information is a crucial player in physical systems and processes. Indeed, a current trend, initiated by John A Wheeler of Princeton University, is to regard the physical world as made of information, with energy and matter as incidentals." (Beckenstein, 2003)

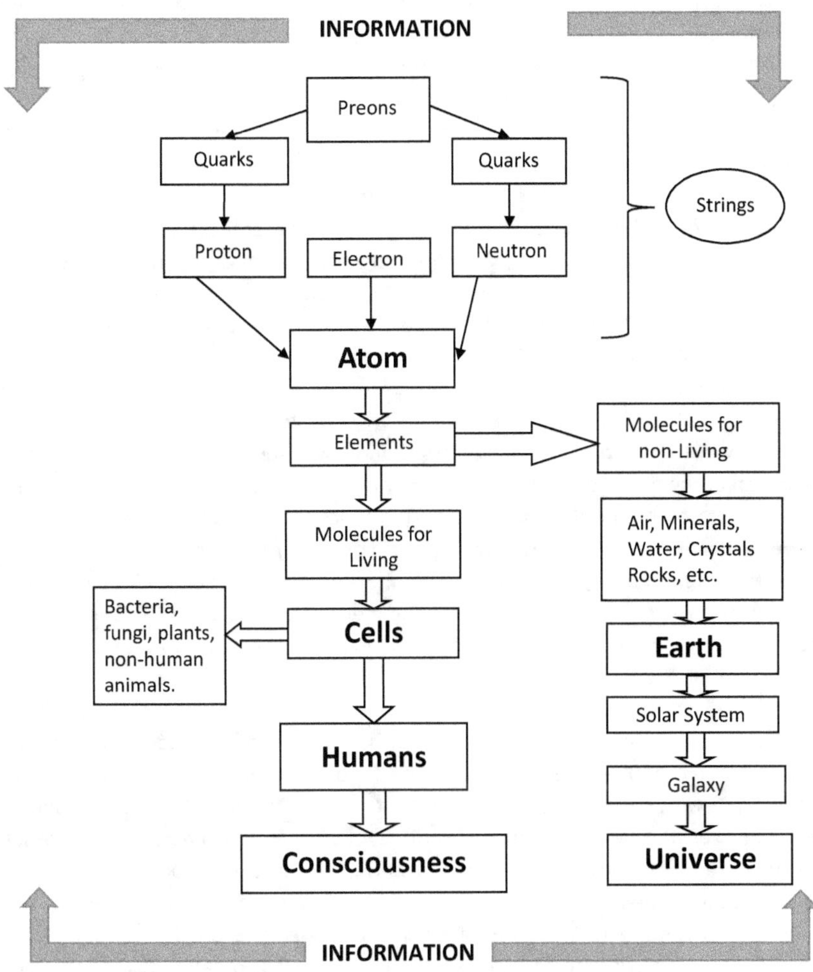


**Fig: 1**

The journey I will bring you on will examine why we are where we are now, and this will be followed by a proposal of what we need to do now. I will use experts in the various disciplines to develop my case. In many areas their reference may be based on accepted facts or their best informed opinion. Other experts in their field may not agree with them but you will hopefully see why I have taken a particular direction. The notions of entropy, quantum theory and consciousness are not easy for some to grasp, but nor was learning to talk, walk, or ride a bicycle and I suspect you accomplished these when you were only a child.

Much of the journey to 'where we are now' may change your idea of reality. Indeed, it may seem at times that I am using 'science fiction' instead of science in my discourse. But taking the blinkers off and facing reality is a major step onto the positive fork in the road. On this journey we discover that everything in the universe appears to be terminal. Galaxies, stars, planets, cities and even life lasts only a certain period of time before all dies and/or disintegrates, scattering off into complete disorder. This is known as high entropy. I will dedicate much discussion to entropy, but at this point consider it as the 'breakdown of orderliness' of matter (the more the loss of orderliness the higher the entropy). Or if you like, think of it as the 'loss of information' that kept matter at ordered states and therefore the loss of information means disorder. Living things, and human beings in particular, can and do keep entropy at bay for the period of their life by consuming low entropy nutrition. Evolution helped life first in this regard by insuring, on an on-going basis, the survival of the fittest towards a more complex or ordered existence. When human beings developed their consciousness, they did not have to rely on evolution alone but could, through intelligent thought, develop better processes to enhance life. The result is that human beings wage a constant battle to enhance order for themselves for others and their environment against the inevitable slide into disorder. Disorder in general has many faces such as, wars, pollution, hunger, poverty, environmental damage, global financial crises, etc. etc. And on an individual basis, such things as gluttony, laziness, cheating and harming ourselves and others.

Many of the things we do as individuals is based on the selfishness of our genes to survive and replicate. However, by following this natural programme we are rewarded with pleasure and high satisfaction. The result is that we are inclined to overindulge, whether it be with food, drink, excessive consumerism or excessive greed in spite of its detrimental effects on the environment or society. "Our genes may instruct us to be selfish, but we are not necessarily compelled to obey them all our lives." (Dawkins, 2006, p. 3) Evolutionary biologist Richard Dawkins, is telling us then that it is the gene that is selfish but that does not mean that the individual person is selfish.

Order though, is a bit of hard work, and one form of such work for orderliness is the work of being employed. Unemployment, on the other hand, is a beacon for disorder, of the individual, business, and society at large. For business in general, the more people unemployed the fewer customers there are. Yet we know that a commercial business has an obligation to be profitable and it achieves this by maximizing sales and minimizing expenses. Employees are an expense, so business has to employ as few people as possible and remunerate them with as little as possible. In addition, there is an increasing contemporary pressure on employment with the implementation of robotics and innovative technology. Also, as evidenced by the global financial crisis (GFC) 2008, when deregulation was allowed to spin out of control, there resulted numerous disasters not least being massive amounts of unemployment. What all this means for business is, that of itself, it is self-destructing via its diminishing customer base. It may be likened to overfishing the oceans without replenishing the stocks. In addition, while over the past few hundred years, we have achieved much in science and economic know how, the wealth of the world is distributed unequally while the gap between rich and poor appears to be widening. These serious problems, although accepted, are not being fully addressed by current remedies and indeed are exacerbated by current capitalism ideology.

It is my intention to attempt to expose the source, development and implementation acceptance of these indigenous anomalies within capitalism, and based on such offer a programme for positive change. My proposal for this programme entails three elements which will hopefully be activated through an innovative contemporary process. The three elements to be activated are, (1) regenerate employment, (2) regulate banks, and (3) redistribute value. Each of these elements I call a 'beneficial economic multiplying entropy' (BEME). In each chapter in *Brilliantbranes* I will endeavour to introduce ideas and facts that are relevant to our contemporary world and as such will have a bearing on my proposals.

In chapter 2, I will examine the Universe as a whole from its beginning and follow through from the birth of particles to atoms and on to the stardust that not alone makes up our planet but also ourselves. In addition we will have some insight into other aspects of our world such as the strange oddity of black holes[7]. I will take the reader on a journey from the beginning of life, through the evolutionary process in chapter 3, up to the world of classical physics, with which most of us are familiar, as it is how we see things around us and how we expect all forms of matter including people to physically act and react. Then we will visit the world of quantum physics which is certainly closer to reality than is the classical world we believe we are in. Indeed, in the world of quantum physics you may think we have entered the world of science fiction, but I can assure you the reality of quantum mechanics is far more entertaining. The following chapter then examines information but as we have introduced the concept of information from the book's beginning it will just be a matter of extrapolation.

---

[7] The term 'black hole' was coined by John Archibald Wheeler (1911-2008). This is but one of the many, many, contributions that this extraordinary man made to the world of physics. In addition he was friend and collaborator with many of the past great scientists, not the least being Albert Einstein. He was also the teacher, mentor, and guide to many other notable physicists, just one of note being Richard Feynman.

Then comes some anatomy and physiology of the human body followed by a visit to another part of being human namely, our consciousness, and just like the quantum world, this is mind blowing (no pun intended). I will then present a chapter on human behaviour and hopefully we will see, based on previous chapters, why we act in certain ways. Technology follows, with its current outburst of innovation and the expectations these may bring. The business process is next and how it works together with the conflicting self-destruct mechanism of 'buyers' vs 'employees'. We then enter the financial world, together with its intrigues, and also how it can get things very wrong, mainly due to vested interest. Economics will then be scrutinized with regard to its historical role and its effects on the current business model. In the second last chapter 'E-capitalism 1' I will propose the BEME as an economic replicator. Just as genes are biological replicators and memes[8] are cultural replicators, economies also require in-built replicators for reproduction, protection and universal distribution. BEME implementation, the core of E-capitalism 1, also represents a new approach in economic implementation methodology.

I do not intend to put you through a long journey of historical 'rattle tattle' before you find out the punch-line at journey's end. Rather, I will set out my stall below giving you the overture, so to speak, and this hopefully will tempt you to stay for the full concert.

I wish to have nothing less than a revolution within capitalism and create the next natural capitalist system. This revolution will be bloodless, and enacted by harmoniously neutralising the self-destructing mechanisms within the current capitalist model for the new. In order to have a successful systemic revolution the following 10 elements are required:

1) The process or system to be revolted against has to be corrupt, inefficient, unfair or any combination of these.
2) The corruptions, inefficiencies and unfairness has to be completely exposed and transparent.
3) The revolutionary goals have to address the current issues and initiate a superior process or system.
4) The revolutionary goals have to be completely articulated, understood and transparent.
5) Information will be the arsenal, and technology the vehicle for the charging revolt.

[8] The notion of the MEME as a cultural replicator was introduced in 1976 by Richard Dawkins in his book *The Selfish Gene*. An example of a meme is an oft repeated joke or song.

6) Participants in the revolution must, (a) understand how and why the current system evolved, and (b) how and why the new system is progressive for the further evolution of human beings and their nature.
7) Sufficient numbers of people and organisations have to be recruited to ensure success.
8) Motivation/benefits to participate are essential.
9) A high profile of the revolution's anticipated positive outcomes will assist with general motivation for participation in a feel good exercise.
10) It will be a bloodless revolution within current market economic capitalism.

The publication in 1543 of *'On the Revolutions of the Celestial Spheres',* by Nicolaus Copernicus gave the word 'revolution' a new meaning. The meaning of revolution in his publication referred to the planets revolving around the sun. This was a new way of understanding our earthly position in the scheme of things as against the accepted positioning. The accepted thinking at the time was that planets and the sun revolved around the earth. So, this new approach became known as 'revolutionary' from the book's title. The word itself 'revolution' then came to represent any upheaval or major change in a given circumstance. We know of course that revolutions can be bloody as in political and/or national revolutions but they can also be bloodless as in scientific revolutions e.g. Albert Einstein's theory of relatively. The revolution I propose is not against capitalism but a revolutionary mechanism to ensure its future.

In order to facilitate the above ten elements I need to go back to the beginning of everything and trace the development of human beings and their environs. In other words, why we and our surroundings are the way we believe we are today? I say believe because many of the things we believe to be reality may in fact not be. In addition, we need to understand why we make the decisions we make, and do we actually have a free will in making these decisions?

Greek philosopher Plato (circa 427-347BC), in his great work 'The Republic' relates the poignant story of the, 'Allegory of the cave'. It may be understood as follows: Since childhood, some slaves are held immobile, chained by their legs and necks fixed, facing a wall in a cave. Behind them is a raised walkway upon which people walk along carrying items. A big fire is burning on the other side of the walkway. The result is that the slaves cannot see the raised walkway or the people but only the shadows on the wall, cast by the fire. They also hear the echoes off the wall of the sounds made by the people as they walk along. The shadows and echoes, we are told are what the prisoners believe is reality. The Allegory of the cave is, to be sure, a sorrowful tale, but Plato is telling us that we are all subject to our own cave, or our own world, which is made up of information from our inherited attributes together with life experiences.

Erwin Schrodinger, Austrian Physicist puts it as follows: "The world is a construct of our sensations, perceptions, and memories..... Its becoming manifest is conditional on very special goings-on in very special parts of this very world, namely on certain events that happen in a brain." (Schrodinger E., 1967)

Vlatko Vedral, Professor of Information Science, Oxford, sums this notion up in one line, "Our reality is ultimately made up of information" (Vedral, 2010). And should that information be incorrect then our reality is questionable.

Understanding information as the essence, from its fundamentals together with its dissemination to its technological applications, is an essential factor for the intended revolutionary process. Not least will be the application of information in business, finance and economics. Consequently, once this book has been read, and its analysis and proposition understood, it will be up to you, the reader, as to whether or not you desire to participate and implement, in a simple and non-confrontational way, the revolutionary processes I believe will benefit us all.

## The Key:

While information is the universe's most fundamental ingredient, it is information relating to the classical universe with which we are most familiar. For example, information with regard to the classical physical universe tells us that it began as a dot, smaller than the tip of a pin, and inflated out like a balloon over billions of years to its present size. Indeed, even today this expansion continues. If the universe was a balloon its boundary would be its skin. This classical deterministic world is the world in which we feel comfortable as it works conveniently for our logical thoughts. For example, if we throw a ball up in the air, depending on the force of the throw, at some point in time thereafter the force of gravity will pull it back down to earth. Prior to throwing the ball our logical thoughts tell us that this scenario will occur, it fits in with our logical thoughts. However, it is now more acceptable to consider the origins of the universe together with its current state to be 'quantum physical' rather than 'classical physical'. This quantum physicality as such represents a fuzziness of possibilities rather than the specifics of classicality.

In addition, a recent proposition known as the 'Holographic principle', which physicists mostly accept, also sheds light literally on our universe. It follows the notion that everything we sense in the universe including ourselves is a hologram. In this proposition specific informational architecture/outcomes of our classical holographic world is projected from the quantum possibilities at the universe's boundary. This architecture/outcomes, is collapsed from the quantum physical possibilities to the classical physical specifics of the world we know and take for granted. The collapsed outcomes take the form of a matter/energy (information) hologram, within which, we, together with everything else in the universe exists. The universe itself is considered to be a quantum computer which downloads the holographic information. From the universe's beginning the collapsed outcomes have followed a natural path of least resistance to fit the classical physical world, and while these outcomes display all the hallmarks of classical physics, they remain inherently quantum physical. The hologram itself of course, as noted, is made up of the matter/energy, from which everything is constructed. This whole process will become clear as we proceed.

Once the matter/energy is collapsed into the classical physical world it follows automatically a deterministic path whether it be animate or inanimate. This means that human beings are also part of the automatism. In other words, everything a human being does is predetermined, unless of course, such automatism is overridden. Make no mistake however, this cannot be achieved by so-called 'free will', as the evidence is clear that 'free will' as we know it does not exist. Indeed, parts of our brain have already begun the process for us to do something seconds before we consciously make the decision to do it.

Everything in the classical physical universe will eventually decay and disintegrate to a state of what is known as 'high entropy' (highly disordered/low information). However, biological entities, e.g. human beings, may temporarily slow-down the natural flow to 'high entropy' by extracting sufficient 'low entropy' (highly ordered/high information) from the environment. This occurs firstly, so there is enough time for natural replication and secondly, to gain enhancements for superior replication. Unfortunately, biological entities, humans in particular, may also speed-up the natural flow to 'high entropy', by damaging and/or extracting excessive 'low entropy' (highly ordered/high information). These two human 'pull' forces, that is, slowing down or speeding up entropy are facilitated by what I will describe as the human need/desire 'S' drives, namely; 'Survival', 'Sex', 'Status', and 'Symbolism'. Delicate management of the 'S' drives therefore will be essential in order to strike the right balance to achieve the most beneficial societal outcomes for today and the future. In this regard we need to understand what high and low entropy means in practical terms.

(A) High entropy/highly disordered/low information: An example is pollution and regressive disintegration of the self, the environment, and the economy.
(B) Low entropy/highly ordered/high information: An example is protection and progressive replication of the self, the environment, and the economy.

For a progressive world, (B) above has to constantly attempt to out-perform (A).

The notions of protection and replication of the self-environment, (health, education and reproduction), and the planet-environment, (laws against pollution, ecological education, and renewable energy sources), are well established, if perhaps not yet fully implemented. Unfortunately, protection and replication in the economic realm is another matter. This is further exacerbated by the fact that unless this is addressed fully, the other two namely, the self and the planet environments will remain under threat.

Many text books, albeit older ones, define economics generally as the study of the distribution of scarce resources. My own definition below, I believe is probably more accurate for market economies in the contemporary world. *Economics is about the distribution of value by way of allotment, or 'who gets what'? Such allotment depends on the laws, rules, regulations, conventions and economic power drivers operating within economies*. Regarding protection and replication of the economy, it is fair to say that governments provide some protection, within the law, so markets may operate with the appearance of a level playing field. For example, specific laws such as, 'antitrust', and 'Insider trading' protect consumers and investors. But is there enough protection? Certainly not enough to stop repeated financial crises. Managed replication of economies, on the other hand, is virtually non-existent as the 'laissez faire' philosophy is preferred by the major economic power brokers. To be sure many governments, with political pressure, give incentives for investment and indeed also gives protection to major industries, particularly the financial sector. However, economies, just like people, nature and the environment in general, also needs protection together with the ability reproduce themselves on an on-going basis.

It is my contention that market economies require, as noted above, three in-built replication processes/BEMEs which I believe need repeating here namely, (1) Regenerate employment, (2) Regulate Banks, and (3) Redistribute value. The sentiment of each is well known and often pursued by government politicians together with other interested parties. However, the root causes for which they are required are not fully apparent, understood, or deemed important enough for radical remedial action. An exposé of these root causes together with a modern and non-confrontational BEME implementation methodology, will, I hope, provide the motivation for such remedial action.

In the next chapter we will meet some of the extraordinary people who have informed our minds, with their amazing discoveries and insights, on the wonders, complexity, and magnificent beauty of our universe. Indeed, without these discoveries and insights BEME remedial action would not be possible.

# CHAPTER 2
# The Universe

## Historical Enlightenment:

The story of the universe is a fantastic tale of extraordinary events. In this story we find astronomical and cosmological blunders, amazing discoveries of enormous proportions, and equally amazing discoveries of tiny proportions. If that is not enough the universe contains literally mind blowing mysteries that have us, not alone, question our grip on reality, but question reality itself. With this in mind I suggest the reader sit back and enjoy the journey of a lifetime. That is the universe's lifetime, from which we emerged by way of progressive evolution, to have the consciousness to now contemplate the universe itself. This surely, is a most wondrous thing.

People today are divided, due to their particular beliefs, about the universe's beginning and also its future. This makes for plenty of speculation. But it is also fair to say that there is general agreement, among the scientific community, on the universe's origin, in that it burst into existence about 14 billion years ago and then rapidly expanded. The future however, is less certain.

Since the earliest times in human evolution we have contemplated the visible world around us, together with our place in it. Different cultures developed myths of the creation of the world in this regard. One such myth is the Biblical Universe. I do acknowledge that some people still cling to the creation story in 'Genesis', however, scientific evidence to the contrary is now well established. Those cultural belief systems though, with designer gods at their centre, served the enquiring minds of our ancestors well, and helped them/us develop rules to live by. More scientists than not for all that, it would appear, do not believe in the notion of a personal god as evidenced in an article in "New Scientist", The God Issue, Victor

J Stenger, emeritus professor of Physics at the University of Hawaii and adjunct professor of philosophy at the university of Colorado at Boulder, advises, "In 1998 the US National academy of Sciences issued a statement asserting, 'Science can say nothing about the supernatural. Whether God exists or not is a question about which science is neutral.'...Yet according to a survey the same year 93 per cent of the members of the academy do not believe in a personal god." (Stenger, 2012). And indeed, two prominent British scientists, Stephen Hawking and Richard Dawkins, whom I reference in this book are certainly not neutral, and are, in fact quite vocal in their assertion of a godless world. Historically however, whilst most early reflective humans believed in a god/gods, some of the more inquisitive thinkers began to look for practical reasons for the way their world worked. Let me consider just some of these individuals together with their contributions.

I'll begin with what was probably one of the greatest astronomical blunder's that continued for around 1400 years. This astronomical error had its origins with two revered Greek thinkers, Aristotle (384 - 322 BCE) and Ptolemy (90 - 168 AD) both of whom had the notion that the earth was the centre of the universe with the other celestial bodies circling it. As a result, the early Roman Church adopted this 'Geocentric' model as part of their dogma, purely because it believed strongly in the sacred positioning of human beings to God, and therefore could/would not accommodate any other position, but the centre, for our species. Once adopted, any other proposition was deemed a heresy. It was the church's dogma, as such, that allowed the blunder to prevail even though another Greek, astronomer Aristarchus (310 -230 BCE), believed and let it be known, that the sun was the centre of the universe and the earth etc. revolved around it. This is known as the 'Heliocentric' model which we now know to be nearer the truth.

Religious dogma itself is claimed sometimes to be divinely dictated e.g. Moses receiving the Ten Commandments directly from God. Or indeed it may be divinely inspired. Such inspired beliefs, truths, rules etc. are written down in symbolic books and other documents, e.g. The Bible, The Koran, and Book of Mormon etc. Some of this literature was written in ancient times for the societies existing then. The result of this is that while many fundamentalists hold to the original text, many others interpret the writings in light of contemporary knowledge or norms. New knowledge or developments are then explained by existing or reinterpreted dogma, or the new knowledge/developments are accepted as additional or extending dogma, or else rejected outright. A difficulty with religion raises its head here, inasmuch as the religion acts as a proxy to God. In other words if you dispute the religious dogma you are disputing God. If God is omnipotent and omniscient then His or Her religion is also, to a certain extent.

This flawed dogma of our place in the universe however, was seriously questioned some 1400 years later by Polish astronomer, Nicholas Copernicus (1473 -1543), who produced a major work that once again put the 'Heliocentric' model as a most likely scenario. Although he did not allow the publication of his proposition, until after his death. This major work titled, 'On the Revolutions of Celestial Spheres' was considered so radical, at the time that it was, so to speak, as referred to earlier, revolutionary. It did nonetheless, begin the move for dogma change. Indeed, in all probability Copernicus spurred on an even more famous Italian physicist, mathematician and astronomer, Galileo, who was certainly more public in his adoption of the 'Heliocentric' model. But his disregard in this for the Church's teachings did see him arrested, made to recant, and suffer house arrest until his death in 1642. The Vatican did eventually see the error of their ways, and gave him a full pardon in the year 2000. The 'Heliocentric' model however, had taken root during Galileo's lifetime and a contemporary of his, a Lutheran, Johannes Kepler developed the model even further. Kepler, due to his religion, probably cared less about the Catholic Church, and he not only embraced the Copernican revolution, but replaced the circular movements around the sun with ellipses.

So, all was ready now for the next great development, a la English mathematician Sir Isaac Newton (1643-1727). His theory of gravity is legendary and the mere mention of the word immediately conjures up his name and the apple falling from the tree. The story of course is probably not true, but his proposition was a gigantic step in our understanding of the Universe. Newton's gravitation law is based on the notion of every object attracting other objects with a force depending on their size and proximity. His law of gravity relates to the force that keeps the planets in orbit around the sun and the moon in orbit around the earth.[9]

Following Newton's exposé, scientific endeavour flourished with various experiments producing new knowledge. Indeed, in this regard another Englishman, Thomas Young (1773-1829), introduced us to the notion of light moving as a wave via what is known as the 'interference' or 'double slit' experiment. This same experiment was to become a major player in confronting the quantum world, as we will see later on. Continuing with investigation into light around this time, it was estimated that light travelled at 300,000 Km per second, a measure that turned out to be extremely close to what we know now as the exact measure, 299,792, Km per second. Then in a master stroke, the great Scottish physicist, James Clark Maxwell (1831-1879),

[9] Newton explained this by way of a cannon ball being fired (say from a great height) on the earth. Depending on the force of the cannon shot, it would do one of three things. Firstly, too strong a shot and it would keep going straight ahead miss the curve of the earth and go straight into space. Secondly, too weak a shot and it would eventually, due to gravity, fall to earth. But thirdly, and just at the right shot force it would follow the earth round in a falling motion but never actually fall because of the curve of the earth.

succeeded in combining electricity and magnetism, (electromagnetism), from which he predicted a whole spectrum of radiation (different forms of light). However, it was not just the Brits producing scientific advancement, as German physicist, Heinrich Hertz then expanded Maxwell's work to what we now know as the 'Light radiation Spectrum' that ranges from radio waves to gamma waves as follows: Radio waves—Microwaves---Infrared light—visible light—ultraviolet light—X-rays---Gamma rays. Further insight into this notion is provided by physicist Steven Manly, "Visible light, gamma rays, X-rays, radio waves, ultraviolet radiation, infrared radiation, and microwaves are all electromagnetic waves. They differ only in frequency. Each of these categories is made up of a range of frequencies of electromagnetic waves. Visible light..... exists in a range of colors, or frequencies, from red to violet............. waves of different frequencies interact with matter in very different ways." (Manly, 2011, pp. 56-57) (See Fig: 2-1 below).

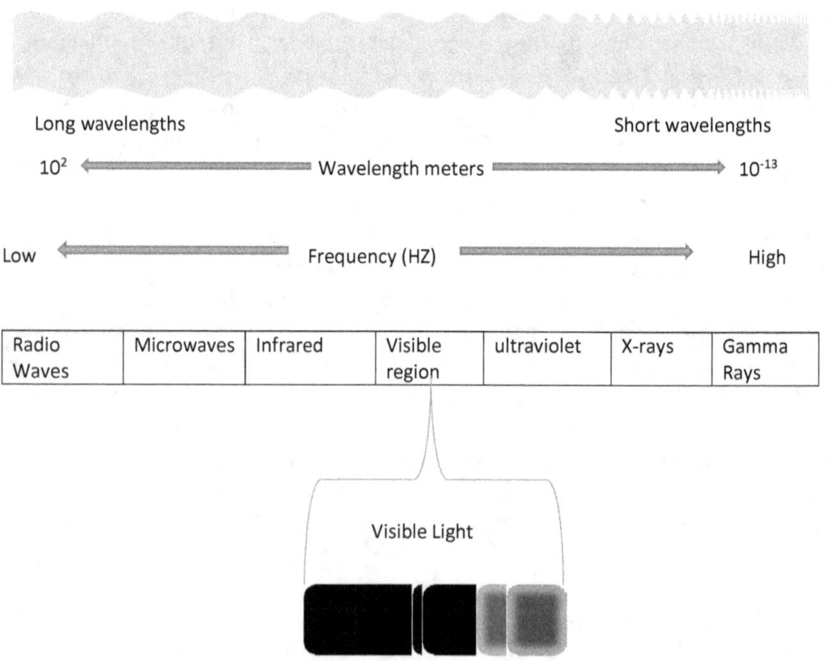


**Fig: 2-1**

The beginning of yet another scientific milestone came on 14th December 1900 when German physicist, Max Planck introduced the world to Quantum theory. In order to solve what was known as the 'blackbody radiation catastrophe'[10] he proposed that light did not flow in a constant stream, rather, it came in small units (quanta). From this major breakthrough the world of quantum was born and would never be the same again. In 1905 Albert Einstein confirmed that light travelled in quanta (photons) and used this notion to solve another physics mystery 'the photoelectric effect'[11]. Planck and Einstein together then, were the founding fathers of quantum mechanics.

Also, in the same year, Einstein created another milestone in science when he presented his theory of "Special Relativity" detailing what occurs when anything with mass[12] speeds up. This postulated that as objects got closer in speed to 'the speed of light' they got heavier and aged more slowly. Nothing with mass can go faster than the speed of light, as the closer one gets to this approximate 300,000 Km per second, the slower time passes. Indeed, if anything could pass this speed barrier then time would go backwards. A simple explanation of why nothing can travel faster than the speed of light is that the faster and object moves the more mass it takes on, as per Einstein's famous equation $E=MC^2$, and it slows time down all the way, until it stops at the speed of light.

In 1917 Einstein extended 'special relativity' to 'general relativity' that incorporated gravity. Physicist Felix Pirani, puts this simply, "General Relativity is based on the principle of equivalence, which asserts that gravitational and inertial effects are indistinguishable." (Pirani F. R., 2006, p. 96)[13] When Einstein published

---

10 Also known as 'blackbody ultraviolet catastrophe' "Any object when heated, gradually emits radiation. This is the reason why iron gets red hot when placed in a furnace, the hotter the iron, the higher the frequency of radiation it emits. A precise mathematical formula, the Stefan-Boltzmann law, relates the frequency of light (or color, in this case) to the temperature. (In fact, this is how scientists determine the surface temperature of a distant star, by examining its color.) This radiation is called *blackbody radiation.* (Kaku, Hyperspace, 1995, p. 197)

11 "The photoelectric effect generates electric currents in metals when they are illuminated by blue or ultraviolet light, but not red light....Einstein suggested that individual photon bullets hit electrons in the metal into motion to produce the photoelectric effect. Because each photon carries a certain energy, scaling with its own frequency, the bumped electron's energy also scales with the light's frequency. A photon of red light (with a low frequency) cannot carry enough energy to dislodge an electron, but a blue photon (light with a higher frequency) has more energy and can see it rolling. An ultraviolet photon has more energy still, so it can slam into an electron and donate even more speed. Turning up the brightness of light changes nothing, it doesn't matter that you have more red photons if each is incapable of shifting the electrons." (Baker, 2007, pp. 96-97)

12 Mass: A measure of the amount of matter in a body.

13 **Inertia** 'the tendency of a body to preserve its state of rest or uniform motion unless acted upon by an external force.' AZ Collins English e-dictionary

his General relativity theory he believed the universe was static which means that the universe hangs together in a 'stopped' position. To be sure, stars were born and disintegrated etc. but in general the universe was static and was held together by gravity. However, when he did his maths on this proposition he found he had a problem and had to incorporate, in his equations, a 'cosmological constant' in order keep the universe static, so to speak. Put simply, a 'constant' is a number inserted in a calculation to achieve some outcome. An example of a constant is the mathematical number called 'pi' and is denoted as the Greek letter 'ϖ'.[14] Einstein's cosmological constant was denoted by the Greek letter '⊠'. Some years later Einstein would refer to this cosmological constant as 'his greatest blunder' when he had to agree that the universe was not static but was actually expanding. And indeed space itself was expanding. So here then is the great cosmological blunder I referred to at the start of this chapter.

The expanding universe proposition was first presented by George Lemaitre, a Belgian priest and physicist and it was later confirmed in 1929 by astronomer Edwin Hubble. Lemaitre also conjectured that working backwards the universe could be traced back all the way to its beginning, as an extremely high energy condensed atom, or what we now call the 'singularity'[15]. From this 'singularity' the 'Big Bang' burst forth. Some confirmation of this surfaced in 1948 when George Gamow, a Russian physicist, who basing his work on 'blackbody radiation' claimed that the 'Big Bang' would have left background radiation in its wake. But this was not ratified until 1965 when two Bell Labs radio astronomers, Allan Penzias and Robert Wilson, upon hearing static on their radio, thought it was caused by bird droppings. Then they realized that this was background radiation, the echo of the Big Bang. On this discovery, physicist Michio Kaku tells us, Penzias and Wilson are said to have exclaimed, "Either we've seen a pile of bird s—t, or the creation of the universe!" (Kaku, Hyperspace, 1995, p. 198)

A final note on this section is that while we have looked at the universe as originating from a 'singularity' Big Bang, we have not considered how such a start may have emanated quantum physically. This we will examine in the chapter on the quantum world.

---

[14] $\pi$ is the number of times the diameter of a circle may be divided into its circumference that is 3.14159. This holds good for all true circles.

[15] Singularity: A "point of infinite density and zero volume" (Clark, 2010, p. 85)

## Contemporary Enlightenment:

Since confirmation of background radiation to the Big Bang was established, telescope technology and satellite investigation has added to the information about our origins. For Example, we are now fairly sure the universe was born 13.75 billion years ago. The standard version of a Big Bang beginning, is based on Einstein's general theory of relativity, where everything, including time, is pushed back to one point and from this point, called a 'singularity', the universe commenced. Physicist Paul Davies explains, "The best way to think about singularities is as boundaries or edges of spacetime..........A boundary to spacetime says that spacetime cannot be continued through it." (Davies P., The Goldilocks Enigma, 2007, p. 79). What this means is that before the Big Bang, it is believed there was nothing, nil, a big zero, a '0', and then there was a singularity, a '1'[16]. From this singularity then, the Big Bang burst forth, with the creation of everything in the universe, even things that are physical that we may not intuitively think of as physical, e.g. space and time[17], and information[18]. Stuart Clark, sums it up, "everything that we see in the universe today was squeezed into a tiny dot, smaller than an atomic nucleus. The four fundamental forces of nature — gravity, electromagnetism and the strong and weak nuclear forces — were indistinguishable from one another, and the 'dot' was already expanding. (Clark, 2010, p. 88).

The closest time to the Big Bang that science can project back to is $10^{-43}$ seconds[19] after its birth. By then the four fundamental forces, we believed were once combined, had probably broken away from each other and the universe, still extremely hot, rapidly inflated like a balloon. Within this balloon, of extremely high temperature, emanated the 'Higgs field'[20] together with a lumpy type of elementary soup. The inflationary period finished at around $10^{-32}$ seconds and things began to cool down. Then at around the first second of universe's life the make-up of fundamental particles and energy began. Significant of these elementary particles

---

16 It is interesting that it all began with the symbols of information namely, 0 and 1.

17 "Space and time...., they are *physical* things, mutable and malleable, and, no less than matter, subject to physical law." (Davies, About Time, 1995, p. 16)

18 "(As Rolf Landauer said, 'Information is physical.') When the electron moves from here to there, its bit flips. In other words, whenever a physical system changes its state–whenever anything at all happens–the information that the system registered is transformed and processed. Information processing is also physical.)" (Lloyd, 2007, p. 157)

19 This is known as the Planck time/era and is the earliest time that physicists can reach back to. Named for, Max Planck, father of quantum theory.

20 The existence of the Higgs field was recently confirmed amid much excitement from experiments at the 'Large Hadron Collider' in Switzerland. It is from this field that particles are believed to get their mass.

were electrons and quarks that would eventually comprise the basic ingredients of atoms. It should be noted that as all particles emerged so did their mirror images, namely anti- particles.[21] But almost immediately then, each particle and its anti-particle annihilated each other. Well, virtually all did, but for some mysterious reason one particle in a billion was spared annihilation, which is just as well or we would not be here today to wonder at it all.

Then from about 1 second to 3 minutes, protons and neutrons come together to form the nuclei of the simple elements of, hydrogen, helium and lithium. Approximately 380,000 years on, atoms formed and this major event was of course the genesis that eventually saw, stars, galaxies, and planets begin to take shape. Our Sun and planet were formed between 4 and 5 billion years ago. And primitive life can now be traced back to 700 million years after the earth's formation. However, the first Homo sapiens did not evolve until 200,000 years ago, where, in Africa, they walked the earth and contemplated the cosmos. Indeed, our contemplation, in this regard, has now produced the following statistics and information (see Table 2-1 below):

[21] Anti- particles differ from their opposite number by way of charge. For example, an electron has a negative charge and its anti- particle, called a positron, has a positive charge.

| Universe Statistics | Year |
|---|---|
| Total number of atoms in the universe | $10^{78}$ to $10^{82}$ |
| Diameter of the known universe | 93 Billion light years |
| Number of stars in the Milky Way | 200-400 Billion |
| How many miles is one light year | 5.87 Trillion |
| Closest spiral galaxy (Andromeda Galaxy ) | 2.5 Billion light years |
| Estimated age of the universe | 13.75 Billion years |
| Estimated number of galaxies | 100 Billion |
| Number of discovered planets in the Milky Way | 350 |
| Closest star to earth (Proxima Centauri) | 4.24 Light Years |
| The part of the Universe that we can see, referred to as the observable universe, is about 28 billion parsecs (91 billion light-years) in diameter at the present time. | |
| Source: Statistics Brain---Lawrence Krauss, NASA | |
| Research Date: March 2nd, 2015 | |

http://www.statisticbrain.com/universe-statistics/ (Retrieved 8/2/16)

**Table: 2-1**

Symmetry[22], it seems, 'underlies the laws of the whole universe' (See Fig: 2-2 below for symmetrical shapes). Other examples of symmetrical shapes are the swastika or a simple square. Physicist Brian Green describes the importance of symmetry in the universe. "During the last few hundred years there have been many upheavals in science, but the most lasting discoveries have a common characteristic: they've

[22] "...the symmetries of an object are the manipulations, real or imagined, to which it can be subjected with no effect on its appearance. The more kinds of manipulations an object can sustain with no discernible effect, the more symmetric it is." (Greene B., 2005, p. 220)

identified features of the natural world that remain unchanged even when subjected to a wide range of manipulations. These unchanging attributes reflect what physicists call symmetries, and they have played an increasingly vital role in many major advances." (Greene B., 2005, p. 219) Another seeming consistent phenomenon is that our universe appears to be mathematically fractal. Fractals delve into things and expose that a small part of it is like the whole. A Fractal is a repeating pattern. As seen below in Fig: 2-3 each small section is the same as the larger sections and the whole.

**Symmetrical Shapes**

**Fig: 2-2**

## A Fractal Image

**The Mandelbrot set**

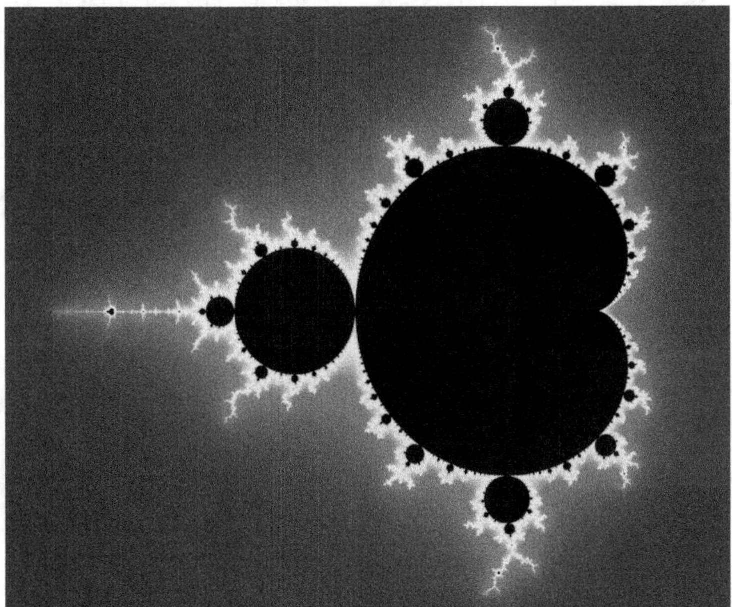

**https://pixabay.com/en/mandelbrot-set-fractal-mathematics-979309/**


**Fig: 2-3**

Yet another all-embracing feature of the universe is its temperature. The temperature throughout is uniform at approximately 2.7 kelvin (-270.3 degrees Celsius). The universe also appears flat, whereas according to Einstein it is curved. Just like the earth seems flat but is actually curved.

There are three specific components making up our known universe, the smallest being 'Atoms', the component from which we ourselves, together with the stars and planets emanate. These atoms account for just 4%. Following in size, is what has come to be called 'Dark Matter' representing 22%. Dark matter, has not as yet been detected but the scientific community believes it is surely out there. Dark matter is postulated to be the component that firstly holds a spinning galaxy together and secondly holds the galactic clusters together. Another dark component, and by far, the most pervasive ingredient throughout, representing 74%, is 'Dark Energy'. This energy is believed to be causing the universe to expand. Indeed, this expansion is accelerating to such an extent that, while astronomers can now observe other galaxies, at some future date such observation will be impossible as these galaxies will have disappeared beyond the horizon.

Atoms, at the other end of the scale, are extremely tiny as portrayed in Fig: 2-4 below: A simple atom consists of electron particles orbiting a nucleus of proton and neutron particles. Regarding an atom's size, physicist Kenneth Ford tells us, "If you are a proton, an atom is very big about a hundred thousand times larger than you. If you are a person, very small, about 10 billion times smaller than you." (Ford K. W., 2011, p. 9)

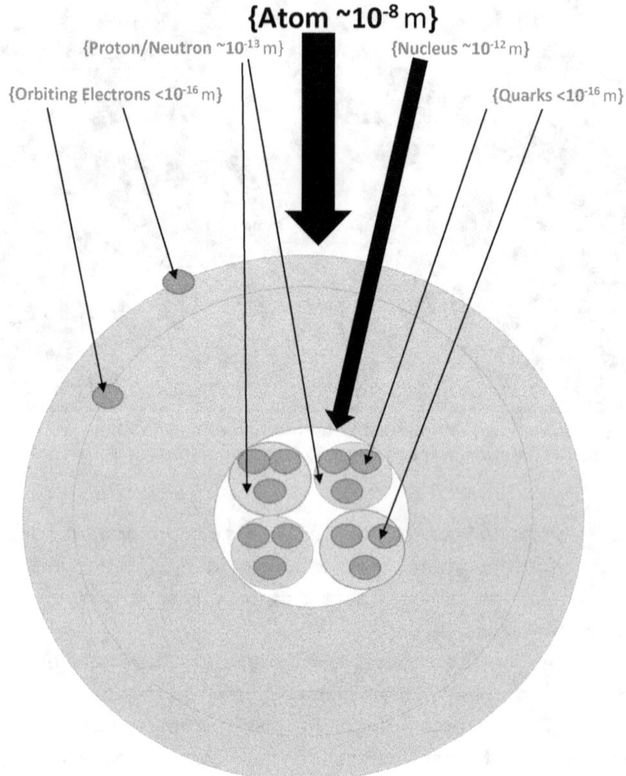


**Fig: 2-4**

There is one other object, of various sizes, throughout the universe that requires out attention and that is the 'Black Hole'. A black hole is a star, the mass of which has collapsed in on itself. Nothing except what is called 'Hawking radiation' can escape from it. It is surrounded spherically by its 'event horizon'. Once anything, e.g. matter and even light passes the event horizon it is pulled in and compressed smaller and smaller with infinite intensity to a single point, a 'singularity'. Indeed some say the same type of 'singularity', from which the 'Big Bang' commenced. Eventually, black holes evaporate and disappear along with everything inside them. Yet, the laws of physics tell us that information like energy cannot be destroyed. And regarding the escaped 'Hawking radiation', physicist and science writer Michael Brooks explains that this contains no information. This dilemma was eventually settled, Brooks explains, "After decades of debate, physicists now believe that the information is encoded in the microscopic structure of space and time at the 'event horizon'. (Brooks, 2010, p. 196)

This revelation on black hole information has led prominent scientists to conclude some astounding hypotheses. For example, we know, that a square 10cm by 10 cm is equal to 100 square cm. So, were we to have a box measuring 10cm wide X 10cm high X 10cm deep we know that its volume would be 1000 cubic cm. The volume then, i.e. the amount inside a container is based on its cubic capacity. Similarly, the volume of a sphere is its cubic capacity. With black holes however, the cubic capacity is the square of its outer surround. In other words to find out the amount of information believed to be sucked into a black hole you calculate it by taking the square of its event horizon. Now, if this is not mysterious enough, scientists have extrapolated this notion for any region in space, and indeed for the whole universe! What this means is that the information pertaining to everything, in our three space and one time dimensional universe, is embedded on its two dimensional surface surround area. This information is then projected from this area to form a hologram[23] that is our universe. This is a serious scientific proposition, known as the 'Holographic Principle'. Indeed, the 'holographic principle' is now becoming accepted as mainstream, as Michael Moyer, a senior editor at *Scientific American,* tells us that...., "although physicists mostly agree that the holographic principle is true...---they know not how the information is encoded or how nature processes (it)." (Moyer, Is Space Digital?, 2012)

Joseph Kasper and Steven Feller, in *The Complete Book of Holograms* explain that, when we look at a hologram, "the scene is not there at all; rather, it is information about the scene, coded in the form *of interference patterns,* that is recorded in the hologram." (Kasper & Feller, 2001, pp. 3-4)

---

23 "Holography is an application of the wave theory of light. In fact it was first conceived as a theoretical possibility on that basis by the British scientist Dennis Gabor in 1947. His idea was to combine two sets of coherent beams of light, to record the interference pattern produced by their interaction in a photographic emulsion, and to do this in such a way that the plate would then contain such complete (or *holo-graphic*) information about a scene that with suitable illumination of the plate a realistic image of the scene could be reconstructed." (Kasper & Feller, 2001, p. 13)

Also, apart from a hologram in itself being an interesting, curious, and even amazing phenomenon, it has another extraordinary feature that is, if a holographic plate/film is cut into pieces, then each piece contains all the information of the whole. In other words if one takes a holographic image of a cricket ball or baseball and then divides the film in half, each half contains the information pertaining to the whole ball. Indeed, the film/plate may be broken into many different sections and again each section will still retain the information for the whole ball image. The more it is sectioned, of course, the less clear the whole image will be projected.

Physicists Stephen Hawking and Leonard Mlodinow say of 'the holographic principle', if the theory, "proves correct, we and our four-dimensional world may be shadows on the boundary of a larger, five-dimensional space-time. In that case, our status in the universe is analogous to that of the goldfish." (Hawking & Mlodinow, 2010, p. 44) I prefer to think of our status in the universe as analogous to that of us in an incubator rather than a goldfish bowl. In addition with the right approach we can perhaps manipulate the information on the outside of the incubator for our further growth, complexity, and prosperity. There will be more on this, as our journey continues.

To conclude this chapter a very important lesson to remember is that we emanated from within a dot that burst forth as the 'Big Bang'. Indeed, when we look at the current vastness of the universe, we are a very small part of the whole. To be sure, we are, or certainly appear to be, a very unique part, and one might even say a very important part. Whatever? We are nonetheless, like everything else, part of the whole. We have also seen that, due to the strong beliefs and/or desires of some, important factual information may be suppressed or hidden, over many generations, to the detriment of many others.

On the universe's vastness we have seen the enormous distances of 'light years' together with the existence of billions and billions of stars, planets etc., while on the small side, there are billions and billions of atomic and subatomic particles playing out their own role in the universe's life and indeed our own lives. But the notion of the 'holographic principle', in that we and everything else are but players in a projected hologram, has got to be a clincher for our amazing world. Indeed, this is especially so when we have seen that this proposition is now becoming main stream in scientific thinking.

We have only touched the surface of our amazing world in this chapter and I sincerely hope I have whetted your appetite for even more incredible revelations to come, and to which, we as individuals, can play a significant part in our own, our children's, and our entire species' future.

The next chapter on evolution will not simply be about the survival of the fittest, rather it will, reveal the power of information with reference to biological and cultural replication. In addition, I hope to show how the dominant power of some genes over others assists, positively or negatively, in making us what we are in physicality and it seems to some degree in intelligence.

## CHAPTER 3

# Evolution

In many ways this chapter is a continuation of the previous one, as the story of evolution begins with the origin of the universe. Everything we are, emerged from the small dot that erupted in a Big Bang and inflated. From within, life began its biological journey, against the overall pull of entropy, toward on-going complexity. The evolution story itself is also coloured with extraordinary events, many of which are unique. In addition there are many mysteries that, in spite of our current scientific sophistication, we appear to be a long way from solving. We will commence the story of evolution with some definitions, and then attempt to present its process, with some insights, hopefully, to assist our understanding.

Evolution is defined by the Oxford dictionary of Biology as: "The gradual process by which the present diversity of plant and animal life arose from the earliest and most primitive organisms." After the emergence of the first microbial cells, the evolution process began in earnest with their transformation to multicellular animals, and then to vertebrates e.g. fish. At which point, some of these vertebrates made the move from water to land[24], becoming what we now know as Amphibians, Reptiles, Mammals, Primates, Apes and finally Humans or if you prefer, Homo sapiens. Such then being the various evolutionary stages to the present state of play, a background

---

[24] Bringing us right up-to date, as reported by Ian Sample- (Guardian service) in the Irish Times 14/1/14, "The fossilised remains of an ancient beast have revealed how prehistoric life hauled itself from the water and took its first unsteady steps along the path that led to four-legged land animals....Clues to the seminal moment in the history of life were found in the bones of Tiktaalik, a 375-million-year-old freshwater creature that grew to three metres long and had aquatic features mixed with others more suited to life on land....the animal had a large pelvic girdle, a prominent hip joint and long hind fins." (Sample, 2014)

to their developmental processes is essential for a better understanding of the *Brilliantbranes'* theoretical proposition.

In the 'Introduction' chapter of this book I referred to entropy as the breakdown of orderliness or the loss of information that makes ordered matter. Such ordered matter is, for example, a human being. Self-replicating human beings, over generations, have been assisted in their own orderliness, with the occasional 'positive' organic mutational variation. Self-replicating human beings, (a) require protection of the replication process for natural replication, and (b) require positive enhancement for superior replication.

A simple example of (a) is keeping the body in a healthy condition to ensure healthy natural replication. An example of (b), on the other hand, is the occasional positive/enhanced organic mutational variation.

The process of (a) and (b) above enables the continued increase in orderliness and is often referred to as a journey towards greater and greater complexity. Indeed, Pierre Teilhard de Chardin, French philosopher, palaeontologist, and Jesuit, called it the law of 'complexification'. In fact he proposed in his, *The Phenomenon of Man,* that this complexification of human beings is a journey, towards a specific end, from the Alpha to the Omega. The Omega end point, as explained by Evolutionary biologist Sir Julian Huxley, in the 'Introduction' to Teilhard de Chardin's work, is the point where knowledge of the universe at large is combined with the increase of psychosocial pressure on our planet to achieve the final condition of 'hyperpersonal' organisation.

My interpretation of this is that we must acquire as much knowledge (information) as possible of our world, and with this raise our consciousness/ social consciousness to reach the ultimate in organization. What that might be unfortunately we do not know? To be sure, this concept is not easily understood and I particularly have avoided using the notion of 'a road towards perfection', as of course 'the road to perfection' is a theme of many religions. However, *The Phenomenon of Man*, according to Teilhard de Chardin himself, should not be read, "as a work on metaphysics, still less as a sort of theological essay, but purely and simply as a scientific treatise." (Teilhard de Chardin, 2008, p. 29) The work itself, on his request, was not published until after his death in 1955 as he wished to avoid possible repercussions from the Vatican.

The journey toward greater complexity is however an extremely fragile one, as natural and/or manmade events can and often do suspend, or revert the journey. Indeed, it is also possible that such an event e.g. unstoppable deathly virus or nuclear holocaust, could stop the journey completely by a total human race wipe-out. Thankfully we have, so far, avoided such disasters. This complexity journey however, it is now clear, follows a path of human evolution over billions of years, from the first simple cells, to our present state and hopefully beyond. Such being evidenced by contemporary genome sequencing. Yet there are still many who refuse to accept this, in spite of increased communication and education and even with the endorsement of major religions.

The Darwinian theory of evolution itself is almost 160 years old and before that there were certainly others who more than dipped their toe in the warm pond where life supposedly began. In 1809 for example, one of the first was Frenchman, Jean Baptiste Lamarck. He based his proposal on the idea of inherited traits i.e. the use of a body part to satisfy a need, like the neck of a giraffe extending to feed off high tree branches. Such extension, he believed, could be and were inherited. This theory however, was not sufficiently demonstrated and the concept lost favour. Although the emergence of 'epigenetics'[25] has once again, in some circumstances, given credence to this notion. Another evolutionist of note was, Alfred Russel Wallace who, in 1858, published a paper titled, *On the Tendency of Varieties to Depart Indefinitely from the Original Type.* In fact Wallace sent a copy of this to Darwin, knowing of his interest in the subject. Charles Darwin himself however, is the man we mostly associate with the exposition of evolution and his name alone conjures up such notions as, 'Survival of the Fittest', 'Natural Selection', 'Descent from Monkeys', 'The Missing Link' etc.

Darwin, who published his own work *On The Origin of Species* in 1859, disagreed with Wallace in that he, Darwin, according to biologist and philosopher, Francisco J Ayala, "did not accept that evolution would necessarily represent progress or advancement, nor did he believe that it would always result in morphological change overtime; rather, he knew of the existence of 'living fossils', organisms that had remained unchanged for millions of years.... (Ayala F. J., 2012, p. 16). There is no doubt though, that it is Darwin's version of evolution that is the more accurate and the greater contributor to the progress of science and knowledge. Now, whilst we know *On The Origin of Species* only takes off once 'life' has commenced, Stuart Clark advises that, "In 1871, Charles Darwin wrote a letter in which he described life's origin as taking place in a 'warm pond, with all sorts of ammonia and phosphoric salts, lights, heat, electricity, etc. present so that a protein compound was chemically formed ready to undergo still more complex changes'." (Clark, 2010, p. 125) Clark adds that such a scenario, with our present knowledge, may be a long way from the truth. That said, we still do not know, scientifically, how life actually began nonetheless, we have a fairly good idea of how it is made up chemically. But, in order to understand this let us look at some basics.

---

[25] Science editor of 'The Times' Mark Henderson explains: the "phenomenon known as epigenetics, by which the genome appears to 'remember' certain environmental influences to which it has been exposed...Some can alter sperm and eggs, to be inherited by future generations. Acquired characteristics, it turns out, can sometimes be passed on after all." (Henderson, 2008, p. 189)

All matter including all living matter is made up of atoms as we have seen already. Atoms consist fundamentally of positively charged protons (each having three quarks) and no charge neutrons (each also having three quarks) combining to form the nucleus, and this nucleus is orbited, so to speak, by negatively charged electrons. Whatever the number of protons there are in an atom, there is an equal number of electrons. This being the case, the negative electrons cancel out the positive protons, and with the no charge neutrons the results is that the atom has no charge overall. Electrons also play an important part in chemical bonding as we will see below.

A chemical element is an atom distinguished by its number of protons. For example, Hydrogen has one proton, whereas Oxygen has eight protons. There is a table of chemical elements known as the 'periodic table' and on it each element is numbered by its number of protons. (See Table: 3-1 below)

## Periodic Table

| 1 H | | | | | | | | | | | | | | | | | 2 He |
|---|---|---|---|---|---|---|---|---|---|---|---|---|---|---|---|---|---|
| 3 Li | 4 Be | | | | | | | | | | | 5 B | 6 C | 7 N | 8 O | 9 F | 10 Ne |
| 11 Na | 12 Mg | | | | | | | | | | | 13 Al | 14 Si | 15 P | 16 S | 17 Cl | 18 Ar |
| 19 K | 20 Ca | 21 Sc | 22 Ti | 23 V | 24 Cr | 25 Mn | 26 Fe | 27 Co | 28 Ni | 29 Cu | 30 Zn | 31 Ga | 32 Ge | 33 As | 34 Se | 35 Br | 36 Kr |
| 37 Rb | 38 Sr | 39 Y | 40 Zr | 41 Nb | 42 Mo | 43 Tc | 44 Ru | 45 Rh | 46 Pd | 47 Ag | 48 Cd | 49 In | 50 Sn | 51 Sb | 52 Te | 53 I | 54 Xe |
| 55 Cs | 56 Ba | 57-71 | 72 Hf | 73 Ta | 74 W | 75 Re | 76 Os | 77 Ir | 78 Pt | 79 Au | 80 Hg | 81 Tl | 82 Pb | 83 Bi | 84 Po | 85 At | 86 Rn |
| 87 Fr | 88 Ra | 89-103 | 104 Rf | 105 Db | 106 Sg | 107 Bh | 108 Hs | 109 Mt | 110 Ds | 111 Rg | 112 Cn | 113 Uut | 114 Fl | 115 Uup | 116 Lv | 117 Uus | 118 Uuo |
| | | | | | | | | | | | | | | | | | |
| | | 57 La | 58 Ce | 59 Pr | 60 Nd | 61 Pm | 62 Sm | 63 Eu | 64 Gd | 65 Tb | 66 Dy | 67 Ho | 68 Er | 69 Tm | 70 Yb | 71 Lu | |
| | | 89 Ac | 90 Th | 91 Pa | 92 U | 93 Np | 94 Pu | 95 Am | 96 Cm | 97 Bk | 98 Cf | 99 Es | 100 Fm | 101 Md | 102 No | 103 Lr | |

**Table: 3-1**

On the periodic table, the first element number 1 is Hydrogen, whilst the eighth number 8 is Oxygen. A combination of the same and/or different elements, with the help of electrons in bonding, produces a molecule. Therefore, combining two Hydrogen and one Oxygen elements, produces the commonly known water molecule H2O. Life itself, we believe consists of the following elements: Hydrogen

(H), Oxygen (O), Carbon (C), Nitrogen (N) accounting for the major components with a little Sulphur (S) and Phosphorus (P). Putting them together to produce new life however, remains a mystery.

There is a standard text book version26 on how life got started but as noted no-one has ever managed to replicate the process. This being the case it is now generally accepted that the start of life was unique. Teilhard de Chardin for example, believes the beginning of life was spontaneous and a one-off, and will never be repeated unless in a laboratory. Other scholars now suggest that a quantum physical process may be a better fit. However, this notion cannot be appreciated until we examine quantum theory later on.

But let us return to Darwin and see what shaped his views. He was born 1809 in Shrewsbury, England, where a striking statue of him sits outside the Shrewsbury library. He was educated first at Edinburgh University and then at Cambridge where in his theology studies he read and reportedly was impressed by William Paley's Natural Theology. In this book Paley presents the beauty and design of living things as proof of a designing God. He is probably most famous for his 'watch maker' analogy in which he proposed that the solar system was designed like a giant clock, as well as the notion of finding a watch in a forest, opening it up, and coming to the conclusion that it just did not happen there, but is a designed piece. Darwin interests however, soon shifted to concentrate more on the study of natural history and in 1809 he set off around the world on a five year survey of plants and animals. As a consequence of this his theory of evolution was developed. No doubt the notion that man evolved over generations rather than, being created by a designer God as related in 'Genesis' made him reluctant, especially with his theological background, to publish for many years. The catalyst to go to print therefore was when Wallace made the first move. One other individual's influence on Darwin's thinking was clergyman and scholar Thomas Malthus, who argued in his *Essay on the Principle of Population* that population multiplies on a geometrical basis while food does so only on an arithmetical basis. Darwin acknowledges Malthus' theory in the introduction to 'The Origin's' sixth edition, "the Struggle for Existence amongst all organic beings throughout the world, which inevitably follows from the high geometrical ratio of their increase, will be considered. This is the doctrine of Malthus, applied to the whole animal and vegetable kingdoms." (Darwin, 1880, p. 3). The doctrine may have

[26] "It is often known as the Oparin-Haldane hypothesis. In the beginning, so it goes, the earth's atmosphere was rich in Hydrogen, methane and water vapour. When these components were exposed to various sources of energy, such as lightning, solar radiation and volcanic heat, the gases combined to form a mixture of simple organic compounds. Over the course of millennia, these compounds would have accumulated in the ocean to form a warm, dilute primordial soup that eventually yielded a new kind of molecule, one that could replicate itself, *the primordial replicator*." **(Mc Fadden, 2000, pp. 85-86)**

assisted in the development of Darwin's theory but for Malthus it was a disaster as it failed to anticipate future advances in food production, costs, and distribution.

Darwin was of course aware of the process of 'breeding selection' for superior plants and animals, and he stressed the difference of this to his 'natural selection' theory. That is, natural variations occurring over millions of years would either enhance or reduce life's opportunities to produce an offspring. Enhancing life's opportunities results in 'the survival of the fittest'. Ayala quotes Darwin from the first edition of The Origin of Species, "Can we doubt.....that individuals having any advantage, however slight, over others, would have the best chance of surviving and of procreating their kind? On the other hand, we may feel sure that any other variation in the least degree injurious would be rigidly destroyed. This preservation of favourable variations and the rejection of injurious variation, I call Natural Selection." (Ayala F. J., 2012, p. 28) Some examples of positive natural variations would be, superior physical attributes, bigger brains, better working immune systems.

How and where these natural variations actually took place within the life form was a great unknown during Darwin's life. There was one gentleman though, who had discovered the basis for this unknown, but unfortunately he was for the most part ignored. Gregor Mendel (1822-1884), an unknown Austrian Augustinian monk and scientist, worked to improve the peas in the St. Thomas' monastery garden located in Brno. His findings, on laws of inheritance in his peas, he presented and published in 1865/66. There was little or no interest shown in his theory until about 16 years after his death, when his work was rediscovered. This work was the beginning of what we now know as genetics.

So what is genetics all about? Well obviously, it has to do with genes and to understand genes we need to first understand cells. All forms of life or organisms, if you like, such as, Bacterium, Plants, Animals and therefore humans, are composed of one or more cells. There are differences as well as similarities between animal cells and plant cells. We will concentrate however, on animal or human cells. These cells are surrounded by a membrane and inside there is a lot of different tiny biological working structures. In addition within, there is the cell's nucleus, also surrounded by its own membrane. Genes27 are made up of DNA28 molecules that determine our make-up. Long strands of genes, known as chromosomes, and inherited from our parents, are housed within a cell's nucleus. In fact 23 pairs of chromosomes are inherited, each pair consisting of one from each parent and each containing both,

---

[27] A gene consists of a combination of four chemical bases that are, Adenine, Cytosine, Guanine and Thymine, designated as A, C, G, and T.

[28] Deoxyribonucleic acid.

DNA (the heredity substance/information), and protein that is the essential building block of all organisms.

To clarify then, within the cell's nucleus are housed 46 Chromosomes (23 pairs)29 each one containing DNA and Protein. DNA is, as stated, the hereditary substance, while protein, comprising of amino acids, is the essential building block of humans and indeed all organisms.

A major breakthrough in genetics occurred in 1953 when two Cambridge University scientists, Francis Crick and James Watson, discovered how genes are copied and the information is passed on to the offspring. For this they both won the Nobel Prize.[30] Rosalind Franklin, chemist and X-ray crystallographer also contributed greatly in this regard, but was not included in the prize, and this has remained a controversy to this day. The discovery of DNA itself caused somewhat of a controversy and dilemma, with regard to the beginning of life, simply because DNA contains the information to manufacture proteins, while at the same time proteins are required to make DNA. This chicken and egg situation is now believed settled, with RNA31, known as a messenger of DNA, thought to have set life in motion. Science journalist, Michael Marshall writing in New Scientist tells us that when it was discovered that RNA could fold like a protein it suggested an answer to the dilemma. "RNA replicators would have no need for proteins. They could do everything themselves." (Marshall, 2011)

In his ground breaking book first published in 1976, *The Selfish Gene*, Richard Dawkins argued, "that the fundamental unit of selection, and therefore of self-interest, is not the species, nor the group, nor even, strictly, the individual. It is the gene, the unit of heredity. (Dawkins, 2006, p. 11). This stance has now been modified slightly by his, "feeling now that not only are some individual organisms better at surviving than others; whole classes of organisms may be better at *evolving* than others. Of course, the evolving that we are talking about here is the same old evolution, mediated via selection on genes." (Dawkins, 2006, p. 269).

Just to recap on what we have learned so far, 'Self-replicating human beings, (a) require protection of the replication process for natural replication, and (b)

---

[29] Pairs of chromosomes crossover and the DNA is mixed from each parent making for a unique offspring, except in the case of identical twins.

[30] **Mark Henderson, Science editor of *The Times* explains, "The DNA molecule is composed of two linked chains of bases. Each base is joined to its natural partner—A to T and C to G—by a hydrogen bond, and held at the other end by a sugar and phosphate backbone. The pairing system means that two DNA strands coil around each other in a double helix, like a twisted rope ladder. Each strand is the mirror image of the other—where one has an A, its partner will always have a T, and vice versa.** (Henderson, 2008, p. 35)

[31] RNA is Ribonucleic acid.

require positive enhancement for superior replication[32].' The gene itself also requires protection, following its establishment, by way of the human carrier for natural replication. For superior replication, the gene requires enhancement, before establishment, by way of positive mutational variation. Mutations it seems, mostly occur during DNA replication.

Regarding genetics in general, science has now reached a stage where genetic manipulation is common practice. Indeed, controversial as it may be, genetic engineering could well assist the passage towards greater complexification. Of course the opposite view is that it may well be a hindrance. There is no doubt, that apart from mutations occurring and changing our make-up, other things have assisted or hindered complexification. This is comprehensively demonstrated by Biologist and Professor of Physiology, Jared Diamond, in his book, *guns, germs and steel.* (Diamond, 2005) He makes the point that different peoples of the world progress, positively or not in their lives, depending on their ability to, win wars (guns), develop superior products (steel), and avoid major health issues (germs).

But a big question we still wonder at is, how and why we are so well suited to this particular world? This question is examined by science under what is known as the 'Anthropic Principle'[33]. Put simply, is the environment finely tuned to allow for life? If so, who or what finely tuned it? Darwin showed however, that there was no need for a creator once life got started. Nature was the creator of the complex human beings we are today. As a summary of our biological evolution, two prominent biologists, John Maynard Smith and Eors Szathmary, identify eight major transitions that took place as detailed in table: 3-2 below:

---

32 When I talk of 'superior replication' in any sphere I intend this replication to be two-fold, firstly, the gene/meme/beme itself is enhanced and secondly, its numbers may also be enhanced.

33 The principle that the constants of nature are tuned to allow for life and intelligence. The strong anthropic principle concludes that an intelligence of some sort was required to tune the physical constants to allow for intelligence. The weak anthropic principle merely states that the constants of nature must be tuned to allow for intelligence (otherwise we would not be here), but it leaves open the question of what and who did the tuning. Experimentally, we find that, indeed the constants of nature seem to be finely tuned to allow for life and even consciousness. Some believe that this is the sign of a cosmic creator. Others believe that this is a sign of the multiverse. (Kaku, 2005, p. 381)

## Major Transitions

| | |
|---|---|
| Replicating molecules | Populations of molecules in protocells |
| Independent replicators | Chromosomes |
| RNA as gene and enzyme | DNA genes, protein enzymes |
| Bacterial cells (prokaryotes) | Cells with nuclei and organelles (eukaryotes) |
| Asexual clones | Sexual populations |
| Single-celled organisms | Animals, plants, fungi |
| Solitary individuals | Colonies with non-productive castes (ants, bees, and termites) |
| Primate societies | Human societies (language) |

Source: (Smith & Szathmary, 2009, p. 17)

**Table: 3-2**

Smith and Szathmary also noted that in their opinion all the transitions were unique, with the exception of two, namely; origins of multicellular organisms and colonial animals with sterile casts. In addition they think the origin of life itself entailed a unique sequence of events.

It is probably appropriate here to insert a note on the evolution of consciousness. In a *Scientific American* article, 'Origin of the mind' by Marc Hauser[34], an editorial key concept states, "Charles Darwin argued that a continuity of mind exists between humans and other animals, a view that subsequent scholars have supported. (Hauser, 2009) Indeed, the human mind, as well as its inherited aspects, also developed to recognise the use of simple tools and then the application of skills to specifically make them. Following on from this was the sharing and cooperation, for common good, via communication/language with on-going education and its application.

This notion in turn leads to the often debated question of, is intelligence inherited or learned? To attempt an answer to this I have extensively used Francisco J Ayala enlightenment in *Evolution (The Big Questions)*. The question itself requires an understanding of what intelligence actually is, or might be? We all have a 'feel' for what it is, but not a lot of agreement of what it is? Let us say it is about a cognitive or mental ability, which is made up of various levels of numerous specific abilities.

Now we know that we inherit genes from our parents that are responsible for specific traits, this is known as our 'genotype'. Whereas, our appearance, make-up

---

[34] Marc Hauser is a professor of psychology, human evolutionary biology, and organismic and evolutionary biology at Harvard University.

and behaviour of these traits, is known as our 'phenotype'. So, to put it simply, certain genes are given, but how they are manifested depends on their dominance and mix within the gene pool, and that determines the 'phenotype'. Let us take an example of genes for brown and blue eyes. If we get genes for both eyes of the same colour then that colour will dominate. But if we get a blue gene for one eye and a brown gene for the other, we might end up with either two blue or two brown eyes depending on which one is the most dominant. Of course on rare occasions some people have ended up with one of each colour. Then there is the mix of genes for different traits that may or may not show in the phenotype due to dominance of other genes, but this may change overtime or under certain circumstances. Such circumstances may be with education or experience of something, or to put it another way, the environment our gene traits occupy.

So, how much intelligence is gene inherited and how much is environmentally sourced?

IQ (intelligence quotient) tests have been developed to measure 'cognitive abilities', and scores are related to what has been determined as the 'average' and this is given the number 100. Scores over 100 are designated as higher than average and below 100 lower than average. These tests over the years have been hailed as wonderful, discredited, had popular bursts and even treated with distain, nonetheless, they are, to some extent, an indication of our cognitive abilities. But how much of the IQ score can be attributed to our genes? Ayala tells us, "Estimates of IQ heritability obtained in different studies vary, but usually within a relatively small range around .70....Within any given population, it seems that 70 per cent of the variation in intelligence is due to genetic factors and only 30% due to environmental factors." (Ayala F. J., 2012, p. 148) Of course this applies only if we are confident in the IQ measurement tests and scoring! We will have a lot more to say about mind/consciousness in a later chapter.

It is now time to move on to the notion of our cultural evolution, and for this it is necessary to have some insight into the world of 'memes'. In *The Selfish Gene,* Dawkins introduces us to the notion of 'Memes' which he proposes are cultural replicators and these too are part of the evolutionary process. He explains, "Examples of memes are tunes, ideas, catch-phrases, clothes fashions, ways of making pots or building arches, Just as genes propagate themselves in the gene pool by leaping from body to body via sperms or eggs, so memes propagate themselves in the meme pool by leaping from brain to brain via a process which, in the broad sense, can be called imitation." (Dawkins, 2006, p. 192). Culture itself, may be defined as particular shared ideas that cause groups to act alike. Culture may also be grouped into e.g. systems like, the financial system or the legal system of a community.

Memes do, in general, run the whole spectrum from good/beneficial to bad/ damaging. That is they can have positive or negative effects in their implementation. But beyond doubt is the fact that from an evolutionary view point they are much faster acting than genes. Gene mutation while immediate can require several steps over many years to demonstrate a specific change in the host vehicle namely plant or animal. Whereas, meme replication such as the use of some new technology may take just weeks to become firmly established. Positive memes are those that appear to bestow advantage, for example, the rules of the road can be considered advantageous as when implemented this meme can saves lives. Negative memes on the other hand bestow disadvantage, for example, a culture of Saturday night 'binge drinking' by groups of young people, can end in addiction, or other major health issues.

In general there is a tendency for memes to change over time, however in some static units be they e.g. national societies or religions, changes will be much slower than in non-static units such as western societies where positive change is encouraged and even negative change is tolerated. Physicist David Deutsch, advises that meme change occurs with criticism and creativity but, "static societies always have traditions of bringing up children in ways that disable their creativity and critical faculties. That ensures that most of the new ideas that would have been capable of changing the society are never thought of in the first place." (Deutsch D., 2011, p. 382). Indeed, powerful groups may use their power, within non-static societies, to stifle a new idea or a criticism that does not suit their ends. Memes of course may also be designed as strategies to achieve specific ends, for example, marketing strategies to sell products. A leading authority on memes, Richard Brodie[35] illuminates, "Advertising works by altering your perpetual filter to pay more attention to, or have better feelings toward, the advertiser's product. Politicians with their slogans and rhetoric hope to infect your mind with memes that make you perceive them as a good choice to vote for." (Brodie, 2009, p. 30) Memes also are often referred to as a virus, but I believe this is to convey their vigour in transmission rather than the negative perception of a virus. So, it is important to keep in mind that positive memes, have in the past, changed history for the good. Typical of these would be with communication memes and how the use of mobile (cell) phones took off via imitation/replication. Even more interesting in this regard are the memes of social networking like 'Face Book', and 'Twitter'.

---

[35] Richard Brodie is one of the world's leading authorities on memetics-the study of the self-replicating aspects of culture. The creator of Microsoft Word and Bill Gates' personal assistant, he is also a professional poker player and an aficionado of the internet and its role in society. www.memecentral.com

A meme must first be established and then protected by facilitating its replication. An example of a meme that is not 'protected' is a popular song that lasts in popularity (replication) for a certain period of time but unless protected/archived, or the like, it eventually is forgotten and lost. A meme that is a song or even a product, can, by innovative enhancement and or advertising, achieve superior replication. An example of a meme, on the other hand, that is protected, is a cultural sport that is regulated, managed, monitored on an on-going basis. Its replication is assured and its progress is also on-going, with innovative enhancements, to accommodate future contemporary needs and developments.

Evolution then has brought us from the lowest form of life to the complex body/brain/mind individual and social creatures we are today. We are the pinnacle of this on-going transformation. Now however, that we have reached this level of sophistication we are in a position, through our cognitive abilities, to assist or hinder further complexification. With this in mind I will conclude this chapter with four lessons from the evolutionary process.

(1) While the universe itself is on a journey towards inevitable entropy/disorder, we, as a species, are on a different, somewhat fragile, journey towards greater complexity/order. With regard to this the great thinkers, investigators and publicists featured in the previous chapter, together with Darwin, Mendel and Dawkins featured in this chapter have all adhered to Teilhard de Chardin's quest, to 'acquire as much knowledge (information) as possible of our world and with this to raise our consciousness/social consciousness'. We should all strive to do likewise no matter how insignificant we believe our contribution might be? In this way our accountability and responsibility for all our actions will be joyfully borne.

(2) The importance of information: Firstly, biological life itself is information based as we have seen how it is replicated through our genes. Secondly, cultural life is also information based, as each meme competes to put information into our brains. Thirdly, information may be supressed by outside influences or oneself e.g. Darwin perhaps holding off on publication of his masterpiece for his own or societal reasons. Fourthly, information may be lost or ignored, a la Gregor Mendel's exposition of genetics.

(3) Nature/evolution has presented us with a simple yet essential message on all aspects of life. The message being that all kinds of replication require protection and enhancement. For example, the fish and other life forms in the sea need protection for natural replication and then innovative enhancement via management restocking etc. for superior replication. Likewise, the environment itself needs protection and management,

restocking of forests etc. This notion also applies to memes and one meme in particular, capitalist market economies, need protection firstly, in order to replicate naturally. However this meme also needs innovation of its methodological processes for superior replication. More on this in a later chapter.

(4) This lesson can be summed up in two words, 'Healthcare' and 'Education'. Because natural processes cannot operate unless the replicator is healthy, and superior replication cannot take place unless there is enhancement and such is best served with education for information.

In the next chapter, 'The Classical World' or if you prefer the world with which we are most familiar, we will examine gravity the fundamental force that keeps the planets going around the sun and the moon going around the earth, yet it is the weakest of the four fundamental forces. In addition, we will visit the notion of Albert Einstein's relativity looking at the relationship between time and space and how matter and energy are interchangeable. Plus, what we think of as gravity may in fact be something else entirely.

## CHAPTER 4
# The Classical World

With the arrival of the first lifeform and its evolution, what it is that we are is now established in the world, and let us not forget, it is a world to which we are most suited, a la 'The Anthropic Principle'. We, did play an on-going part, via positive mutational variation selection, to ensure the best fit. In other words, biological evolution continuously selected out the best environmental fit. In addition, cultural evolution, via positive conscious variation selection, did likewise. However, negative conscious variation selection, intended or not, has impacted also on the general environment. By environment here I am referring not to just climate etc. but also to ourselves, together with general societal processes e.g. political and/or religious ideologies, and economic systems.

So, having arrived in the world, with years and years of history and information behind us, we believe we have reached the stage where we can distinguish between what is real and what is not? For example, if I pick up a stone and throw it into the sea, it will, depending on the force of the throw, travel a certain distance and then crash into the sea. We may even say that once the force of the throw decreases to less than the force of gravity, then gravity itself pulls the stone into the sea. Such a stone throwing exercise is what we expect to happen and therefore is part of our reality. Conversely, if we throw another stone with the same expectation, but this time it stays floating in the air above the sea for a while then turns at right angles, travels on a bit and then drops into the sea, we would call this incredible, amazing and unreal. Why, because it breaks our reality expectation. Our reality expectation of what will physically happen to the stone is based on what is now called, 'classical physics'.

Classical physics, up to the middle of the twentieth century, was for everyone but a few scientists, the only understandable and practical physics there was. From the 1950's onward however, the use of quantum physics' processes in everyday life has grown considerably. Nonetheless, in spite of the use of quantum physics in virtually all of the new technology we never notice the quantum world in action and only directly recognise the classical. The reason for this is that the quantum world processes are too small for us to notice. Physicist, Kenneth Ford describes classical physics as, "the physics of force and motion (mechanics); of heat and entropy and bulk matter (thermodynamics); of electricity and magnetism and light (electromagnetism). Albert Einstein's twentieth—century theories of relativity—special and general—are also classical because they are nonquantum." (Ford K. W., 2011, pp. 7-8) We will look at each of these in turn now starting with mechanics. In this regard two 17th century thinkers, Galileo Galilei (referred to as Galileo) and Rene Descartes laid the groundwork.

The Italian physicist, Galileo, if you remember, agreed with Copernicus that the earth and planets went around the sun and for this suffered the wrath of the Catholic Church. It was he who perfected the telescope to investigate the stars and planets. Together with this, he also discovered or developed various mechanical processes. The result of all his investigations was that he believed the world to be mathematical. Rene Descartes (1596—1650), French Philosopher and Mathematician, also believed the world to be mathematical, however, he went further claiming that all of nature was mechanical.[36] It was Descartes who developed the algebra notation using lowercase a, b and c for known quantities and x, y and z for unknown quantities. He also introduced a methodology that used algebra to describe geometry, and in addition, created or at least made popular, "superscript notation for showing powers or exponents (e.g. $2^4$ to show 2 x 2 x 2 x 2)."[37] However, Descartes is probably best known as a philosopher with his notion of 'Cogito ergo sum' ('I think therefore I am') which probably could be described as his mantra. Nonetheless, his contribution to the evolution of mathematics was quite significant as it helped in the development of 'Calculus,' which Newton and Leibniz[38] both separately created. It is also noteworthy that he, Descartes, delayed the publication of some of his work following the condemnation of Galileo in 1633. An indication of Descartes' influence was evident, as Cambridge was abuzz with his writings, when Isaac Newton first arrived there. Newton would therefore have had ample opportunity to study these works and of course considered them when formulating his own thoughts and

36 It is important to note that it is believed that physics can only be fully understood through its mathematical computations. Such mathematics are for the many difficult. However, I believe we can appreciate music without being a musician or art without being a painter. So, physics in this regard will be no different.

37 Descartes—17th Century Mathematics–The Story of Mathematics (2010 Luke Mastin) http://www.storyofmathetics.com/17th_descartes.html (Retrieved 22/1/2014)

38 German Mathematician, Gottfried Leibniz (1646—1716)

propositions. Indeed, Newton's thoughts and propositions were to prove to be one of the most profound and lasting contributions to scientific knowledge.

By far the greatest of Newton's works however, and probably the most well-known was, 'Mathematical Principles of Natural Philosophy'. In this he presented his theories of the *laws of motion* and *universal gravitation*. Put simply, its publication in 1687 began what we now know as classical physics, which is the physics upon which we base most of our understanding of reality. Not alone did Newton take science into a new paradigm with these laws but in order to do so he invented a new mathematical process called 'Calculus'.[39] The same mathematical process was, as I mentioned above, separately created by Leibniz.[40]

Historian, William Rankin in *Introducing Newton* explains the three axioms of Newton's *Laws of Motion* as follows:

*"Axiom 1.* *Every body continues in its state of rest, or of uniform motion in a straight line, unless it is compelled to change that state by forces impressed upon it.*

*Axiom 11.* *The change in motion is proportional to the motive force impressed.*

*Axiom 111.* *To every action there is always opposed an equal reaction: or the mutual actions of two bodies upon each other are always equal and directed to contrary parts."* (Rankin, 2007, p. 122)

We are all well aware of the consequences of gravity, but what is it exactly? It is a force, one of the fundamental forces of nature and one of the two with which we are most familiar. The second one with which we are familiar is the electromagnetic force. The other two being, the strong and the weak nuclear forces with which we need not trouble ourselves. So, gravity being an attractive force keeps our feet firmly on the ground and indeed everything else around us as well. Outside the earth, gravity keeps the moon orbiting us. It also keeps the earth itself, with the moon in tow, together with the planets orbiting the sun. How this is achieved is explained in chapter 2 note 20 with the 'cannon ball' analogy. Beyond our solar system gravity also keeps the stars in the galaxies and the galaxies in clusters. An extraordinary force to be sure, but nonetheless, the weakest of the four forces. For example, think how easy it is to lift a feather off the ground.

So, did Newton have that 'Eureka' moment with the apple falling onto his head while sitting under the tree? It would be nice to think so but it is probably not true,

39 Calculus for those interested is the study of functions using limits to explore rates of change (differentiation) and sums or areas (integration).

40 Leibniz also created what we now know as 'binary' numbers, as used in computers.

although he himself is reported to have related that observing an apple fall from a tree did give him the idea for his 'Universal Law of gravity'. This is nicely summed up by Felix Pirani as being "that every object attracts every other object with a force proportional to their masses and inversely proportional to the square of the distance between them." (Pirani & Roche, 2006, p. 90)[41].

There are five lessons we need to remember regarding Newton laws:

1) His laws are set in three dimensions.[42]
2) Objects/bodies communicate with each other directly or by way of one connecting to the other e.g. via a force such as gravity. This is known as locality.
3) Newtonian laws are reversible. This means that if you have e.g. the structure of a church made up of bricks, and you take it apart and then construct a house with all the bricks, the whole process can be reversed by deconstructing the house and rebuilding the church.
4) 'Classical', also now known as 'Newtonian' physics is deterministic. An example of this determinism was summed up by French mathematician, Pierre-Simon Laplace who roughly said, 'give me enough information about an object, and I can predict its future state, or how it arrived at its present state'.
5) This notion of determinism is also applicable to human beings, implying that everything about us was already determined. And our future is also already written in the book of nature.

So everything we do, it appears, is automatic! We believe however, that we have choices e.g. we might choose to allow the automatic to prevail and not interfere with it, or we might intervene to stop/change the automatic processes for another choice. We certainly know that much of what we do is automatic and run by our autonomic nervous system. For example, we automatically take in and expel air, our hearts automatically pump blood around our bodies etc. Also, there are other things that we do automatically like driving a car, we may be miles away in thought yet automatically, driving within the speed limit, stopping at red lights and indicating to turn, but such is all happening while thoughts may be on sport, finance, or romance etc. So, certainly much of what we do or happens to us is automatic. But we do

---

41 The inverse square simply means that the attraction between the two objects will weaken as they are separated by the process e.g. if the distance between them is doubled the pull will be weakened by a factor of 4 ($2^2$), or if you triple the distance, the pull will be weakened by a factor of 9 ($3^2$), etc.

42 "the surface of any sphere in three-dimensional space—is proportional to the square of its radius, which in this case is the *square* of the distance between the sun and the satellite etc." (Greene B., 2005, p. 395)

believe we have the ability to decide to change the automatic and that we have a free hand to do so. Such a free hand is more commonly called our 'free will'. Now whilst most of us have no doubt that we have a free will, psychologist Susan Blackmore tells us that in 1985 a consciousness scientist, one Benjamin Libet, carried out a specific brain experiment producing, at that time, extraordinary results. The experiment showed that when a person flexes their wrist, "the brain processes planning the movement began over one-third of a second before the person had the conscious desire to move. In brain terms this is a very long time." (Blackmore, 2005, p. 87) This experiment then indicated that we do not have a free will! So, here is a dilemma of major proportions, the least not being legal issues. Example, should we be responsible of our decisions/actions if we have no free will?

Libet himself offered a sort of solution, as he noted that sometimes his experimental participants said they had stopped the movement (flexing the wrist) just before it occurred. So, he carried out a further experiment and following this he argued, that while consciousness did not initiate the action (flexing the wrist), it could stop it from happening. In other words no 'free will' but 'free veto'. This might appear to solve the problem but it is easily argued that the veto itself is part of the deterministic automatism.

Further experiments into this dilemma have been carried out but only exacerbated it. Kate Douglas reported on such in *New Scientist*, "We now know the unconscious decision happens even earlier. In 2008, John-Dylan Haynes at the Bernstein center for Computational Neuroscience in Berlin, Germany, found activity up to 10 seconds before a conscious decision to move (Nature Neuroscience, vol 11, p543)." (Douglas, 2010) So, is there any solution to this? Or are we merely robots acting out some play in a holographic film presentation? In this play on the one hand, we have nothing to contribute by way of change to the performance, while on the other, we are neither accountable nor responsible for our actions within it. There might however, just might, be an answer to give us back some self-respect, in the scheme of things. But first some insights into other prominent contributions to classical physics.

Apart from gravity the other fundamental force in nature, with which we are very much aware, is the electromagnetic force. In this regard, it was the great Scottish physicist and mathematician, James Clark Maxwell (1831—1879), who not only combined electricity and magnetism as a singular force, but also described the various phenomena associated with electromagnetism and this he did with just four mathematical equations. These phenomena include things like, light always travels at the fixed and non-changing speed of light, approximately 300,000 Km per second. Also with light, being a form of radiation, it moves in waves of various lengths from extremely long radio waves to extremely short X-rays. See Fig: 2-1.

In addition, Maxwell also developed a kinetic theory of gases and heat. The energy of a moving object is its kinetic energy. The hotter the gas the more its atoms jiggled about. This we can observe when we see the jiggling of boiling water in a pot. Maxwell developed these propositions even before atoms had been fully accepted and confirmed, so it shows the foresight of the man. His aim was to show that the statistical behaviour of microscopic units predicted the properties of their combined macroscopic body. Continuing with the notion of heat, another luminary, James Joule (1736-1819) in the 19th century showed, that a certain amount of heat could produce a certain amount of work. In this way heat was recognised as energy and indeed we now measure quantities of energy in 'Joules'.

From there then developed the first two laws of Thermodynamics[43] as presented in 1850 by Rudolf Clausius (1822-88).

The First Law is the conservation of energy. This means that if some energy is used in one place it will appear again in another. We cannot create any more energy, what we have, is all there is and it is conserved. The energy information in one place may however be created into a different form, with new bits of information, someplace else.

The Second Law was called 'entropy'. Kaku explains; "the total amount of entropy (chaos and disorder) in the universe always increases. In other words, everything must eventually age and rundown. The burning of forests, the rusting of machines, the fall of empires, and the aging of the human body all represent the increase of entropy in the universe." (Kaku, 2005, p. 289). In order to get a feeling for this entropy, let us visualise an exercise as follows; we have a large water tank divided into two compartments by a barrier down the middle. The left compartment we fill to the top with extremely hot water while the right hand compartment we fill to the top with extremely cold water. We would then say that each side alone has low entropy. But when we remove the dividing barrier the water of both temperatures mix during which they are gaining more and more entropy. Eventually when they reach the point of total equilibrium they have reached maximum entropy. The same outcome will occur if initially one side is filled with water and the other side with black ink, only this time the equilibrium or maximum entropy will present as a grey liquid.

Extrapolating this to the whole universe everything then, people, animals, plants earth, moon, planets, stars, galaxies, will all disintegrate until the universe reaches its complete equilibrium of maximum entropy. So, as far as science was concerned there was no going back. It was a one-way ticket. It was impossible to separate the hot and cold water molecules, likewise the water and ink molecules or indeed

---

43 Thermodynamics is simply the movement of heat.

reorganise the maximum entropy of the universe into its original parts. Entropy then was irreversible, whereas Newtonian laws of motion were reversible. This was a conundrum that concerned Maxwell together with another physicist, Ludwig Boltzmann (1844—1906). Boltzmann addressed this, with the help of Maxwell's theory of gases and input from two other scientists[44], by developing what was to be called 'statistical mechanics', a precursor of quantum mechanics. With this he was able to demonstrate that entropy was not completely irreversible. His statistical mechanics would show that there was the probability, albeit extremely small, that entropy could be reversed.

So, let us think visually about how Boltzmann's notion of entropy might work. On this occasion think of a large tank again divided down the middle. Only this time suppose we could colour a specific number of atoms and have exactly half red and the other half black. We now put the red in the left hand side and the black in the right hand side, knowing that atoms jiggle about or fluctuate. Again each side is in a situation of extremely low entropy. We then lift the barrier and of course the jiggling atoms mix up until again we can expect that the most probable outcome will be equilibrium or maximum entropy. Boltzmann showed however, that based on a probability distribution, there was an outside chance that with their movement they could in effect wiggle their way back to their original compartments. It might take a very long time for this to eventuate, maybe even the lifetime of the universe, but the probability was there. His formula[45] for entropy is so famous that it is written on his tombstone in Vienna.

By this time it had been shown and was generally accepted that light/radiation moved in waves but, based on this notion, a concerning mystery showed up within classical physics known as the 'blackbody ultraviolet catastrophe'[46]. This had to do with the calculations[47] of radiating heat coming from e.g. a stove. German physicist Max Planck worked on this problem and eventually, in 1900, using Boltzmann's statistical analysis, he proposed a fix with new calculations based on the notion that radiation was emitted and absorbed in small pieces that he called quanta. The scientific community were not quick in accepting this theory and it probably didn't help that Plank himself had little confidence in it. Nonetheless, his discovery was rewarded with a Nobel Prize in 1918.

---

44 Josiah Gibbs (1839 –1903) and Max Planck (1858 –1947)

45 S=K. Log W

46 A Blackbody is, "An idealized object that absorbs all heat and energy and radiates it back in a manner determined solely by its temperature." (Randall, 2006, p. 460) See also note: 21 Chapter 2.

47 "..classical calculations predicted that far greater energy could be emitted in high-frequency radiation than physicists had seen and recorded." (Randall, 2006, p. 120)

Indeed, Planck's discovery contributed to Albert Einstein (1879-1955) receiving the Nobel Prize in 1921. Einstein received the prize, not for his relativity theories but for his 1905 work on the *photoelectric effect.* Physicist Kenneth Ford explains how Einstein, progressing on from Planck, "argued that light is not only emitted and absorbed in bundles, as Planck had proposed, it *exists* in bundles." (Ford K. W., 2011, p. 27) These bundles would later become known as photons. The photoelectric effect has to do with how photons can knock electrons from a metal sheet. It matters not the number of photons fired at the metal, what matters is the energetic strength of the photon. Think of some photons as feathers and other photons as steel balls, both trying to knock rocks out of a circle. Lots of feathers will not do the job but one steel ball does the trick. It was in this then that Einstein began his major contribution to quantum theory with his use of photons, and he probably started the uneasy notion that light was both a wave and a particle. But more about that in the next chapter. We now need to look at Einstein's theories of relativity.

An earlier experiment had shown that no matter which direction on earth light took, east-west, west-east, north-south, south-north, it always travelled at the speed of light. When we talk about the speed of light we always infer the time element. For example, a light year is the distance light will travel in, the time of one year. And that is pretty far when we consider that the speed of light is 300,000 Km in the time of one second. It was with this in mind that Einstein began his 'special theory' of relativity. This showed that while the speed of light does not change, the faster one moves in space, up to the speed of light, the slower time ticks away. In fact if you could actually reach the speed of light, then at that point, time itself would stop. And if you could go faster than the speed of light you would actually go backwards in time. Einstein proposed that the speed of light was different from the speed of other things. For example, if you are travelling on a bus at 100 Km per hour and a car passes you at 120 Km per hour you feel it is like they pass at 20Km per hour. But it makes no difference to your bus or the car, if light passes you while you are in motion it will always pass at 300,000 Km per second. In addition, suppose you are in a Rocket ship and getting close to the speed of light, the nearer you get to that speed the more mass your rocket, you etc. will take on, eventually making it impossible to reach light speed. Yet, if someone is observing you say from the earth, while you will feel no difference, they will observe that your spaceship and you etc. have contracted in size. Another consequence is that should you be a twin and send your twin, or someone with your date of birth, off into space travelling for a number of years. Depending on how close they travelled to light speed, when they return you will have aged considerably in comparison to them, due to time slowing down for them as their speed increased.

Indeed, no matter what mode of transport you travel in or at whatever speed, once it is smoothly running your sensations will feel normal like you are not in motion. For example, should use a computer, take a toilet break, or drop your ticket it will occur as if you are not in motion. Put another way, were you to throw your book into the air, thus travelling, it will drop back on your lap, not somewhere behind you due to your speed.

With 'special relativity' Einstein introduced us to his famous equation namely; $E= Mc^2$ with E being energy, M, stands mass, and $c^2$ for the speed of light squared[48]. So, energy is equal to mass, and simply put mass is matter, therefore matter is energy. Such enormous energy is unfortunately well known in e.g. hydrogen atom bombs, and neutron (from the nucleus of the atom) bombs. In addition nuclear energy, like it or not, contributes significantly to our energy needs. It goes without saying then that 'Special Relativity theory' had enormous consequences for our world, unfortunately not all good. Nonetheless, its insights are without doubt astounding. But Mr Einstein was only warming up. In 1915 he amazed the world once more with his 'General theory of Relativity', in this he shows that gravity is the same as inertia. Inertia being the resistance of a body to acceleration. Science writer Martin Gardner explains, "At the heart of Einstein's general theory is what he calls the principle of equivalence. This is nothing less than the staggering assertion....that gravity and inertia are one and the same. This does not mean merely that they have similar effects. *Gravity and inertia are two different words for exactly the same thing."* (Gardner, 1997, p. 65). He was basically saying that the gravitational pull one feels of the earth is the same as the push-back one feels when a car suddenly accelerates.

Unlike Newton, Einstein was not satisfied with three dimensional space he added a fourth dimension namely time, the result was the creation of space-time. We can visualise three dimensional space but space-time is another matter! Nonetheless, it is now a generally accepted phenomenon. This he extended to a curved space-time, often referred to as a type of fabric that permeates the universe. Einstein's insight was that the presence of stars, planets etc., together with energy, all warped this fabric into lumps bumps and valleys. Indeed, while this fabric exists in four dimensions, we can get some idea of how it works as follows: Imagine a steel

[48] c, is the notation used and accepted for the speed of light. Regarding why it is squared; David Bodanis explains, in the early 18thC "Willem 'sGravesande, a Dutch researcher who'd been letting weights plummet onto a soft clay floor.....found. If a small brass sphere was sent down twice as fast as before, it pushed *four* times as far into the clay. If it was flung down three times as fast, it sank *nine* times as far into the clay....Why is squaring the velocity of what you measure such an accurate way to describe what happens in nature?..One reason is that the very geometry of our world often produces squared numbers. When you move twice as close toward a reading lamp, the light on the page you're reading doesn't simply get twice as strong. Just as with 'sGravesande experiment the light's intensity increases *four* times." (Bodanis, 2001, pp. 64-67)

ball, the size of a soccer ball, sitting on a trampoline. The steel ball, placed in the middle, will make a dip in the fabric of the trampoline. Now roll a golf ball across so it passes close to the steel ball and you will see the golf ball dip into the incline as it passes the bigger ball. It is this warping of the four dimensional fabric that we feel as gravity. Ask most people however what it is that keeps their feet firmly on the ground and the chances are the answer will not be, 'the warping of Space-time'. Some of the valleys predicted by Einstein's equations, in the space-time, were more than mere valleys, they were deep holes or black holes as they are known today. These black holes pulled everything inside that came near to them, including light (hence 'black holes'), to eventually form a 'singularity' as discussed regarding the formation of the universe.

Newton's gravity still remains in our psyche and works well for us in everyday life, but the more accurate and superior is Einstein's version. Martin Gardner gives an example, "The major axis of Mercury's orbit wheels around the sun at a rate close to 5,600 seconds of arc per century. Newton's equations for gravity, after taking into account the influence of other planets lead to an expected rotation of about 43 seconds per century *less* than what is actually observed. Einstein's equations give the tiny planet an additional relativistic push, so to speak, of just the right amount - 43 seconds of arc per century." (Gardner, 1997, p. 93) However, combining gravity with quantum mechanics has proven to be a most difficult task. It was this attempted amalgamation that Einstein seriously worked on up to his death in 1955. To date there is no agreed solution to this endeavour. But there are indications that it might not be far away.

An interesting afterword occurred with the 'General theory', in 1919, Theodor Kaluza, a little-known German mathematician extended Einstein's equations and discovered that space had an additional (space) dimension. From this Brian Greene advises, Kaluza *"had found a framework that combined Einstein's original equations of general relativity with those of Maxwell's equations of electromagnetism."* (Greene B., 2005, p. 361)

This chapter has left us with many strange developments that I will now summarize. Firstly, there is the mechanics of determinism that leads to our automation and appearance no 'free will'! Secondly, the notion that entropy always increases but there is a minute but virtually impossible 'probability' of it being reversible! Thirdly, the strange phenomenon of light/radiation, its speed and its relationship with time. Also its wave and quanta duality. Fourthly, matter simply being another form of energy.

A final note on the world of 'classical physics'. This was the physics of reality for most people up to the middle of the 20$^{th}$ century, but at this point in time that quantum processes began to have an input into our lives. However, even today when most of our new technology uses quantum processes, we still live our lives within the classical realm, because it is the reality of our perceptive environment simply because we have evolved into this environment and for us it is predictable. Some examples of this predictability are; what goes up must come down; cats are not green; cats are alive or dead; dogs cannot use our ability to speak; people cannot walk through walls; and to communicate over distances requires a connection[49]; if I push someone they will move; I feel wet from the rain and warmth from the sun; people have sex and produce an offspring; an offspring will survive with protection and nourishment to eventually die and disintegrate; everything will eventually disintegrate.

It is often said we can change the rules or even introduce new facts but it is much more difficult to change convention based on previous beliefs. How much more difficult is it then to change a perception of reality, that has been established, at a compounded rate, over billions of years of evolution. Indeed, it is even more so when a more enlightened reality is, for the most part, not perceived. I am of course referring to quantum reality which we will endeavour to come to grips with over the next two chapters.

[49] By this I mean the connection must be physical in the sense of connected by something like a wire or a field, e.g. a gravitational field of influence, or within the range of radio waves etc. Such connection is called locality by physicists.

## CHAPTER 5

# The Quantum World

The major problem in attempting to explain quantum physics, as the most accurate physics to date, is that, as we have seen from the previous chapter, our reality is grounded in the classical world. Because of this the quantum world, or quantum reality will appear to be strange, weird, mysterious, and counter-intuitive. However, allow me to suggest that the best adjective to describe it is 'wondrous'. For convenience I will use the terms quantum-world/realm, quantum-theory, quantum-mechanics, and quantum-physics as all meaning the same thing. At times in this chapter, you, the general reader, may find the information a bit full-on. But I encourage you to persist as the information is here as a reference for future chapters. In other words you do not have to confine it all to memory, rather know that it exists to refer back to if required.

It was Einstein's use of quantum in the 'photoelectric effect' that helped establish more fully the new form of physics. But there is no doubt that it was Max Planck who introduced quantum physics to the world. It was his mathematical equation, regarding the radiation from hot bodies that was the key, and in particular it was the mathematical constant, within the equation, that differentiated quantum physics from classical physics. It may seem extraordinary that this constant, now called the 'Planck Constant', and denoted by the letter *h,* could have had such a profound and changing effect, on the world of science in particular, and society in general[50]. Indeed, it is extraordinary alone because of its size.

---

[50] The constant fits in when it (*h*) is multiplied by the radiation frequency to give the energy (*E*) result for the quantum unit or photon. With radiation frequency denoted as (v) the formula for the energy of a quantum is then $E= hv$. The reason Planck's discovery profoundly affected society in general is evidenced in that the modus

Planck's constant, or $h$ = 0.000 000 000 000 000 000 000 000 006 626

From this constant two other important measurements evolved namely; The Planck length which is about $10^{-35}$ metres, and Planck time $10^{-43}$ seconds (the time it takes to travel one Planck length).

It is often stated that the quantum world is the world of the extreme small, notwithstanding the size of Planck's constant, and the classical world is the world of the big. The world of the big being everything we can see, feel and sense. In spite of this it is now generally accepted, scientifically, that the universe and everything in it is 'quantum based' even though it appears as 'classically based'. Due to this enigma though, knowing where the boundary is between both worlds is, to say the least, fuzzy. Kenneth Ford gives some historical perspective. "The great Danish physicist Niels Bohr was one of the first to grapple with the seeming conundrum that quantum physics, although totally different from classical physics, does not overturn it. In 1913 he introduced what he called the *correspondence principle*, which states that as the increments between one quantum state and the next become relatively smaller and smaller, classical physics becomes more and more accurate." (Ford K. W., 2011, pp. 7-8).

An understanding of the quantum world requires it, as far as possible, to be explained classically as the classical realm is our reality setting. I will endeavour to do this as we proceed. In this regard, I will commence the quantum examination with the next paragraph as 'nice to know' information, as well as to highlight a start of the strangeness of the quantum world. So, don't stress out on it! Rather, soldier on and know it is there for reference, if required.

Although not entirely correct, think of the quantum world as pertaining to unseen and extremely small entities such as molecules, atoms, and subatomic matter and force particles. Subatomic matter particles are called 'fermions' e.g. quarks', 'protons', 'neutrons', and 'electrons'. And subatomic force particles are called 'bosons' e.g. 'photons' and also the 'Higgs boson' (being the force particle of the Higgs field). Fermions and bosons are also differentiated from each other by an intrinsic component called 'spin'. This intrinsic 'spin' should not be confused with a rotation about, similar to the earth's rotation[51], rather, physicist Lisa Randall tells us that when a particle has intrinsic spin, "it interacts as if it were rotating, even though in reality it is not." (Randall, 2006, p. 146) Fermions have intrinsic spins of half numbers e.g. ½, $^3\!/_2$, etc. while the intrinsic spin of bosons are either zero or whole numbers e.g. 0, 1, 2, 3, and so on. A weird thing about the fermion half numbers is

---

operandi of cell phones, TVs, computers, medical scanners, communication devices, and all electronic devices etc. is all enacted by the manipulation of quantum physics.

51 Particles may also rotate, similar to the earth, such as an electron rotating around the nucleus of an atom.

highlighted by Paul Davies. He advises us that it is possible to rotate the spin axis of subatomic particles by applying a magnetic field. Then if you rotate, "an electron (or any spin ½ fermion) you have to rotate it through 720°—i.e. *two* entire revolutions—before it returns to its original state!" (Davies, 2007, p. 122) This strange double view of the world is not, it seems, shared with bosons.

Matter particles, i.e. electrons, protons and neutrons (each proton and neutron having three quarks) are found mostly in atoms. There are numerous other particles that we do not need to bother with at present, however, it is important to know that each matter particle has a partner called an antiparticle. Whereas, in the case of force particles they are usually also their own antiparticle. Matter particles however have specific antiparticles e.g. the antiparticle for an electron is called a 'positron'. The difference between a particle and an antiparticle is the charge e.g. an electron has a negative charge while a positron has a positive charge. 'Opposite' charges attract while 'like' charges keep away from each other.

We have already noted that all matter is made of atoms. So, what are atoms exactly? Well, mostly empty space it appears. Science journalist Piers Bizony elaborates, an atom is, "about a tenth of a millionth of a millimetre across.... If all the atoms in your body could be squeezed down to get rid of the empty volume inside them, you would weigh the same, but would be as small as a grain of salt. Almost all of you---almost all of everything in the entire cosmos---is *nothing*.....The atom is not a hard-edged 'thing'. It's a ghostly shimmer." (Bizony, 2007, pp. xv-xvi) The nucleus of an atom is surrounded by layers of electron shells, of different energy levels, like an onion. For example, the outer shell can have up to 8 electrons. These electrons are manifested, for example, when you kick a stone with your shoe, and the stone bounces off, the reason your foot doesn't go through the stone is because the negative charge in the electrons in your shoe hits the 'like' negative charge of the electrons in the stone, and shoe and stone bounce away from each other. Electrons, we have also seen, act as bonding devices between atoms.

Apart from electrons and quarks one other particle had quite a lot of publicity some few years ago, and that was the 'neutrino[52]'. The neutrino appears to be the most numerous subatomic particle of the lot[53]. Trillions of neutrinos, mostly coming from the sun, pass through us every second or so. We don't feel this in any way but they travel at a very fast speed. In the press in 2011 it was reported that some neutrinos were believed to have travelled to earth faster than the speed of light, but

52 "All in all, there are more neutrinos than any other particle we know, certainly far more than the electrons and protons that make the stars and all visible matter such as you and me...All we know is that if you had some subatomic scales, it would take at least 100,000 neutrinos to balance a single electron. Even so, the vast numbers make it possible that, in total, they outweigh all the visible matter of the universe." (Close, 2012, p. 2)

53 Neutrinos, it appears, emanate from beta decay of atomic nuclei.

this proved to be untrue, so Mr. Einstein was correct. Although some things were even beyond him as for many years he was convinced there was, what could be called, 'A Theory of Everything' underlying the nature of the universe. Indeed, he spent the latter part of his life trying to find this but to no avail. Such a theory, now known as a 'Grand Unifying Theory', would be where the four fundamental forces could be unified to a single fundamental force. Some progress has been made in this endeavour as by the mid-1970's the Electromagnetic, Strong and Weak nuclear forces had, to all intents and purposes, been stitched together mathematically, and this is referred to as the 'Standard Model'. Unfortunately, to date, it is not complete as it was found impossible to add in the Gravitational force[54]. It appears however, that gravity may well be accommodated with the other forces within what is called 'String Theory', and this will be examined in the next chapter.

We know Newton believed that light flowed in particles which he called 'corpuscles', and this notion persisted until Thomas Young (1773-1829) demonstrated it was something different. Early in the 19th century, Young, set up a 'double slit'[55] experiment that was to show light travelled in waves and not particles. The experiment consists of cutting two slits in a sheet of, say metal, and shining a light through these slits. Behind the sheet is a detection screen that records the pattern of how the light, coming out of the two slits, lands on the screen. The light in fact lands on the screen in light and dark bands, a result indicating an 'interference pattern' of light travelling in waves. See Fig: 5-1 below.

---

54 *"The notion of a smooth spatial geometry, the central principle of general relativity, is destroyed by the violent fluctuations of the quantum world on short distant scales."* (Greene B., 2000, p. 129)

55 The experiment was to prove its on-going worth in quantum experiments up to the present day.

**Double-Slit Experiment**

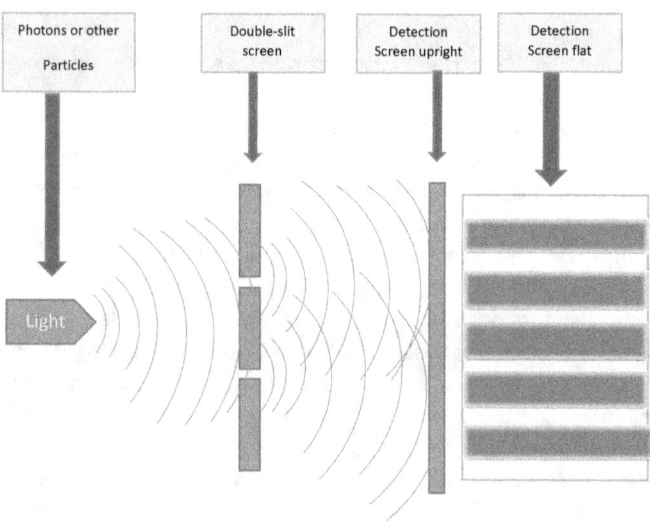


**Fig: 5-1**

This was the reason that Maxwell, as with most of the scientific community at the time, believed light travelled in waves. Indeed, it was later revealed that not only photons of light, but other particles (Fig: 5-1) e.g. electrons, protons and even atoms and molecules could all be demonstrated, within this experiment, to travel as waves. Yet this was questioned by Planck's and Einstein's notion of light travelling in quanta (pieces/particles). But probably the most important revelation of the 'double slit' experiment was that it exposed what came to be known as the 'measurement problem' of quantum mechanics. Certainly, this problem is, one of the weirdest, if not the most fundamental exposures, of the quantum realm. I will now attempt to describe it.

Suppose we set up the experiment as above with the sheet with two slits and behind it a detection screen. Now suppose the two-slit sheet is bullet proof and we fire a series of bullets from a machine gun at this screen, some bullets would go straight through the slits some would graze the sides/top/bottom of both slits and arrive on the detection screen in an expected distribution of single entities (not as waves) as demonstrated in Fig: 5-2 below.

Now we also know that subatomic, atomic and even some molecules, when fired at the double-slit sheet, arrive at the detection screen displaying light and dark bands indicating an 'interference pattern' of light travelling in waves as in Fig: 5-1 above.

It has also been demonstrated, within this experiment, that when one of the slits, say the left, was covered and light was shone through just the right slit, it arrived at the detector screen as particles just like the bullets. The same result occurred when the right slit only was covered and light shone through the left slit. Then should the results of the two separate slit firings be combined, the particles displayed on the detection screen had the distribution similar to particles/bullets as in Fig: 5-2. So, let us restate this again to be clear. When light or other particles are sent through both open slits, they arrive showing the interference pattern of a wave. Yet, when sent through either slit with the other covered they arrive as particles on the detector screen as one would expect bullets to arrive.

**Double-slit experiment with light as particles/bullets**

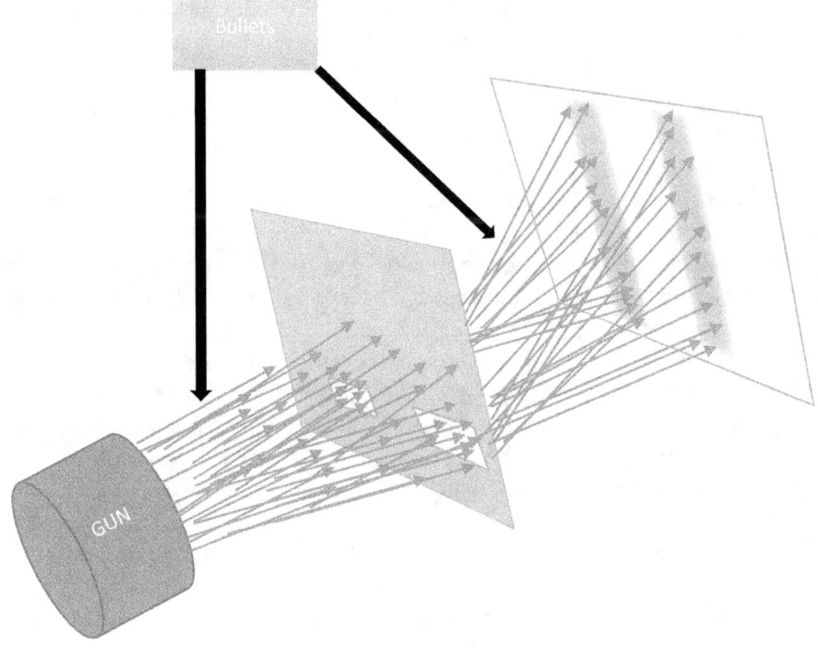


**Fig: 5-2**

Following this discovery, physicists were stumped as to which slit each particle, via waves, went through when they were both open, so they put a checking (measuring) device on one of the slits. This device revealed that a number went through the measured slit okay, but another number went through the other slit arriving at the detector screen as if they had gone through separately like the bullets. There was no interference pattern. The conclusion then was that when it was measured, that is knowing which slit the beam or stream went through, it became a particle, but unmeasured as to which slit, it became a wave. And so, the notion resulted that they were both waves and particles at the same time, known as the wave/particle duality. Biologist Johnjoe McFadden advises, "The experiment with two holes reveals the wave particle duality of both matter and radiation. Photons may be emitted as particles, they may be detected as particles, but when unwatched, they travel through space as waves." (Mc Fadden, 2000, p. 157)

Let us recap here and think of the stream of photons, electrons, atoms, or even some molecules flowing towards the two-slits and suppose we know that we have exactly 100 such items say 100 electrons for the experiment. We send them off towards the two open slits and they arrive on the detection screen displaying the interference pattern of a wave. Next, we close e.g. the left slit and send the electrons off through the right open slit, the result is they arrive at the detection screen with a distribution as one would expect individual bullets to arrive. The same process with the same result is carried out closing the right slit and leaving the left open. So, were we to combine both sets of particles, that arrive via the single open slits, they show only what would be expected if we fired bullets.

The next step is to put a measuring device on top of the one slit and that will tell us which of the one hundred electrons actually goes through that slit. Then with both slits open our measuring device should tell us that perhaps 50 go through the measured slit and therefore presumably the other 50 go through the other slit. But extraordinarily the result on the detection screen shows no interference pattern, rather it is the same as if we sent 50 through each slit separately. From this it was concluded that we collapsed the wave function, with observation (by looking at, or with a measuring device), either directly or indirectly. We also learn, it appears, that putting a measuring device on just one of the slits, somehow, tells the electrons going through the other how to act! In addition we do not know why each electron goes through one slit or the other?

The experiment has now got to the point that it is possible to carry it out by slowing electrons down to just one at a time going through the slits and it seems each goes through both slits at the same time via the wave function. Indeed, it has also been carried out with three slits and the results all come out the same. On top of this there are other bizarre outcomes within this experiment with the turning on and off or moving the position of the measuring device. One of such was proposed by John Wheeler and is known as the 'Delayed choice experiment'. With this, the experiment is set up the same, except that we do not observe the which- slit or have not set up a measuring device to find out the which-slit, until after the particles have gone through the slits. In this a case for example, the measuring device would be near the detection screen. This experiment has been tested and shows that once the measuring device is switched on well after the which-slit decision is made the wave function collapses. Stephen Hawking and Leonard Mlodinow point out that, "Wheeler even considered a cosmic version of the experiment, in which the particles involved are photons emitted by powerful quasars billions of light years away. Such light could be split into two paths and refocused towards earth by the gravitational lensing of an intervening galaxy. Though the experiment is beyond the reach of current technology, if we could collect enough photons from this light, they ought to form an interference pattern. Yet if we place a device to measure which-path information shortly before detection, that pattern should disappear. The choice whether to take one or both paths in this case would have been made billions of years ago, before the earth or perhaps even our sun was formed, and yet with our observation in the laboratory we will be affecting that choice." (Hawking & Mlodinow, 2010, p. 83).

It must be pointed out here that this 'delayed choice' experiment is not saying that we can change the past and so affect the future, rather it is saying that doing something in the present can have an effect on the past. In other words, the past or history accommodates present activities. In effect we can undo the past.[56] This notion has some significant questions to answer regarding the way the past exists for us in the quantum world. We will revisit this at a later time.

When particles are acting as waves it is known as the 'wave function' or the 'superposition of position states'. Physicist Steven Manly advises that "Physicists call this complex, potentially infinite-dimensional space in which the quantum

56 Brian Greene elaborates, "What if, just before the photon hits the detection screen, you eliminate the possibility of determining through which slit it passed by erasing the mark imprinted by the tagging device?..............In an experiment carried out by Raymond Chiao, Paul Kwiat, and Aephraim Steinberg...with a new erasure device inserted just in front of the detection screen....the eraser works by ensuring that regardless of whether a photon from the left slit or the right slit enters, its spin is manipulated to point in one and the same fixed direction. Subsequent examination of its spin therefore yields no information about which slit it passed through, and so the which-path mark has been erased. Remarkably, the photons detected by the screen after this erasure *do* produce an interference pattern. When the eraser is inserted just in front of the detector screen, it undoes—it erases—the effect of tagging the photons way back when they approached the slits. As in the delayed choice experiment, in principle this kind of erasure could occur billions of years after the influence it is thwarting, in effect undoing the past, even undoing the ancient past." (Greene B., 2005, pp. 192-193)

mechanical states are specified *Hilbert space*". (Manly, 2011, p. 77) Put simply, the wave function is the realm of potentialities and possibilities until it is collapsed into the classical world we understand. McFadden elaborates, 'superposition', "When a photon travels through the screen, the photon is said to exist as a quantum superposition of a photon going through the left slit *and* one going through the right. Neither possibility (photon passing through the right or left slit) is entirely real on its own. Quantum superposition is a basic ingredient of quantum mechanics. It may, as we have seen, refer to a superposition of position states (a particle in two places at once) but it can equally describe a superposition of momentum states, energy states, angle of polarization, angle of spin, or indeed any property of a quantum system." (Mc Fadden, 2000, pp. 157-158)

A superposition of all position states literally means all states, whatever they could be? It should be noted here that quantum states persist in all matter, from particles to elephants, but in the bigger objects we cannot see them. McFadden explains, "The principle of quantum superposition of states knows no size limit. It is perfectly valid in standard quantum mechanics to describe my being in two places at the same time or doing two things at once......it is only the *evidence* for *quantumness* - the interference effects - that have vanished from the world. Individual particles still exist, as quantum superpositions; we just don't see them. The quantum weirdness is hidden, but is still there." (Mc Fadden, 2000, p. 164 & 215)

There were numerous contributors to quantum theory in the early part of the 20th century for example, Werner Heisenberg and Erwin Schrodinger both developed theories in different ways[57], but both represented the same thing. Heisenberg also developed what is known as the 'Uncertainty Principle'. This means that at a quantum level there are certain limitations to information, e.g. it is not possible to know the position of a particle precisely if we know its speed precisely and likewise we cannot know the speed precisely if we know the position. These are things we can establish easily in the classical world but not in the quantum world. In fact the nearer you get to be precise about one the less you get to be precise about the other.[58] Eugenie

---

57 Heisenberg's 'matrix mechanics' and Schrodinger's, probability wave equation. Niels Bohr developed the standard interpretation while John von Neumann developed the mathematics.

58 "And so we are faced with a quantum-mechanical balancing act. If we use high frequency (short wavelength) light we can locate an electron with greater precision. But high frequency photons are very energetic and therefore sharply disturb the electron's velocity. If we use low frequency (long wavelengths) light we minimize the impact on the electron's motion, since the constituent photons have comparatively low energy, but we sacrifice precision in determining the electron's position. Heisenberg quantified this competition and found a mathematical relationship between the precision with which one measures the electrons position and the precision with which one measures its velocity." (Greene B., 2000, pp. 112-113)

Reich writing in *New scientist* tells us why, "Measuring one makes the other more uncertain. That's because individual particles are considered parts of a probability 'wave', in which many possible combinations of position and momentum exist simultaneously." (Reich, 2009) The more precisely you measure one the more the wave of the other spreads out in space. Indeed, we can cite the uncertainty principle then as the reason, within the 'double slit experiment', we cannot determine which slit a particle goes through.

Erwin Schrodinger also contributed further by bringing to light the notion of 'Entanglement'. This occurs when two particles interact with each other and then separate with the result each separate particle has an innate understanding and connection with the other. This situation prevails even if each are on either side of the universe. Einstein was not at all happy with this notion and referred to it as 'spooky action at a distance'. Philosopher David Albert and scientist Rivka Galchen writing in *Scientific American* note, "Entanglement may connect particles irrespective of where they are, what they are and what forces they may exert on one another—in principle, they could perfectly well be an electron and a neutron on opposite sides of the galaxy. Thus, entanglement makes for a kind of intimacy amid matter previously undreamt of." (Albert & Galchen, 2009)

Irish physicist John Bell devised a method to see if this 'entanglement' was true, as it raised the problem of information seemingly being transferred, from one entangled particle to the other, faster than the speed of light. To date, a number of experiments have shown, via the John Bell process, that it appears there is 'spooky action at a distance' where the properties of one particle are known to the other.

The next two paragraphs are again for 'nice to know' information, as well as to highlight more of the strangeness of the quantum world. The important thing to take from these paragraphs is that, at the quantum level, there is a constant fluctuation/interaction with particles together with the decay of some particles into others and indeed, the spontaneous arrival of others, out of nowhere, only to vanish just as quickly.

An important aspect of the quantum world is quantum field theory. Quantum fields are somewhat different to e.g. gravitational fields etc. of the classical world. Lisa Randall explains, quantum fields, "create or absorb elementary particles. According to quantum field theory, particles can be produced or destroyed anywhere and at any time." (Randall, 2006, p. 158) Throughout empty space at a temperature of -270.3°c there is still a buzz of quantum fluctuations with particles and antiparticles popping into existence and then annihilating each other. Quantum activity appears to slow down the nearer it gets to absolute freezing -273.15°c but this temperature is non-reachable[59] (just like the speed of light).

A quantum field theory discovered by Nobel physicist, Richard Feynman, called quantum electrodynamics (QED), is the quantum field theory applied to electromagnetism. He explains, it is a "fundamental theory of the interaction of light and matter, or electric field and charges. (Feynman, 1998, p. 37) This is the fundamental electromagnetic force at work exchanging its force carrier, the photon, in its interactions. Regarding the interactions of the other three fundamental forces, gravity's force carrier is thought to be the 'graviton' while the weak and strong nuclear forces use different force carriers. The result is a constant activity of interaction at the quantum level. In addition more interactions within atoms were proposed when Nobel-prize winning physicist, Murray Gell-Mann and others proposed a quantum field theory called quantum Chromodynamics (QCD) describing interactions in the atomic nucleus with quarks[60]. We have already have seen that the more heat there is, the more jittering it causes to particles. But even if we take the temperature right down to just above absolute freezing we still get fluctuations of particles. Such fluctuations[61] entail the exchanges in quantum fields plus the decay of some particles into others and indeed, the spontaneous arrival of other particles, out of nowhere, only to vanish just as quickly.

Apart from quantum manipulation pervading current 'information technology', there is also research and development into the production of working quantum computers. The results of this R & D is still in its infancy but major breakthroughs are imminent. An ordinary computer works on 'bits' (binary digits 1 and 0) of information whereas a quantum computer works on what are called qubits. Vlatko Vedral elaborates, "As we know, classical bits, by definition, exist in one of two different states at any given time—a zero or a one. With quantum mechanics, however, we are permitted to have a zero and a one at the same time present in a physical system. In fact we are permitted to have an infinite range of states between zero and one—which we call a qubit. The number of states a qubit could occupy is infinite because in principle we can tweak the ratio of probabilities in which the states 0 and 1 occur

---

59 Should absolute freezing be possible to reach quantum activity would stop. This is known as **the Third Law of Thermodynamics.**

60 Gell-Mann got the word quarks from reading James Joyce's *Finnegan's wake* 'Three quarks for Muster Mark! /Sure has not got much of a bark/

61 *Everything* is subject to the quantum fluctuations inherent in the uncertainty principle—even the gravitational field. Although classical reasoning implies that empty space has zero gravitational field, quantum mechanics shows that on average it is zero, but that its actual value undulates up and down due to quantum fluctuations. (Greene B., 2000, p. 127)

to any desired accuracy. When with certainty we have either 0 or 1 then this reduces to the classical case." (Vedral V., 2010, p. 137)

Richard Feynman of QED fame was one of the first in 1982, to put forward the notion of a universal quantum simulator (a quantum computer). Developing this further, David Deutsch, in 1985 proved that under quantum physics there is a universal quantum computer, and has noted that, *"quantum computers* can perform computations of which (no) human mathematician, will ever, even in principle, be capable." (Deutsch, 1998, p. 132) Then in 1996, Quantum mechanical engineer at MIT, Seth Lloyd, "showed that conventional quantum computers were themselves universal quantum simulators." (Lloyd, 2010, p. 150) And in Lloyd's book *Programming the Universe* he equates the universe itself to a quantum computer. "Because the universe can perform quantum computation and a quantum computer can simulate the universe, the universe and a quantum computer have the same information-processing power: they are essentially identical." (Lloyd S., 2007, p. 149) I will have more to say on this in later chapters.

With quantum reality we can now consider two major universal phenomena in a different light. The first of these is the beginning of the universe itself and the second is the beginning of life itself! Regarding the universe, we saw earlier that the 'Big Bang', was based on a single point (the singularity) and this represents a classical basis. A quantum basis however, would mean that the singularity point was not clear, rather it was a probabilistic situation in the superposition of every universe type possible. Paul Davies tells us that John Wheeler, was first to propose this notion, "in the 1960's, (it was he) who argued that quantum uncertainty would fuzz out the singularity, replacing the infinite curvature of spacetime with something gentler and more complex". (Davies, 2007, p. 86) Then there is a notion that life itself probably emerged from the quantum superposition of states, of the required compound chemicals, to collapse into the first classical life form.

## String Theory:

To delve further into the world of quantum, a brief examination of 'string theory' will add to the quantum interpretation picture.

String theory began life based on the idea that each particle is not a dot but an extremely small string, or to put it more precisely the vibration of an extremely small string. In other words, if you take the string on a violin and pluck it you will get a specific vibration, pluck it harder to get another vibration. Each vibration, according to string theory, represents a different particle, depending of its energy. To have an idea of the size of strings, think first of the size of an atom. Piers Bizony tells us the atom is, "about a tenth of a millionth of a millimetre across.....The width of the finest hair is longer than the span of one million carbon atoms stretched out in a row." (Bizony, 2007, p. xvi) The nucleus of an atom is more than 10,000 times smaller than the atom itself, and we know that the nucleus is made up of protons and neutrons. Now consider that the strings of string theory are actually some hundred billion times, smaller than a proton. Regardless of the string size, however, string theory, as stated earlier, is thought to accommodate the unification of the four fundamental forces of nature and therefore finally create the 'Theory of Everything'.

There were five different models of string theory constructed during its development each of which required additional space dimensions to be added to our accepted three dimensions of space and one of time. John Gribbin notes, that in addition there was a sixth theory, known as supergravity, which required eleven dimensions However, in 1995 physicist Ed Witten, showed that the different models were all part of the same thing, "(and that included eleven-dimensional supergravity)" (Gribbin J., 2009, p. 152) Most of the dimensions are impossible for us to see due to their small size but the eleventh dimension may in fact be a much bigger brane[62], attached to our 'three space one time' brane, but impossible to travel to.

Strings are purported to come as either open or closed. An open string is a simple two ended string, each end can attach to a particular brane and therefore to its dimensions. A closed string is a loop. The 'Graviton'[63] is a vibration of a looped string, that is, both ends are attached to each other. This means that they are not attached to a particular brane and its dimensions. Therefore it can move or slide from one brane to another. This is believed to be the reason that gravity is such a weak force, compared to the other fundamental three, in our spacetime as it leaks its strength, or some of it, to other branes. So it seems strings may or may not be connected to particular branes. Nonetheless, we are confined to our own brane of three space and one time dimensions. However, there is the possibility of communication between branes. Physicist Lisa Randall explains "bulk particles could interact with particles on one brane and subsequently interact with particles on a distant brane, thereby permitting the particles that are confined to separated branes to communicate indirectly." (Randall, 2006, p. 327)[64]

---

62 It was when I read Physicist Lisa Randall's informative popular science book, 'Warped Passages' that I first got interested in branes. She makes the point, "Branes took the physics community by storm in 1995, when the physicist Joe Polchinski of the Kavli Institute for Theoretical Physics (KITP) in Santa Barbara established that they were essential to string theory". (Randall, 2006, pp. 50-51)

63 The hypothetical force carrier of gravity (not yet confirmed).

64 "Unlike a brane, the bulk extends in all directions. The bulk spans every dimension, both on and off the brane." (Randall, 2006, p. 53)

The theory overtime also had name changes, going from 'string' to 'superstring' theory, and finally M-theory[65]. This present status M- theory, requires 10 space dimensions and 1 time dimension a total of eleven dimensions in all. The reason it was called superstring was because in the 1970s additional particles were discovered[66]. All fermions (matter particles) were found to have a super boson (force particle) partner, or if preferred all bosons were found to have a super fermion partner. This doubled the number of particles believed to exist. So here were particles with different 'spins' combined in partnership that, as physicist Michael Brooks tells us, "will behave the same in any experiment" (Brooks, 2010, p. 188). Now we know that the universe is symmetrical as discussed in chapter 2, but here was a case of 'supersymmetry'. This meant that the strings in 'string' theory itself were supersymmetrical and so were named 'superstrings'. M-theory with its branes and strings is the big hope to at last bring the four fundamental forces together. Indeed, it should be noted also that within string theory there appears to be a realization of holography! But more on this later.

In conclusion then Shakespeare was right on the button when he made the observation in Hamlet that 'there are more things in heaven and earth etc.' Certainly, the quantum world, prior to its enlightenment, was not dreamed of by classically based scientists, as in it we have seen that waves of particular things are superpositions of every possible state. Things act as waves while at the same time act as particles. Other things are in two different places at the same time. Some things don't appear to be there unless we look at them. Indeed, even when we look at some things, other like things know what we are doing. When we do something in the present it can undo the past. When we try to get a measurement on one thing another related thing is impossible to measure accurately. There is 'spooky action at a distance' of which the greatest scientist of the 20th century could not conceive. Indeed, this action at a distance, emanating from the concept of entanglement, gives credence to the notion of the 'whole' inasmuch as when we know that two particles are connected no matter how far apart, so also must all particles have been connected in the one dot that Big Banged. But we have only skimmed the surface of quantum physics as there is much I have ignored for convenience. Nonetheless, the information presented will suffice to assist us as we proceed.

Two final notes, (1) regarding the quantum world and holograms, Japanese brain scientist Mari Jibu and theoretical physicist Kunio Yasue tell us, "The principle

---

65 Thought to stand for 'Membrane' or even 'Magical' theory.

66 These additional particles were additional to the antiparticles noted in the previous chapter. If we took an analogy of particles being animals then particles and anti- particles would be male and female or vice versa. However, regarding the fermion and boson partnership, still with the animal analogy, one would be a chicken and the other a crocodile! No wonder this partnership was considered 'super'.

behind the optical holograph, that is, the stereoscopic image, is neither too sophisticated nor difficult to understand. It uses the **interference** effect of waves, as in the double-slit experiment for electrons or photons." (Jibu & Yasue, 1995, p. 133) And (2) on quantum theory itself, Physicists Bruce Rosenblum and Fred Kuttner advise it "is the most stunningly successful theory in all of science. Not a single one of its predictions has ever been wrong. Quantum mechanics has revolutionized the world. One-third of our economy depends on products based on it." (Rosenblum & Kuttner, 2007, p. 3)

Now that we have had some exposure to the world of quantum we will turn, in the next chapter, to how some of it may be interpreted. In this, the amazement of the quantum continues, but in a higher gear.

## CHAPTER 6

# Quantum Interpretations

There are numerous interpretations and attempts to explain the quantum phenomenon. Let me now give you my understanding of some of them.

### Copenhagen Interpretation:

I'll start with the so-called 'standard' or Copenhagen interpretation, a la Niels Bohr (1888-1962). This put simply states that an object does not exist until it is registered i.e. observed/measured. The observation brings it into existence. That is, it collapses the wave function or superpositions. This interpretation is dependent of course on consciousness. But what was the case before life had consciousness? John Wheeler, went so far as to believe we lived in a 'participatory universe' "wherein the universe depends for its existence on conscious observers to make it real, not only today but retrospectively right back to the Big Bang!" (Mc Fadden, 2000, p. 195).

Erwin Schrodinger thought this interpretation was ridiculous, and so he devised a thought experiment to make his point. It is known as 'Schrodinger's cat' experiment, and has become quite famous, or infamous as far as Stephen Hawking is concerned. Hawking is believed to have said something like, 'If I hear about that cat once more I'm going for my gun' presumably to shoot the cat. But let me take the risk and give you a flavour of the experiment.

*A metal box contains a cat, along with a Geiger counter, some radioactive material and a bottle of poison (the bottle of poison has a hammer attached poised to smash the bottle). The radioactive material, according to quantum mechanics, has the probability or not to decay within say one hour. Should it decay it will cause the hammer to break the bottle and so poison the cat to death.*

*The experiment involves the box being closed so nothing inside can be seen or heard. At the end of the hour one may only find out the fate of the cat by observing/ opening the box. Prior to opening it the cat can either be alive or dead.*

The Copenhagen interpretation, Schrodinger pointed out, would have us believe that the cat was both alive and dead at the same time prior to opening the box, and it was only the observation of opening and looking inside that determined the cat's fate.

## Hidden Variables Interpretation:

Einstein was not at all happy with The Copenhagen interpretation and in fact, he and his friend, physicist David Bohm, preferred to believe that there was something in the process that was hidden and not yet apparent or discovered. This would then account for the weirdness of the quantum realm. Bohn advises that e.g. "Newtonian mechanics was thought to be of completely universal validity...., but this had to give way to the theory of relativity..... (Then) in its turn classical mechanics had to give way to quantum mechanics. (Bohm D., 1980, p. 105) Quantum mechanics then, will have to give way to something else that is currently undiscovered. Bohm's 'hidden variables' he called 'the quantum potential'. In his theory, the wave function is a 'pilot wave' or 'radar wave' that guides the particle that is there all the time but hidden.

Physicist Basil Hiley, a long standing collaborator of Bohm explains the thinking behind this in a BBC interview with fellow physicist Paul Davies. His example would be to think of, "a ship which is guided by radar waves; the radar waves are fed into the ship's computer, and the ship then adjusts its direction depending upon the information it receives from the radar waves." (Davies & Brown, 1993, p. 138) In this interpretation the wave function is sometimes called the 'pilot wave' and it exists simultaneously with the particle. The pilot wave conveys the measuring device's presence to the particle that is always there but hidden. In other words the particle does not pop into reality by way of observation it is there all the time but hidden. It is an attempt to interpret the process as deterministic. The radar/pilot wave guides the ship/particle.

This interpretation should have been received as one valid approach to the 'measurement problem'. It did not however, because, the famous John von Neumann wrote a seminal mathematical book in favour of the Copenhagen interpretation and therefore it became the accepted 'standard'. Indeed, according to astrophysicist John Gribbin, Neumann's book, also contained "what seemed to be a mathematical proof that no hidden-variables theory could ever properly describe the behaviour of entities in the quantum world." (Gribbin J., 1996, p. 154) It turned out though that von Neumann, one of the most respected and renowned mathematicians at the time, got the maths wrong and John Bell later showed that hidden variable theories can be made to work in the quantum realm. But unfortunately, the Copenhagen interpretation remained standard for many years.

Another reason Bohm's theory may not have been accepted, into so-called main stream scientific society, was political. Bohm, when at Princeton University was an assistant professor, and while there he worked with his friend Einstein. However, in 1949 he was called before the House of Un-American Activities Committee to testify against other friends and colleagues who were suspected communists. Bohm refused to testify, taking the 5th amendment. The result was he was sacked from Princeton and had to leave the US. He eventually settled in the UK, where he somehow got to be branded as a mystic, further downgrading his scientific standing.

Speaking to Paul Davies in the same BBC programme noted above, Bohm explains that quantum mechanics suggests "that phenomenal reality comes about from a deeper order in which it is enfolded. Reality unfolds to produce the visible order and folds back in." (Davies & Brown, 1993, p. 121) Enfolded he called the 'implicate order' and unfolded he called the 'explicate order'. Indeed, one of the extraordinary things he did was to liken this notion to a hologram which he called the 'Holomovement'. He confirmed to Paul Davies, how his notion was like a hologram in that "we see that a pattern is enfolded into a photographic plate, and when you shine a light on it it's unfolded into a visible image. Each part of the photographic plate contains information about the whole. So the whole is unfolding from each region." (Davies & Brown, 1993, p. 122) This is especially extraordinary as Bohm's holomovement theory was detailed in his 1980 publication, whereas the notion of the 'holographic principle' was not proposed until the 1990s.

## Many worlds interpretation:

Just to clarify, this 'many worlds' notion may also be referred to as the 'multiverse' or 'parallel universes'. The interpretation is very popular among physicists as it leaves observation and consciousness out of the equation, so to speak. However, different people explain this concept in different ways. One thing it is not, and that is a notion of universes begin by breaking off from other universes to form multi universes similar to a bubbles breaking off from a bigger bubble.

This 'many worlds' interpretation of the quantum phenomenon proposes that what we think of as a collapse of the wave function is simply a branching off into a particular universe from the myriad of universes that exist. So, we neither see nor feel anything different we just go in a different direction. Think of it as going along a road and you come to a fork, one branches off to the left and the other to the right. What happens is you decide to go left and off you go, but another you, goes on to the right in another universe! There are different approaches to this interpretation. Hugh Everett, the originator of the theory, was a student of John Wheeler when he first proposed the notion of every time a choice is made, in a quantum system, the world branches off to follow that choice. Wheeler was concerned with this radical interpretation, and in his autobiography written with Kenneth Ford he tells us that, "An oversimplified way to describe the outcome of his (Everett's) reasoning is to say that all of the things that might happen (with various probabilities) are in fact happening" (Wheeler & Ford, 2000, p. 269). Wheeler tells us that he spent many hours working on this paper with Everett and when it was submitted for publication to *Reviews of Modern Physics,* he himself also sent in a paper entitled "Assessment of Everett's 'Relative State' Formulation of Quantum Theory". Wheeler also tells us that it was his friend, fellow physicist Bryce DeWitt who chose to call the Everett interpretation the 'many worlds' interpretation. Wheeler was not happy with this title and preferred his own title of 'relative state' formulation. Nonetheless, 'many worlds' and 'parallel universes' have become almost standard when referring to the Everett theory.

Philosopher David Chalmers, tells us, "The splitting view is frequently attributed to Everett (largely due to the expositions of Everett's work by DeWitt (1970, 1971), but cannot be found in his writings..." (Chalmers D. J., 1996, p. 347). A very strong advocate of this theory is Oxford physicist, David Deutsch and in an interview with fellow physicist Paul Davies (same BBC programme as above) he gives his view, "The idea is that there are parallel entire universes which include all galaxies, stars and planets, all existing at the same time, and in a certain sense in the same space. And normally not communicating with each other." (Davies & Brown, 1993, p. 83). Deutsch believes these other universes may be inferred due to processes of what he terms tangible particles and shadow particles leading to a tangible universe and shadows universes.[67]

The many worlds interpretation is also sometimes extended to what is called a 'many minds' interpretation. There seems however, to be some confusion as to what this 'many minds' interpretation actually is. Steven Manly advises thus, "As far as I can tell, the many-worlds theory and the many-minds theory really differ in ways that would interest a philosopher more than a physicist. In both cases the fully unitary evolution of the universal wave function happens. In many worlds, different streams

[67] For those interested in Deutsch's thoughts on this see 'Shadows' chapter in *The Fabric of Reality* (Deutsch, 1998)

of reality evolve separated in Hilbert space and there is no way for an observer in one stream to perceive what is happening in a different stream. In the many minds view, the splitting is one of our perception. We are only able to perceive particular streams that correspond to the classically accepted potential realities that are the emergent streams in many worlds." (Manly, 2011, pp. 84-85)

From this many worlds/many minds interpretation, it is my contention that our choices produce outcomes and every choice we make actually changes the world and this is happening over and over again. There is no doubt that this scenario can be difficult to accept, however, a look at 'Chaos Theory' may help us appreciate the concept a little better. In this regard most of us will remember the following Rhyme from Benjamin Franklin, or at least a story in the same context.

*For the want of a nail the shoe was lost,*
*For the want of a shoe the horse was lost,*
*For the want of the horse the rider was lost,*
*For the want of the rider the battle was lost,*
*For the want of a battle the kingdom was lost,*
*All for the want of a horseshoe-nail*

The message is clear; small things often can and do have enormous repercussions. I am sure most readers will also have heard of the 'Butterfly Effect' as often quoted when referring to 'Chaos theory'. What it is saying basically is that if a butterfly flaps its wings in Japan, this can have an effect on the weather on the west coast of Ireland, or for that matter anywhere.

So, let me bring this back to the parallel or many worlds situation. If I live in my world in Sydney and I have to make a decision to take a bus, or drive to the beach, then whichever way the decision goes it will affect my own world and or the worlds of numerous others. Of course a decision I make in Europe or Australia may have little, or no seeming effect on something/person living in California in the US, but in reality, at the minutest level it does, although it cannot be felt. Yet, some choices have enormous effects for example, if some country leader decides to declare war on another country. Or even, if a government decides to change their economic policies, this can have major effects on its citizens and indeed on other countries with which it does business. All decisions and choices have effects and these effects have other effects, all the time changing the decision maker's world and the world of everyone else. Parallel worlds are constantly being created. Deutsch believes, "Physical reality is the set of all the universes evolving together, like a machine in which some cogwheels are connected to other cogwheels; you cannot move one without moving the others. So the parallel universes are connected as inextricably as the universes of the past and the future. (Davies & Brown, 1993, p. 89)

The many worlds interpretation of quantum mechanics is a way of keeping the act of observation out of the measurement problem. It claims there is no collapse. Rather, there is a smooth, unfelt transition from an existing world into another. Such worlds are all around us but we cannot communicate with them, nor they with us. However, Deutsch believes they do have effects on us via interference. I will visit this interpretation again when discussing choices in the chapter on 'Consciousness'.

## Richard Feynman Interpretation:

This interpretation, proposed by Richard Feynman, is based on the notion of many histories. How this works, it seems, is that prior to measurement we are faced with many histories or paths to arrive at our measurement point. This is not just the history that we are familiar with but it is all possible histories. It is explained by the following example; suppose you are in a room and you want to get to the other side, from point A to point B, by the quickest path. Obviously, according to classical mechanics the straight line/path from one side to the other would be the way to go. But with the quantum 'many histories' interpretation of reality, Kaku explains, "as odd as it may seem, every time you walk across the room, somehow your body 'sniffs out' all possible paths ahead of time, even those extending to the distance quasars and the big bang, and then adds them up". (Kaku, 2005, p. 164) With the many histories interpretation, we can take numerous paths that bring us various ways around the room before we get to our objective point on the other side. Indeed, Feynman tells us we can even take off out of the room and go via the other side of the universe before returning and reaching our destination. By mathematically adding up every option/history, Feynman reached the probability path to take, and in most cases this averaged out as the same path as the classical process would have predicted.

## Decoherence Interpretation:

In this interpretation the term 'decoherence' may be used the same as the term 'collapse' of the wave function. Decoherence/collapse occurs when particles that are so-called coherent (quantum-like), within the quantum system, interact with other particles that are not coherent e.g. classical or already collapsed particles. This interaction causes the coherent particles to become decoherent or classical-like. In other words decoherence happens due to the classical environment the quantum particle finds itself in. The classical particles are, so to speak, the measuring devices. Remember, particles are constantly interacting with each other. We know this happens all the time with particles above absolute freezing, and indeed the warmer it gets the more jiggling takes place and the more interaction there is. McFadden explains that, "(Polish Physicist) Wojciech Zurek working at California's Institute of Technology has proposed that the reason why the entire world appears classical to us is because of decoherence. Just as an electron beam may be bombarded with photons, so any open system is continually bombarded with photons, electrons, atoms, and other particles. The quantum system will eventually become entangled with the fate of billions of particles in its environment, and this entanglement will cause decoherence. Interference effects will be erased, so that the world will appear classical. The environment will *measure* the quantum system." (Mc Fadden, 2000, pp. 214-215). This interpretation is extremely popular, indeed probably the most popular amongst scientists, as it, like the many worlds, interprets the move from quantum to classical without conscious observation.

Seth Lloyd refers to decoherence as the creation of information, in that it, "effectively creates new bits of information, bits which previously did not exist. In other words, quantum mechanics, via decoherence, is constantly injecting new bits of information into the world. Every detail that we see around us, every vein on a leaf, every whorl on a fingerprint, every star in the sky, can be traced back to some bit that quantum mechanics created. Quantum bits program the universe." (Lloyd, 2010, pp. 99-100) Indeed these bits emanate from the periphery/horizon of our universe. Now remembering, as stated above, the notion of particles 'that are confined to separated branes being permitted to communicate indirectly' there is the possibility that the information for the programming may in fact be initiated from a higher dimensional brane!

Questions have been raised by many prominent scientists on how decoherence naturally collapses to one state and not another? Is chance involved in nature's choice from so many possibilities? Mathematician Max Tegmark advises in this regard, that continued work on decoherence by Wojciech Zurek, has shown that, "not only does it explain why large objects never seem to be in two places at once, but it explains why conventional states (such as being in only one place) are so special: out of all the states that quantum mechanics allows for large objects, these conventional states are the ones that are most robust to decoherence, and therefore the ones that survive. It's a bit like why deserts tend to have cacti rather than roses." (Tegmark, 2014, p. 211) In other words not alone is decoherence caused by the jiggling of the environment, but it decoheres into a state to fit the environment.

From as far back as we know decoherence has made up the classical world we live in. So, decoherence follows the environment set out before it and fits in. For example, a rock would not decohere to have no gravity or a flower does not decohere to speak! Rather decoherence follows into conventional states, or natural classical states. But how does it know what the environment is or what to decohere? The simple answer is entanglement. From the beginning of the universe as the fuzzy singularity everything was together/entangled as one and once entangled all particles/information have instant quantum communication abilities faster than the speed of light. However, it may well be that there is also a contrived decoherence, and this we will examine further in the chapter on consciousness.

To conclude this chapter then it now seems that there is an objective reality out there, without our conscious observation, caused by decoherence. But of course we cannot truly know this! The reason is simply that, as far as we are concerned things only exist for us if we are conscious to experience them.

Each of the above interpretations has its followers and indeed its own logic of sorts. The 'Copenhagen' interpretation has its merits in that for us to appreciate anything we must have conscious experience of it. Measurement by observation certainly collapses the wave function so this interpretation is not without a certain credibility. The 'hidden variables' interpretation is not unlike the Copenhagen, replacing the wave function with a pilot wave. For this reason it had some of the credibility of the Copenhagen but it also has an element of hedging one's bets for future developments. In addition now, with the correction of the original maths that excluded this interpretation as a legitimate contender, together with Bohm's attractive holographic proposition, it is a definite credible interpretation. The 'many histories' interpretation is somewhat similar to the two above as the histories arrive as perhaps a bunch of wave function superpositions! The 'many worlds' along with the 'decoherence' interpretations do not require a conscious observer as there is either, a smooth branch off for the former, or the environment itself causes the collapse, of informational bits, into the classical world for the latter.

# CHAPTER 7
# Information

In many ways this is the pivotal chapter of the book. It is where the previous chapters have been leading us, and it is from here that the final chapters will take their positions. I have noted from the beginning, and illustrated in Fig: 1-1 that the most fundamental property of our universe and therefore nature itself is information. It is the essence from which everything else comes. John Wheeler was one of the first to recognise this and simplified it in his 'It from bit' statement. It should also be noted that apart from Information technology (IT), giving rise to the 'Information Age', many scientists, economists, and numerous experts from other disciplines all now refer to information to convey procedures and developments emanating from their field.

Prior to our examination of the nature and processes of information however, it is probably appropriate to have a quick review on some of the pertinent information we have gleaned thus far on our journey.

The universe itself has evolved from the Big Bang to reach the vast expanse it is today. Within this expanse is a planet called earth, that, for whatever reason, had the chemical wherewithal and environment to spawn the first simple life-form. Life then evolved progressively to its most sophisticated complex form, the human being. Human beings, apart from natural evolution also acquired physical and cognitive skills that were used for further progress. No matter what the progress however, there was and is no escaping the entropy of complete disintegration and disorder of ourselves and everything else[68].

[68] Except for Boltzmann's extreme outside possibility of the contrary.

The skills and knowledge acquired however, have also shown that natural progress, together with progress from acquired skills and knowledge, are based on mechanical automatism. Nonetheless, with our intuitive belief that we do enact conscious choices and actions, the human species instigated further progress in knowledge, with the discovery and application of quantum physics, M-theory, and quantum computation. Indeed, this knowledge has led us to conclude that the universe is a quantum computer that programs itself with bits, by the process of decoherence that is projected holographically. In order to reach such a stage of scientific and societal sophistication though, human beings have had to strive to progress as noted above against the tidal pull of entropy.

Two lessons arise from this brief review; (1) There is an inherent growth desire within humans to progress for self and loved ones, and (2) this desire enables obstacles to be overcome to reach the progress goals.

To understand more fully how information plays such a fundamental role in nature we must revisit the Second Law of thermodynamics. Remember the Second Law was entropy ('everything disintegrating into a state of disorder to eventually reach maximum equilibrium'). We have seen that Boltzmann's 'Statistical mechanics' moved the notion of entropy on a notch. If you remember it was noted that Boltzmann's entropy was based on a probability distribution. For example, if you had a large box divided into two sections one side filled with high energy gas and the other side filled with low energy gas. Then you remove the divider and the two gases mix until they reach a point of equilibrium namely maximum entropy. Now because the gas molecules/atoms move about bashing off the walls and the top and bottom of the box and indeed banging into each other, there is a probability that at some point all of the gas could end up in one side, or back to where they started, i.e. high energy one side, low energy the other. We know, feel and expect that neither of these situations are likely to happen, but there is always the probability that they might, due to their indiscriminative movements.

It is similar to a fresh uncooked egg falling off the table and splattering onto the floor. We know in our hearts and minds that the bits are not going to recombine and lift back onto the table as a whole egg. Perhaps if somehow the room turned upside down and all the atoms in the egg went back to where they were before. Most unlikely but!!!!!! Boltzmann's entropy however, allows for this extreme probability.

There are cases nonetheless, where such entropy can temporarily be slowed down or even stopped and physical things may be put back to their original state. For example when you buy a new pack of playing cards they usually come in an ordered state of four suits, hearts, clubs, diamonds and spades. Each suit comes ordered 2,3,4,5,6,7,8,9,10, Jack, Queen, King, and Ace. Upon receiving these cards we shuffle them causing as much disorder as possible in order to make the game fair (no numbers predictably following each other). In doing this we have caused maximum or almost maximum entropy with the pack of cards. We can however, separate each suit and put them back to their original state of little or no disorder/entropy.

One can say that nature does the same with life, as it bucks the entropy process by temporarily holding it off, up to death. Evolution also helps by assisting towards greater complexity and order for survival. But re-ordering playing cards and extending life-span are only temporary stops. Eventually all cards and all life will finally disintegrate and dissipate into maximum entropy. We know that we delayed and reversed, temporarily, entropy with the playing cards. But how is it delayed with living beings like ourselves? Some further examination of entropy will be required to fully understand the answer.

Perhaps some readers may think, from the example of the playing cards, that human intervention/knowledge could hold and/or reverse such entropy for ourselves on a more permanent basis? James Clark Maxwell, that is he who combined electricity with magnetism, was of the same opinion and dreamed up a thought experiment that was, until relatively recently, to show that this indeed could well be the case. That is that human intervention could hold/reverse entropy. His experiment now known as 'Maxwell's demon' again took the box divided into two compartments full of molecules. Both compartments contained some fast molecules of a uniform speed and some slow molecules of a uniform speed. With this experiment a little 'demon' was perched on top of the divider with the 'information' ability to discern the fast molecules from the slow molecules. In addition, the demon could allow, through a small opening in the divider, individual molecules to go from one compartment to the other. The demon then proceeded to allow all the fast molecules into the left hand side and all the slow molecules into the right hand side, thus creating order out of disorder or if you like reversing entropy. The demon appeared to violate the Second Law of Thermodynamics and caused great concern in the scientific community for nearly 100 years until it was resolved.

Maxwell's demon was so called because it appeared to have the demonic power to circumvent the entropy process and in this regard we need to examine the notion of information, and its relationship with entropy. Or, as we shall see, entropy is information!

To understand this better we will start with the German mathematician, Gottfried Leibniz, whom, independently of Newton, also created the mathematical process of 'Calculus'. Indeed, it is the Leibniz symbolism that is used in the 'Calculus' process today. Leibniz however, also gave us the 'binary'[69] number system, where numbers are represented by either 0 or 1 or a series of zeros and ones.

The next part of the information story requires a visit to an obscure 19th century English school teacher, George Boole, who taught himself mathematics and later became professor of mathematics at what is now University College Cork. He published *An Investigation of the Laws of Thought* in 1854. In this, he reduced all thought via algebra to just Leibniz's two binary numbers, zeros and ones. The outcome of Boole's work has since become known as 'Boolean logic'. Seth Lloyd, tells us that since the publication of the *Laws of Thought,* "it has been known that any desired logical expression, including complex mathematical calculations, can be built up out of NOT, COPY, AND, and OR. They make up a universal set of logic gates." (Lloyd, 2007, pp. 32-33)[70]

The information story continues then with the master himself, Claude Shannon. In the 1940's, Shannon, an executive researcher with Bell Labs in New Jersey, was trying to work out how best to improve communications e.g. down a telephone wire. He wondered firstly, could more than one two-way conversation be sent down the wire. He then wondered about the content of information through the system and realised that it could be condensed to a minimum, using Boolean logic. Mathematician Sarah Watson explains, "Shannon determined the fundamental unit of information as a yes-no situation and considered this expressed in Boolean two-value binary algebra so that 1 means "on" (the switch is closed and the power is on) and 0 means "off" (the switch is open and the power is off). A unit of information could therefore be expressed as a "binary digit" or "bit" (i.e. 1 or 0), with a combination of "bits" being used to express more complicated information...The idea that information could be transmitted by sending a stream of 1's and 0's down a wire, was at the time fundamentally new. Today it is taken for granted that pictures, words and sounds can be transmitted using this method—it's called digital". (Watson, 2008, p. 333)

Michael Brooks further illuminates. Shannon, "developed techniques for 'compressing' information....... but also found fundamental limitations. Shannon discovered that each communications channel has a maximum capacity, and there is also a maximum efficiency with which information can be sent without it getting lost in transmission....The latest mobile phone and satellite TV systems work to within 1 percent of this 'Shannon limit'. However, they cannot get to it, or get past it. It is a little like the speed of light in relativity." (Brooks, 2010, pp. 194-195). Indeed, it is also like being unable to reach or go beyond absolute freezing.

---

69 See 'Measurements' for the conversion of some common numbers base 10 to binary numbers base 2.

70 "Logic gates are devices that take one or more input bits and transform them into one or more output bits." (Lloyd, 2007, p. 32)

Let us think of a communication where the bits 1 and 0 could be used. Suppose I am in the prestige car sales business and I sell brand AB luxury car. I am aware that a CEO of a major corporation changes her luxury car, for a new model, every two years. Unfortunately the CEO always buys the competitor's brand XY. I have tried in the past to change the CEO's choice but she told me not to bother her again as she would not be changing her brand.

Business had been slow recently, so I decide to quote the CEO a competitive price, for my brand AB, together with details of its features and benefits. In the quote I apologise for bothering her and advise that should she wish to buy at the competitive price just communicate a '1' to me, or should she not wish to buy communicate a '0' to me. I believed there was a 95% chance she would communicate '0', so when I received a '1' communication I was really surprised as the probability of a sale was just 5%. Information then is based on how surprised we are at a given outcome. The more surprised we are the more information we have received. However we can and do attempt to predict the probability of information content. An example would be that there is a 65% probability chance that I will go to the movies tonight. There is also 20% probability chance that if I go to the movies I will meet my friend David. The total probability of me going to the movies and meeting David there is the product of both probabilities namely, 13%. On the other hand, the information content received, should both events occur, will add up to a combination of the two individual events. The information content of an event can be mathematically calculated,[71] however, we do not need to delve into the process.

More complex messages can be sent using strings of zeros and ones, however, the more often used letters or words, the less the number of zeros and ones and, the less often used letters or words, the greater will be the number of zeros and ones. This innovation in information was established mathematically and it enabled Shannon to give it a specific formula. Indeed, the story goes that Shannon asked colleague mathematician John von Neumann what he should call his new formula and von Neumann basically replied that it already had a name, and that being 'entropy'. This was because the formula was almost the same as Boltzmann's entropy formula, but not quite because, as mathematician Sarah Watson advises, "In information theory, 'information' refers to a degree of order or non-randomness that can be measured and treated mathematically." (Watson, 2008, p. 333). Whereas, with Thermodynamic entropy we look at degrees of disorder. Taking both types of entropy together, John Gribbin says it's, "a measure of the amount of (dis)order in a system. The higher the entropy, the less organised and more random the system is;

---

71 The "information content of an event is proportional to the log of its inverse probability of occurrence: $I = \log 1/p$." (Vedral, 2010, p. 29)

the lower the entropy, the more organised it is, with a higher information content." (Gribbin, 2009, p. 210) Paul Davies also explains the two and indeed how each is affected by the other; "Entropy (waste heat) and information are closely related (technically, rising entropy is the same as falling information.)" (Davies P., 2002, p. 114). Or, increasing information is the same as falling entropy.

From this point on when we talk of entropy please consider it as information content. It will also, I believe make things a little clearer by designating entropy as either 'Regressive' or 'Progressive'. Therefore the following will apply:

**(A) Regressive entropy** is decreasing or missing information producing disordered degeneration, and on-going increasing disintegration of the self and the environment toward complete equilibrium. Some practical examples of regressive entropy are, natural disintegration as stated, together with ignorance and/or prevention of information. Regarding ignorance, it is either through not attempting to gain information, or 'Wilful Blindness' to information that is available. Prevention has to do with the suppression or hiding of the general information flow specifically to some groups as well as to society at large. This may be enacted either by ideological beliefs, ignorance, selfishness, thoughtlessness, or simply laziness.

**(B) Progressive entropy** is increasing information to produce ordered generation, and on-going increasing integration of the self and the environment toward greater complexity. Huxley says of this, "It is an anti-entropic process, running counter to the second law of thermodynamics with its degradation of energy and its tendency to uniformity. With the aid of the sun's energy, biological evolution marches uphill, producing increased variety and higher degrees of organisation." (Huxley, 2008) Practical examples of progressive entropy are firstly, temporary prevention where possible, or otherwise management, of regressive entropy. Secondly, informing oneself, together with a contribution to the flow of information to society at large, for use, toward on-going complexity. We are now in a position to look at how life avoids for the Second Law or as designated 'Regressive entropy'.

Probably one of the first to address this issue was none other than Erwin Schrodinger. He did this in lectures given at Trinity College Dublin in 1943. The lectures were titled 'What is Life' and a book of the same name has become a classic in its field. In it Schrodinger uses a slightly different terminology i.e. positive entropy and negative entropy. (Schrodinger, 1967, pp. 70-71) However, what he is saying is that we stay alive by using various foods and drink and energy to extract its 'information' via nutrition or heat. By extracting the information from these sources to keep us alive we are therefore increasing their regressive entropy. In this way, while we temporarily delay our regressive entropy to final equilibrium, we cause regressive entropy elsewhere in the process.

So, let me be clear, in order for us to have progressive entropy we have to cause regressive entropy. We do this by extracting progressive entropy from the environment. It is a necessity for sustenance and energy, but we also do it to satisfy desires. Such extraction requires serious management. For this management to operate at its greatest efficiency every single person in the world needs to participate in it to the best of their ability. Therefore everyone needs to understand the consequences, in this regard, of good or bad management. This in turn therefore means that any action/behaviour that facilitates this management contributes to a better evolving progressive entropy. While on the other hand any action/behaviour that hinders this management accelerates the inevitable regressive entropy.

Human beings then, that are healthy, educated and informed, together with those who are self-less, sharing, undiscriminating, and environmentally/societally caring, no doubt contribute to a superior (albeit temporary) progressive entropy. But, I think we would be hard pressed to find many such saints that tick all these boxes. Nonetheless, such must be our goals. Because, human beings that are unhealthy, ignorant, uneducated and uninformed together with those who are greedy, abusive, discriminating, polluting, exploiting, and war-mongering, accelerate regressive entropy. Indeed, if such human condition and behaviour is left unchecked, the result could be the complete annihilation of the species. So, as may be seen in the flow chart Fig: 7-1 below all progressive entropy extracted, from the progressive entropy environment, eventually ends up in the regressive entropy pool. However, on the positive side excess progressive entropy extracted, over and above necessary and comfortable requirements, for ourselves, family, and group can in fact contribute back to the progressive entropy environment. Such, of course will require positive management and direction.

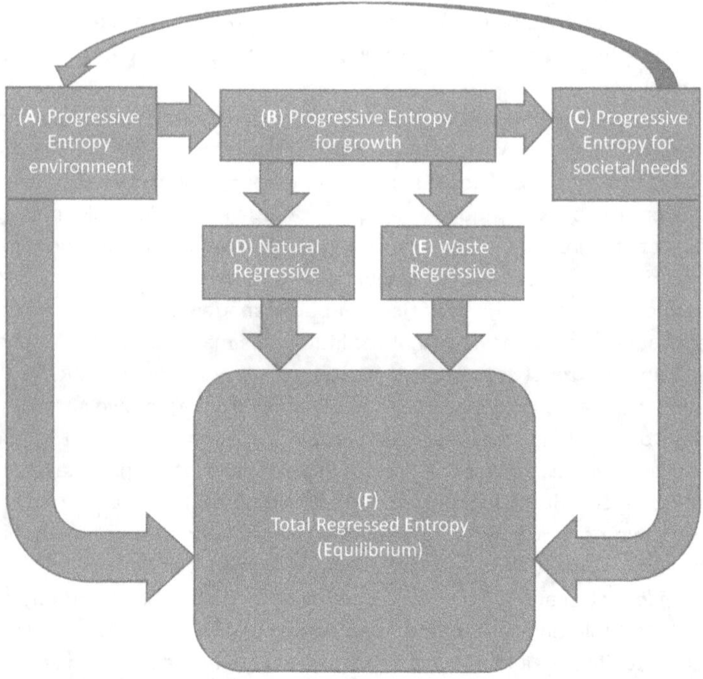


**Fig: 7-1**

## Legend:

(A) This is the environment of progressive entropy available for extraction e.g. food, resources, value etc. Should this not be used/extracted it will automatically disintegrate into (F) regressive entropy.

(B) Here part of the progressive entropy extracted from (A) is used for self and family towards complexity.

(C) This is where excessive progressive entropy is used to enhance the complexity of others, e.g. in employment, health, education, social/public contributions and the Arts etc. In so doing it is increasing/contributing back to the pool of progressive entropy environments.

(D) Here a natural disintegration emanates from that used for self, family etc.

(E) This represents excessive progressive entropy that is basically wasted. This means that it is not used as in (C) or simply accumulated without regard for the need of societal complexity.

(F) Here all progressive entropy used or not will eventually end in total disintegration and equilibrium.

The key to progressive entropy is twofold namely, health and education. There is of course an argument that pervasive good health and education will result in further industrialisation, leading to ever more energy consumption. There are two answers to this argument the first is that good health and education are of themselves contributors of progressive entropy. The second is that just because a state for example, is industrialised it still has the capacity to efficiently manage energy consumption by way of its healthy and educated society. Vlatko Vedral gives examples of different states management skills and or ethical desires in this regard. "If we take GDP (Gross Domestic Product) per capita as a proxy of how developed a society is, then a recent study (2006) shows a very strong correlation between the degree of development and society's energy consumption. At the top of the list we have the USA closely followed by Japan, Australia, UK, France, Germany, and Canada......The shining light in this analysis was clearly Japan, being nearly twice as efficient as the US (in terms of having the same degree of development, but only half the energy consumption)". (Vedral, 2010, pp. 66-67) Greater management of energy usage and sources only comes with education for a better informed society. Then once management is implemented major efficiencies ensue.

## Quantum information:

Is there any correlation with information and quantum reality? I believe there is and in many ways. Different writers favour a specific aspect of quantum mechanics, as the fundamental at its core. So, let me take some of these, with no particular order preference and see how they fit with information.

Firstly, the fact that at its origin remember Planck discovered that quanta were exposed as discrete chunks e.g. photons. In this regard David Deutsch voices the relationship between quanta and information, "It is no coincidence that the word *bit,* meaning the smallest possible amount of information that a computer can manipulate, means essentially the same as *quantum,* a discrete chunk." (Deutsch, 1998, p. 211)

Secondly, regarding the quantum 'measurement problem'. The relationship here is simple enough, that is, in order to gain information on a particle we need to collapse/decohere the wave function by measurement.

Thirdly, 'entanglement' as a fundamental of quantum, it is exposed/expressed in the exchange of information, or knowledge between entangled particles that may be separated over distances as far as one side of the universe to the other.

Fourthly, with Heisenberg's 'Uncertainty Principle', e.g. 'the more information you get on a particle's position the less information you get on its momentum' and vice versa. This may be likened to the notion of the more Regressive entropy the less Progressive entropy and vice versa.

So, we see that information and quantum are close enough to be the same thing! Are they? We will see.

## Biological information:

On the biological side, the connection between 'genetics' and 'information' has already been shown with genes carrying information from parents to offspring detailing instructions for development and continued replication. And the other information machine we are all familiar with is of course the brain, and while we will examine its processes more fully in the next few chapters, suffice to say here that the electrical firing of neurons is the body's pervasive information processor.

## Physical information:

A better understanding of the physical processes of information would help if we considered information itself to be physical and indeed, physicists are more and more accepting this view. A view pioneered by physicist Rolf Landauer (1927-1999) who spent his whole career establishing the physicality information. Science historian James Gleick relates that two of Landauer's most famous papers were titled 'Information is Physical' and, 'Information is Inevitably Physical'. "Whether a bit is a mark on a stone tablet or a hole in a punched card or a particle with spin up or down, he insisted that it could not exist without *some* embodiment." (Gleick, 2011, p. 361) Landauer also proposed that there is a tiny minimum amount of energy necessary to delete one bit of information. This minimum amount is known as the 'Landauer limit' and has now been verified.

We are probably now in a better position to tackle the solution to Maxwell's demon, in as much as the demon has information about each molecule e.g. about the speed of it and where he wants it to go. Therefore it seems that eventually, the demon's memory will be filled up with information and he will have to delete some. To do this will expend energy and therefore cause the erasure of information which in turn increases regressive entropy. This would be similar to the case of having too much information on the hard drive of your computer and having to delete some 'not required' to take on more 'required'. You can actually feel the heat energy being expended by the computer with this action. So on the one hand, regressive entropy is reduced but on the other it is compensated for by an increase.

## Holographic information:

Let me start off here by returning to David Bohm, remember he was the one who had the 'hidden variables' quantum interpretation. Also, as noted in the previous chapter, Bohm anticipated 'The Holographic Principle' and this is demonstrated in his 1980 publication *Wholeness and the Implicate Order.* Here Bohm puts forward the notion that everything is connected as a whole. For example, the human body is the whole of systems, limbs, organs etc. all made from cells/atoms. Likewise, the universe is a whole of interconnected parts and indeed this was how he explained the location dilemma of quantum entanglement. This, you will remember, assumed that when two entangled particles were separated, they still appeared to communicate with each other, no matter what the distance apart. Bohm's theory is that they are not separate, as such, but part of an interconnected whole. He further conjectured that everything in the universe is given birth to from what he called an 'enfolded or implicate order' and what we see, feel, and are is the 'unfolded or explicate order'. This process of enfolding and unfolding is continuous, with particles enfolding and unfolding in interactions even changing their type. In addition, and very importantly for our purposes, he likened his notion of the 'Whole' to a hologram with the enfolding information projecting out to the unfolding holographic reality. In fact Bohm called it a 'holomovement' due to its constant enfoldings and unfoldings.

The principle behind a hologram[72] is the interference effect of waves of photons just like the interference of the waves of photons in the double-slit measurement experiment. Kasper & Feller refer to the hologram as a plate but nothing on the plate resembles the scene. "The plate may be quite clear or somewhat cloudy, or it may have dark swirls and striations...... the scene is not there at all; rather, it is information about the scene, coded in the form *of interference patterns,* that is recorded in the hologram. The coded information itself would have no discernible resemblance to

[72] See Chapter 2 'Universe' footnote 33 for holographic process.

the scene even if you could see it with the naked eye. Actually, the interference patterns are present on a microscopic scale.....It is only when the hologram is suitably illuminated that the information contained in the hologram can be decoded and the scene *reconstructed* or made visible." (Kasper & Feller, 2001, pp. 3-4)

Furthermore, as noted in chapter 2, 'Apart from the hologram itself being an interesting, curious, and even amazing phenomenon, it also has an extraordinary feature, and that is, that should a holographic plate/film be cut into pieces, then each piece contains all the information of the whole'. It appears then that if everything is part of a hologram, it is part of a whole, a la Bohm. Certainly, his notion of a cosmic hologram turned out to have more than a little legs, so to speak, what with its later general acceptance in 'the holographic principle'. The same principle that had its genesis in the problems arising with entropy/information and black holes.

Black holes remember are shaped like a sphere and act like a sink hole in space. Think of a sink hole in the ocean. Should you get caught in a boat, close enough to the pull of the water going into the hole, unless you are a strong rower or have a powerful enough engine you are in deep trouble. The event horizon, i.e. the outer surround of the black hole is such a place of no return. It is so strong once it catches anything, there is no return. In fact it even pulls in light. Hence the name black hole and nothing could escape therefrom. However, in 1970 Stephen Hawking demonstrated that black holes do in fact emit a radiation[73] and eventually evaporate. The trouble was however, as Michael Brooks tells us, "this radiation does not contain any information." (Brooks, 2010, p. 196) John Wheeler was unhappy about with this notion, of all information pulled into black holes with no escape to eventually evaporate, as then their entropy/information was gone forever. But as we have seen earlier information, like energy, cannot be destroyed, so there was a big problem that needed a solution. Jacob Bekenstein, a Princeton student of Wheeler took up this challenge. In this endeavour physicist Leonard Susskind[74] tells us that Bekenstein's great achievement was to show that, "*the entropy of a black hole, measured in bits, is proportional to the area of its horizon, measured in Planck units.*" (Susskind L., 2009, p. 155). A Planck unit being $10^{-66}$ square centimetres. Initially, Stephen Hawking, by then an authority on black holes, was not convinced of Bekenstein's proposition. He was however, eventually able to mathematically confirm Bekenstein's view and demonstrated that not alone, was the entropy proportional to the area of its horizon but equal to it[75]. With this then, the mystery of the information/entropy of black holes was solved, in that it is situated on the event horizon.

---

73 Now known as the Hawking radiation.

74 Susskind was one of the co-inventors of 'String Theory'.

75 Brian Greene explains: "Take the event horizon of a black hole. Hawking instructed, and divide it into a gridlike pattern in which the sides of each cell are one Planck length ($10^{-33}$ centermeters) long. Hawking proved

This outcome itself proved to be strange because when we want to measure what is inside a sphere or a box we look to find the cubic capacity or the volume therein. Simply to do this with a box e.g. we multiply length e.g. 10cm by breath 5cm by height 6cm and this will tell us that there are 300 cubic cm capacity in the box. One can also get the volume of a sphere, once you know the length of the sphere's radius, with a specific formula[76]. But as I stated earlier to find out the amount of information sucked into a black hole you calculate it by taking the square of its event horizon. This extraordinary enlightenment was further extended to apply to any area of space and eventually in the 1990's Nobel prize winning Dutch physicist, Gerard tHooft together with the co-inventor of string theory, physicist Leonard Susskind both proposed that this phenomenon extended to the universe as a whole and so 'the holographic principle' was born. That is to say that everything, galaxies, stars, planets, plants, animals and people within our universe, consisting of three dimensions of space and one of time, has the information pertaining to it printed on its horizon/periphery. In other words it is the square or two dimensional horizon information of the universe that dictates the reality within.

Brian Greene, an expert on string theory, tells us of further evidence of the 'holographic principle'. An Argentinian physicist, Juan Maldacena, working on string theory in 1997 'by considering string theory in a universe whose shape differs from ours but for the purpose at hand proves easier to analyse," produced a result that, *"realized explicitly the holographic principle, and in doing so provided the first mathematical example of Holographic Parallel Universes."* (Greene, 2011, p. 263) "Maldacena's result is amazing. He found a concrete, albeit hypothetical, realization of holography within string theory." (Greene B., 2005, p. 484) Stuart Clark, notes, string theory suggests that black holes are a fuzzy ball of quantum strings that would store fundamental information about objects that had fallen into (it). In this view, matter does not pass *through* the event horizon on its way to the singularity; instead it compresses itself onto the surface of the 'fuzz ball' and merges with the other strings." (Clark, 2010, p. 86) String theory then suggests that black holes do not have singularities but the quantum fuzziness of strings. Michael Moyer, gives us an indication of the state of play as at February 2012, "although physicists mostly agree that the holographic principle is true—that information on nearby surfaces contains all the information about the world—they know not how the information

---

mathematically that the black hole's entropy is the number of such cells needed to cover its event horizon—the black hole's surface area, that is as measured in square Planck units ($10^{-66}$ square centermeters per cell). In the language of hidden information, it's as if each cell secretly carries a single bit, a 0 or a 1 that provides the answer to a single yes-no question delineating some aspect of the black hole's microscopic makeup." (Greene B., 2011, p. 254)

76 Volume of a sphere = $4/3\pi r^3$

is encoded or how nature processes the 1's and the 0's, or how the result of that processing gives rise to the world." (Moyer, 2012)

To conclude this chapter we have found firstly, that the universe is probably a hologram, as is any/all areas of space within, right down to the smallest subatomic space, and secondly, that supersymmetry underlies its laws meaning that unchanging attributes behave the same no matter what the manipulations. There appears to be a confirmation these two 'sameness' attributes of the universe demonstrated by fractal mathematics[77] where each smaller section of space is representative of the whole for any special section right down to even subatomic areas (see Fig: 2-3).

Also in this chapter we have seen that information plays an essential role in everything we are, everything we do, and everything around us. It dictates whether we are progressive or regressive and even appears to programme the universe itself. In this, Stephen Hawking noted we may be as goldfish in bowl. But as I have preferred to believe we are in an incubator, and are moving toward greater and greater complexity. Are we automatons though, inasmuch as we are completely reliant on the peripheral information that naturally/automatically decoheres, or is it possible for us to influence such informational decoherence? To know if such influence is possible or not, we need to examine in depth our species and this we will attempt to do over the next three chapters.

---

[77] Fractals a relatively new branch of mathematics
"Fractals were defined by Benoit Mandelbrot in the 1960s and70s as a way of quantifying self-similar shapes. Short for fractional dimensions, fractals are patterns that look essentially the same at any scale. If you zoom in on a small piece of the pattern it looks indistinguishable from the larger scale one, so you cannot tell what the magnification is just by looking at it. These repeating and scale-less patterns appear frequently in nature, such as in the crinkles of a coastline, the branches of a tree, the fronds of a fern, or the six-fold symmetry of a snowflake." (Baker, 2007, p. 46)

# CHAPTER 8
# Human beings

Human beings may be described as self-serving/self-preserving, conscious and social animals. Firstly, they may be self-serving/preserving with little or no regard for others up to a point, and then, by decreasing levels of selfishness, switching to incremental levels of selflessness up to complete self-sacrifice. Selflessness/altruism however, may be enacted with a view to reciprocal favours. Secondly, humans are thinking beings, in their consciousness of self, others and the environment. They are also thinking beings in their beliefs, shaped by their heredity traits and environmentally acquired experience. Thirdly, humans are social in their need for relationships e.g. love, sex, friendship, and trade. 'No man is an island', some may believe this is untrue, particularly those who live alone and/or in isolation out of choice. However, even such individuals may, from time to time, require social contact, e.g. in sickness.

It is generally thought that the first life forms, from which we human beings originated, began in a suitable chemical environment and from there developed into various biological sea creatures. These sea creatures eventually moved onto land and with the further process of natural selection, one branch of animals reached the level of our major forebears namely, the primates. Monkeys, apes, and humans are all primates. Humans 'homo sapiens', being the most sophisticated product, so far, of the evolutionary process. One of the great apes, the chimpanzee, is the closest primate to us and around 6-7 million years ago 'homo erectus' branched off from the chimpanzee to evolve into the 'homo sapiens' we are today. The difference between ourselves and other primates, Ayala tells us is, "We have bipedal gait, large brains and opposable thumbs that make possible precise manipulation of tools and other objects. Moreover, and most important, humans have superior intelligence and culture, which includes language, advanced technology and complex social and political institutions, as well as ethics and religion." (Ayala, 2012, p. 108)

That life may have begun within the quantum realm should now be better understood since we now know of quantum wave functions and superposition of states. Thus, taking the right combination of required probability life chemicals, from the superposition of probabilities/states, such a combination, given the right environment, would have decohered into the first life form on earth. Remember, while decoherence is environment driven, we have also seen 'conventional states are the ones that are most robust to decoherence'. For example, life particles would have decohered into an environment in which they could form, survive, thrive, replicate and eventually evolve into human beings.

Human beings that are made up of special kinds of cells. Cells come in two basic types; firstly, prokaryotic cells, these were probably the first forms of life as they are the cell found in a single-cell organism. Secondly, there is the eukaryotic cell, and this is found in plants, animals and other multi-cellular organisms. No one knows for sure the actual number of cells in a human being but it is certainly in the billions and billions, and maybe, some even say, trillions. A simple human cell is surrounded by a membrane that encloses a gel-like substance call the cytoplasm. Within the cell is the nucleus, which contains most of the cell's genetic material. There are also other bits floating in the cytoplasm, one of which is the mitochondrion. The mitochondria in cells are the ingredient that supplies the cell's power.

There is no doubt that many of the body's physical features are inherited from our parents. One has only got to look at such things as height, facial features and even gait to recognise such passing down to offspring. Unfortunately, other physical elements may also be passed on, from either parent, such as genetic disorders. Some of these may come from one or the other parent while others require both parents to be a carrier, e.g. the disease cystic fibrosis. Children may also be born with physical problems contracted in the womb and so arrive in the world physically and /or mentally disadvantaged.

So, what is the composition of the human body? Suffice to say here that the body consists of cells making up skin/hair, fat, bones, muscles, sugars, salts, organs, DNA, and blood (see Fig: 8-1 below depicting internal organs). There are numerous other components acting out various jobs within the body and many of these are involved with the body's different systems. Most of the atoms in the body are hydrogen and most of its mass is oxygen. But while the body is approximately made up of 57% water, it is in fact nearly 100% empty space.

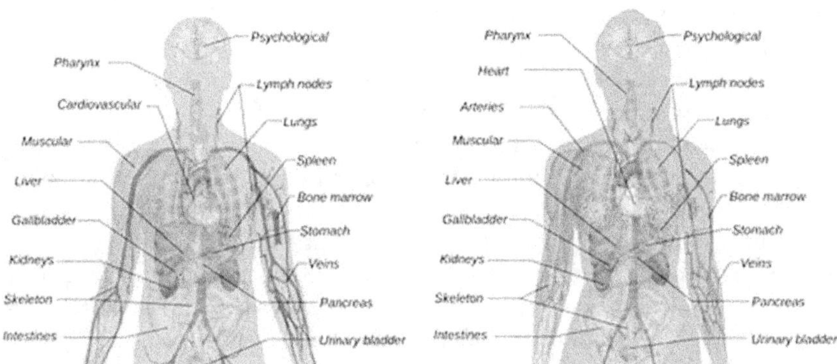


**Fig: 8-1**
Source: https://pixabay.com/en/man-woman-schema-body-anatomy-144378/
CCO Public Domain. Free for commercial use. No attribution required.

As I proposed since chapter 1. the body is driven by what I will call the four 'S' drives, namely, 'Survival', 'Sex', 'Status' and 'Symbolism'. Survival and sex are self-explanatory, while status refers to one's standing in society. Regarding symbolism, for the moment take the symbol of the Nazi swastika or the Christian cross as an example of human drive symbols. These drives I will discuss in greater detail in chapter 10 'Behaviour' but here, I must emphasise that the natural implementation of these 'S' drives may result in an excess of one or the other, way beyond individual requirements. This excess is a natural pursuit and, to a degree, is quite acceptable. However, should such excess, infringe negatively on others then such excess increases, by deprivation, 'regressive entropy'.

To refer back briefly with the entropy theme, please remember each individual born into this world has a unique set of genes that in themselves are a world apart from everyone else. Then with these genes they acquire knowledge and experiences, and through this, by degrees, further develop their own world, as in Plato's cave. As a consequence though they will inevitably infringe on the worlds of others. No matter what their sex, sexual orientation, race, nationality, marital status, ideology/creed/religion, or adult age, they have the natural human right to 'progressive entropy' in sustenance, health and education (information). In addition, it is believed, that by way of their own decisions, they choose their own path, in so far as they can, towards increased complexity. On this path, all information that is available should be accessible if possible. Other humans of course can and do also influence other individual's decisions in this regard both overtly and/or covertly. Indeed, some people/groups may not just influence but force their beliefs/desires on others by use of superior powers.

I will now look at some of the relevant bodily systems that may act alone or in combination and all such systems do, in most cases, assist the 'S' drives.

Firstly, ***the reproductive system:*** We have already touched on this with regard to genes. The system works simply when the sperm from the male testes penetrates the female ovum (egg) in one of the fallopian tubes and from there it goes into the womb proper to grow for nine months at which time the birth occurs through the birth canal. Each person born is in fact a one off e.g. everyone has unique fingerprints and a unique DNA, with the exception of identical twins having the same DNA. Then there are the various features and traits we are born with like, race, skin colour, height, hair colour, facial features etc. etc.

Apart from reproduction being assisted by the survival drive it is also obviously assisted by the sex drive in order to initiate the system. Of course this sounds all quite mechanical, but as we know there is much pleasure and heightened emotion, not alone in the initiation and participation in the sexual process, but also in the nurturing, care, protection and love of partners and their the offspring.

Then there is the ***Gastrointestinal or Digestive System*** that allows us to take the nourishment ('progressive entropy') from food to assist in our growth towards complexity and hold off our own ultimate demise via regressive entropy. By extracting this nourishment however, we also increase regressive entropy of the food to waste via the gastrointestinal system. Vedral reminds us that, "Schrodinger was the first to argue convincingly that life maintains itself on low entropy (i.e. progressive) through increasing the entropy (i.e. regressive) of its environment. Of course, this is not in opposition to the fact that the genome may be getting more complex with time. In fact it may be that you need a more complex genome in order to better utilize the environment and bring yourself to a lower entropy state" (Vedral V., 2010, p. 68). As noted earlier when Schrodinger talks of 'low entropy' this we now call 'progressive entropy', whereas his 'increasing the entropy' will be 'regressive entropy' for us.

Other important systems are, the ***Muscular/Skeletal System,*** which protects the body with its bones, ligaments etc. the skeletal system works with the muscular system helping the body to move, twist and turn, arms/legs movements etc. These movements are voluntary, that is you decide or at least believe you decide the movement. Smooth muscles i.e. those that are within organs are involuntary. Therefore, e.g. the heart/cardiac muscle is involuntary in that it moves of its own accord. The heart muscle is protected by breastbone or sternum. The ***Integumentary system*** consists of skin, hair and nails. It also protects the body, helps with sweat, keeps blood in, and keeps other things out. It is a sensory interface with the outside world. The ***Immune and Lymphatic Systems,*** both act to defend against dangerous infections, viruses or other substances that enter the body. The immune system operates to expel these dangers via e.g. sneezing while the Lymphatic system works a bit like the circulatory system bringing good fluids to the body and taking away bad fluids, linking up with the blood stream. The ***Respiratory System*** operates the intake of air with oxygen into the lungs and expels carbon dioxide. And the ***Urinary or Renal System*** is the mechanism by which waste is filtered through the kidneys and combined with water makes its way into the bladder. Once the bladder is full the body expels the contents as urine.

The ***Endocrine System*** is one of the most important systems for us to understand with regard to the proposition in this book, as it has to do with information the body receives and the action the body does or does not take from this information. This system is best recognised in its hormonal involvement with the testes and the ovaries. It has much to do with glands in general. The pituitary gland, a small gland the size of a pea behind the nose, e.g. secretes many hormones and is greatly involved in sexual development and reproduction. The adrenal gland is also commonly referred to when people say, *they got an adrenalin rush,* when something excited them. This gland is also associated with the fight or flight syndrome. The pineal gland is a small gland in the brain and apart from its secretions, was thought to be the seat of the soul, according to the 17th century philosopher and mathematician Rene Descartes. Other glands in the system include the pancreas and thyroid gland. All the glands bring hormones via the blood stream, to all parts of the body for development and functionality.

The ***Cardiovascular or Circulatory System:*** is probably the most well-known system in the body. It has the heart as a pump pushing blood around the whole body and back again. It is basically the body's two-way transport system. It brings, via the lungs, blood with oxygen, together with other nutrients and hormones, through the arteries to all areas of the body. Once this is achieved it returns the used up blood, through the veins, back to the heart to commence the process once again. The heart itself, being such an important organ, even has its own blood supply known as the 'coronary circulation'. This supplies blood via its own coronary arteries to itself and then exits through its coronary veins. One could say it is running its own business, while at the same time running the business of the entire body.

The ***Autonomic nervous system*** is essential for the cardiovascular system above as it is this that keeps the heart automatically beating. It also regulates digestion, that is the mechanics of how food is pushed through the gut by a process called, 'peristalsis' involving smooth muscle contractions that move the food along. It also includes the sympathetic and the parasympathetic systems, the former kicking in for 'fight or flight', and the latter for relaxation or slowing down.

The ***Peripheral nervous system.*** This assists in carrying the messages to the muscles or glands from the central nervous system. It has to do with the nerves outside the brain and the spinal cord.

The ***Central nervous System,*** for me however, is the system at the core of being human, as without its efficient operation the other systems are under pressure regarding functionality or even meaning. The heart may be running the entire business but the nervous system is directing it, via the brain, the spinal cord, and the nerves themselves. Such is the mechanism by which the body is controlled. Impairment of these and control is lost. The 'nervous system' operates like a trinity in that there are three prongs each contributing to the whole. These are, the central, the autonomic, and the peripheral nervous systems.

Before looking at these we will firstly look at some of the constituent parts of the brain. (See also Fig: 8-2 and 8-3 below)

**Brain**

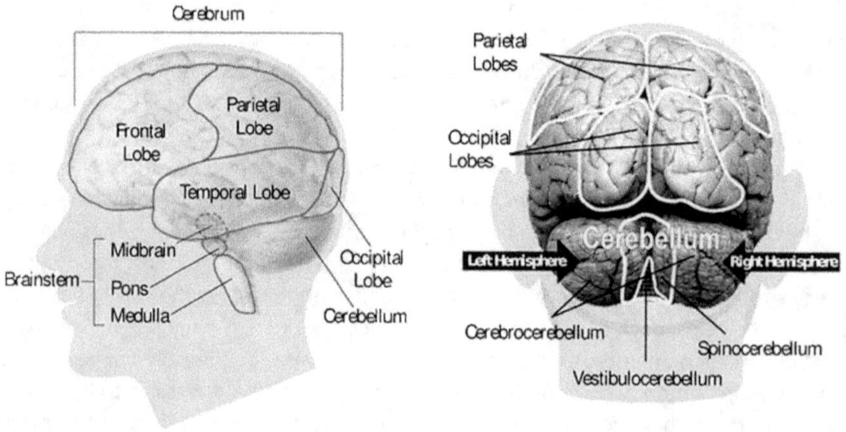

Source: https://pixabay.com/en/brain-human-anatomy-organ-medicine-148131/
CCO Public Domain. Free for commercial use. No attribution required.

**Fig: 8-2**

**Brain**

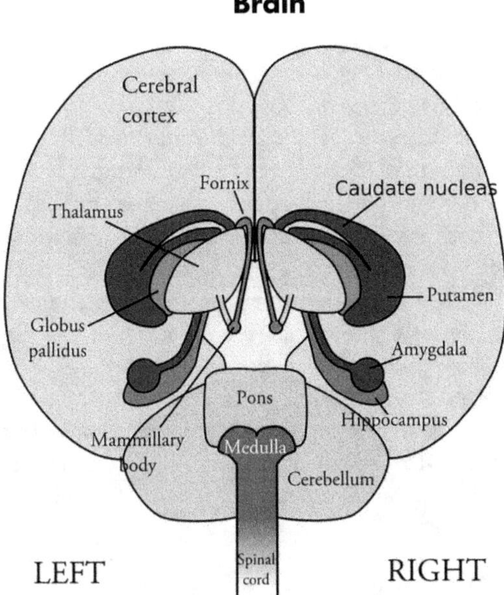


Source: https://pixabay.com/en/brain-anatomy-human-147148/


**Fig: 8-3**

The brain's 'cerebrum' which covers most of the organ has what is called the 'cerebral cortex' on the outside layer. Part of the 'cerebral cortex' is the 'neo cortex', believed to be the area concerned with conscious thought. The cerebrum is divided, by a type of groove, into two sides known as the left and right hemispheres. The 'hypothalamus', by way of the 'pituitary' gland, links the nervous system to the endocrine system. The 'pituitary 'gland along with the 'pineal' gland, mentioned previously, are embedded deep within the brain.

The 'cerebellum' is located below the 'cerebrum' and above the 'brain stem' and is associated with coordinating movement. The point where the brain and the spinal cord connect is known as the brain stem and is sometimes referred to as the 'primitive brain'. It is associated with survival techniques. Science writer Zack Lynch with Byron Laursen tell us, "Much of the time, your newer and more thoughtful brain parts don't realize they're being bossed by the older ones." (Lynch & Laursen, 2010, pp. 47-48) The majority of the cells acting in the brain and other parts of the nervous system are called 'neurons'. McFadden elaborates, "Our brain consists of about one hundred billion ($10^{11}$) neurons and about a trillion ($10^{12}$) non-nerve cells, known collectively as *glia*. A huge amount of evidence has accumulated to indicate that it is within the thin sheet of cells of the brain's cortex.....that most information processing takes place." (Mc Fadden, 2000, p. 282)

A neuron is set up to electrically transmit and receive messages. The best way to think about this is that at one end of a neuron there is an 'axon' (message sender) and at the other end there is a 'dendrite' (message receiver). The axon of one neuron sends a message to the dendrite of another neuron (See Fig: 8-4 below). This message is sent from one to the other across a space called the 'synapse'. Single neurons or bunches of them are constantly sending and receiving messages and interacting with the glia throughout the system. For example, your brain is constantly sparking like a miniature fireworks display. The result of this is that the brain uses approximately 20% of the body's total energy. Medical writer Rita Carter advises, "The brain has 100 trillion connections joining billions of neurons and each junction has the potential to be part of a memory. So, the memory capacity of a human brain is effectively infinite, provided it is stored in the right way." (Carter, 2002, pp. 288-289)

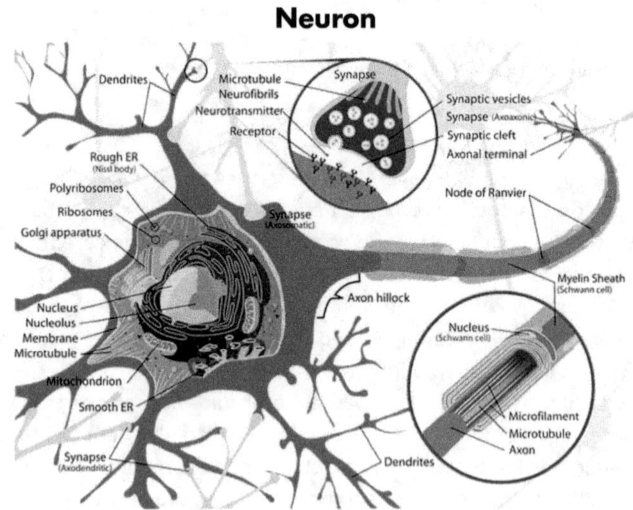


Source: https://pixabay.com/en/drawing-nerve-cell-neurone-732830/
CCO Public Domain. Free for commercial use. No attribution required.

**Fig: 8-4**

Suffice to say the brain, spinal cord, and nerves, send and receive messages for the body's coordination and functionality.

The central nervous system then as a whole carries out analysis and puts together various input information it receives, and then helps with the appropriate body action. Such information will come from the senses. These senses come from without and within the body and indeed, some information from without can and often does cause particular actions within, even if there is not actual physical contact with the body. For example, things we see might cause an angry reaction from us. In addition the senses may cause a particular reaction in one person but not another. Indeed, we may even believe from our senses that a certain process is happening, when in actual fact it is not. For example, we may believe that our eyes record the scene before us, much like a movie camera, but this is not the case. Instead our eyes record a series of snap shots that the brain puts together in a stream.

To conclude then there is no doubt that human beings, as far as we know, are the most complex animals yet to evolve. Certainly, other animals have an almost similar complexity in physical make-up, and actually do some things physically better than us. But with our dexterity, together with our brain power/intelligence we surely win the day.

Nonetheless, no examination of human beings would be complete without an attempt to comprehend what is known as the human mind. Thousands of books have been written on this subject, however, it is worth pointing out that the experts, in the 'mind' field, cannot themselves reach agreement on a universal mind theory. They can, of course, make up their own minds but cannot convince the minds of others So, while probably unqualified for the task, I'll throw caution to the wind and endeavour, in the next chapter, to give you a flavour of what I think it's all about. In this regard, I can promise a 'mind expanding' experience as I believe we take consciousness for granted and don't realise it is an extraordinary and wondrous human attribute for our own and other's progressive entropy.

# CHAPTER 9
# Consciousness

## Part 1 Solo performance:

Just as the physical body evolved, so also in tandem, did its consciousness or mind[78]. We shall see that consciousness may exist in all matter and that it is a fundamental of the universe, and certainly it is in situ in the great diverse animal family. But let me concentrate on the human species and start with the notion that, along with the evolution of the physical body, there was/is an evolution of consciousness. Deutsch advises, "Human brains and DNA molecules each have many functions, but among other things they are general—purpose information—storage media: they are in principle capable of storing any kind of information. Moreover, the two types of information that are respectively evolved to store have a property of cosmic significance in common: once *they are physically embodied in a suitable environment, they tend to cause themselves to remain so.* Such information—which I call *knowledge*---is very unlikely to come into existence other than through the error-correcting processes of evolution or thought." (Deutsch, 2011, p. 78) In addition, we shall see that consciousness is partly inherited from our parents and subsequently, through on-going experience, it evolves us, individually, into a unique and dynamic conscious self. It is unique firstly, by genetic inheritance as we have seen regarding DNA, and secondly, by being constantly adjusted with on-going experience. It is this on-going adjustment of additions, subtractions and manipulative mixtures that also makes it dynamic.

---

[78] Mind and consciousness will mean the same thing throughout.

Regarding its inheritance, psychologist Jonathan Haidt explains (from the work of Baillargeon 1987[79]) "if the infant's mind comes already wired to interpret events in certain ways, then infants can be surprised when the world violates their expectations. Using this trick, psychologists discovered that infants are born with some knowledge of physics and mechanics: they expect that objects will move according to Newton's laws of motion, and they get startled when psychologists show them scenes that should be physically impossible... (And from David and Ann Premack[80]), they found that infants come equipped with innate abilities to understand their *social* world as well. They understand things like harming and helping." (Haidt, 2012, p. 63) Therefore, a baby is born with basic informational discerning abilities. It quickly learns, by using these discerning qualities, what it needs and how to get it, by for example, crying. Such then is the inheritance part of consciousness. On-going experience then kicks in and this information is added to the consciousness data base, thereby extending it. Let us say that a baby needs food, and in conjunction with the need for food it also requires the food to be at a certain temperature. Firstly, it gets the food by crying. Then if it discerns that it is not at the correct temperature, it learns again how to convey this message also, albeit in the same way. Again this is added to the consciousness base. Such continues on through life with the conscious self, using the cumulative conscious experience to add to the existing consciousness for better decision making choices. In other words the conscious self uses itself continuously, to accumulate experience to further enhance itself.

So, how may the notion of consciousness itself be described? In one word, it seems, simply as, 'awareness'. But awareness of what? Awareness, I believe of information! For example, I am aware that my son is in the adjoining room, my daughter is reading by the window, my wife is out shopping, some tomatoes in the garden are ripe and a beautiful red in colour while others are unripe and green. From experience, I am aware that the ripe tomatoes will smell and taste beautiful, and were I to eat the green ones they would taste bitter. These then are just some instances of conscious information. Information that we know has found its way into our awareness via decoherence from the edge of the universe. We have learned that all information, as far as we can tell, whether we are conscious or not, emanates in this way. In fact any and all areas of space, we have learned, operate likewise, down to the smallest subatomic area. This of course also means that some spaces will run into other spaces partly or completely, so e.g. there may be spaces within spaces, within spaces, like layers of an onion. Perhaps they are shaped and packed

[79] Baillargeon, R. 1987. "Object Permanence in 3 ½ - 4 ½ - Month-Old Infants." *Development Psychology* 23:655-64.

[80] "The first work demonstrating that infants have innate abilities to understand the social world, including abilities to infer intentions and react to harm, was done by David and Ann Premack; see Premack and Premack 1994 for review summarizing the origins of moral cognition." (Haidt, 2012, p. 332)

like Russian matryoshka dolls[81] and subject to the same information distribution, via decoherence and the 'holographic principle', following the symmetry that underlies the laws of the universe together with fractal mathematics where a small part is like the whole.

In addition, fractal geometry may also be used on the one hand to measure the uneven or jagged lines that mark the natural world, while Euclidean geometry on the other hand embraces unnatural smooth straight or curved lines. An example of this difference is that when an ordinance survey of the distance around the coast of Ireland is taken the result is 3171 Km. However, were we to apply fractal geometry to the measurement process, something similar to measuring every nook and cranny with a long piece of string, we would find that the distance was 3, 4 or more times the 3171Km, depending on how minutely exact we wished to go. Space likewise is not smooth but pervasively rough with quantum fluctuations. The point to be made here is that 'areas of space' are not necessarily smooth and curved in the Euclidean geometry sense. Rather, such areas may be crinkled with protrusions and nooks and crannies, like for example, the human brain or the human body. Perhaps a more precise term for these 'areas of space' is 'environmental areas of space' because each area will have its own specific environment. Just like the brain, the body, Canterbury cathedral, The White House, the earth itself, and the solar system all have their own environmental make-up.

So, to reiterate, information and specifically conscious information or awareness emanates from the quantum computer universe. This it does, by decoherence from the periphery, to programme the holographic classical world. This holographic world in turn is made up of 'environmental areas of space' each a hologram that may stand alone, overlap, or be layered within each other from the periphery of the universe to the smallest of sizes and each hologram is produced by quantum wave interference. We will revisit this further in 'part 2' of this chapter.

We now have a pretty good idea, based on the holographic principle, of where our awareness information originates, and this information, we believe is in our brain, but how does it actually get there? To get an answer, we need firstly to know, what is this mind that seems to be in the brain, that captures, and uses this information automatically or conscious manipulatively? This mind or consciousness, it seems, certainly means different things to different people. Some people equate it with the soul or religious spirit that leaves the body after death and goes to hopefully, a better place, as the alternative appears to be pretty grim. To others, not of a religious bent, the mind may still be a separate entity from the body/brain. To others still, the mind is no more than a process within the brain that has yet to be fully

---

[81] A Russian matryoshka doll, also known as 'nesting doll' fits into a series of larger dolls.

understood. As human beings we certainly do have the feeling of the self. 'I am me.' 'I am my body or 'I am my brain' or 'I am my whole self'. However, we do feel that we steer the self from within our heads i.e. our brains. We also feel we make this steering action as a result of decisions we make within our brain. These decisions may be the result of some message we received from the body itself, e.g. we get an itch, so we scratch. Or they may be the result of a message we received from without the body, e.g. the weather is extremely hot, so we shed some clothing. In addition, a decision to act in some way may simply be made consciously, due to a desire for the action itself, to give us pleasure and/or satisfaction or for some other reason.

It appears then that consciousness has a lot to do with our senses and desires e.g. reactions to particular sensations or I just want to do something. But I can also remember many things and these memories allow me to make certain decisions. Then there are other things that I can bring to my brain, either by thought alone, or by one of my senses. These are emotions. If we think of some misfortunate happening in our life we may feel extremely sad or maybe we feel happy that we got through it okay. We may also see something that makes us extremely angry or perhaps sympathetic. All of this is part of our consciousness. We are also aware of not just ourselves but others around us and indeed our whole environment is constantly, we feel, interacting with our brain and our brain is interacting with many aspects of our environment.

I mentioned above that we feel we steer ourselves from within our heads but this is not strictly true in three particular processes. Firstly, you will remember from the last chapter that the autonomic nervous system carries out numerous bodily functions on an automatic basis. Secondly, there is a 'zombie' element to our consciousness that allows the body to act without our awareness. For example, when driving a car, particularly when travelling on a frequently travelled route, we are often miles away in our thinking, but at the same time automatically driving and following the rules of the road. Another example is our almost instantaneous reaction when we are exposed to danger e.g. moving quickly out of the way before a potential accident, or reacting automatically, without prior thought, in a contact sport. The third area and probably the most controversial that questions our belief of steering ourselves, is the notion of 'free will'. In this regard, scientific experimentation, as we have seen in chapter 4, is proposing that we are not necessarily in control.

There is also something else that I have to myself and no one else can know my sense or understanding of it. Psychologist Susan Blackmore explains, "All of these are my own private experiences and they have a quality that I cannot convey to anyone else. I may wonder whether your experience of green is the same as mine or whether coffee has the same smell for you as it does for me, but I can never find out. These ineffable (or indescribable) qualities are what philosophers call 'qualia' (although there is much dispute about whether qualia exist). The redness of that shiny red mug is a quale; the soft feel of my cat's fur is a quale; and so is that smell of coffee. These experiences seem to be real, vivid, and undeniable. They make up the world I live in. Indeed, they are all I have." (Blackmore, 2005, p. 3)

When people attempt to define what consciousness actually is, there are basically two camps, the 'materialists' and the 'dualists'. The materialists, believe that everything can be brought back to 'matter' in the human being via reductionism. The dualists, on the other hand, look to mind and matter as separate entities, acting in unison in the individual. There are variations on both of these, as well as the peculiar proposal of 'idealism' a la philosopher George Berkeley which denies the existence of matter altogether. For our purposes though, we will just concentrate on materialism and dualism.

The notion of full consciousness is when we are in an awake state. So, we are not conscious when we are asleep, under an anaesthetic, or unconscious for some reason. I understand also that there are levels of semi-consciousness in all the above. But to be sure, when we die so does the consciousness that was attached to our life. Indeed, this is the major reason the 'materialists' give for having consciousness confined to the brain alone with no 'matter' and 'mind' duality. Materialist, neuroscientist Antonio Damasio believes, mind comes from the brain/within the brain "conscious minds arise when a self-process is added onto a basic mind process. When selves do not occur within minds, those minds are not conscious in the proper sense. This is a predicament faced by humans whose self-process is suspended by dreamless sleep, anesthesia, or brain disease." (Damasio, 2010, p. 8) Yet another materialist, biologist Christof Kosh[82] in his studies of consciousness he teamed up with three prominent scientists, psychiatrist Giulio Tononi and two Nobel Prize winning biologists, Francis Crick, of the 'double helix' fame, and Gerald Edelman. The outcome of their cross-fertilization, is a theory of consciousness by Tononi, which is backed by Lindstrom. It is called *The Theory of Integrated Information.* Koch presents the theory with excellent explanations in his 2012 book *Consciousness.* Tononi[83], the same year, presented the theory himself, with an innovative style, in his beautifully illustrated book *PHI.* The theory is that conscious experience is *extraordinarily differentiated* but also *highly integrated.* So, what does this exactly mean? Well, Tononi uses a metaphor of the body to explain this, in that each part of our body is extraordinarily differentiated e.g. the lungs being different from the heart, but highly integrated into a human entity. Consciousness is like an

---

[82] Christof Kosh is Professor of Biology and of Engineering at the California Institute of Technology and Chief Scientific Officer of the Allen Institute for Brain Science in Seattle.

[83] Giulio Tononi is a professor of Psychiatry, the David P. White Professor of Sleep Medicine, and Distinguished Chair in Consciousness Science at the University of Wisconsin.

onion he tells us, peel away each layer neuron by neuron and each is me, just as the neurons above represent different parts of me, but they have to be integrated for the whole me. "Whether consciousness was present and where it was generated... was determined not by any property of neural cells but by the quantity of integrated information generated by a complex of neural elements." (Tononi, 2012, pp. 179-180) The measure of the extent of consciousness he calls PHI and it is represented by the symbol $\phi$. The total combination is greater than the sum of the parts. Tononi's theory also postulates that consciousness is a fundamental of the universe and therefore not only 'matter' itself, but its constituent parts atoms and their ingredients all have a modicum of $\phi$.

Such are some examples of the materialist stance. It is interesting to note however, that Teilhard de Chardin also believed that consciousness was a fundamental of the universe.

The dualists on the other hand, believe in the separation of mind and matter and this notion goes back in time probably to those who had enough mind to contemplate the self. Certainty Aristotle believed that human beings had a sort of soul, called the psyche, that was separate from the body, and Christianity obviously favoured such a notion. In fact the great 13$^{th}$ century philosopher Saint Thomas Aquinas believed, that apart from ourselves, numerous members of the animal family had souls. Indeed, many contemporary scientists, philosophers and scholars are in no doubt that consciousness abounds throughout the living and some even think it may even exist in non-living matter, albeit in what we would consider insignificant amounts. Dualism then was embraced by Aristotle and the early Christian church, and indeed it was firmly anchored within Western belief by none other than Rene Descartes. In fact he went so far as to banish the notion of consciousness/souls from all other life except humans. Descartes believed, as we have noted earlier, that human beings have the seat of the soul firmly implanted in a particular part of the brain, the pineal gland. Descartes' influence was all the more accepted as his explanation sat comfortably with how people felt regarding mind-body separation. Indeed, his famous 'Cogito ergo sum' (I think therefore I am) has, when first encountered, a reasonable ring to it! But as numerous thinkers have since pointed out, the 'I' presupposes one exists before the 'thinking'. Nonetheless, like his contemporary Isaac Newton, his propositions were to hold sway for many years as, apart from the idea of consciousness being housed in the pineal gland, the notion of it being housed in the brain feels comfortable and right for most of us. Another form of dualism that attempts to solve the consciousness dilemma is called, 'Naturalistic Dualism'. We will confront this shortly.

By far though the 'materialist' interpretation is the most popular among scientists as well as with people who do not have a particular spiritual or religious focus. Materialists rightly hold that we are made up of matter i.e. combinations of different kinds of atoms and molecules and our brains and nervous systems are therefore similar. Consciousness however, they believe, emanates from this matter alone. This assertion is most attractive in its logic, but still leaves us a little uncomfortable, especially as materialists cannot account for certain aspects of consciousness, namely, experience. Experience in consciousness philosophy is what is known as the 'hard' problem.

Australian philosopher David Chalmers[84] differentiated between what he called 'the easy' and 'the hard' problems of consciousness. The easy problems are such things as being able to discriminate, categorize, control behaviour and react to stimuli etc. While these problems are not that easy we can believe that they may be solved with some future e.g. brain scanning device. On the other hand, he tells us, "The really hard problem of consciousness is the problem of *experience.* When we think and perceive, there is a whir of information processing, but there is also a subjective aspect. As Nagel[85] has put it, *there is something it is like* to be a conscious organism. This subjective aspect is experience." (Chalmers, 2010, pp. 4-5) He also believes "The character of our world is not exhausted by the character supplied by the physical facts; there is extra character due to the presence of consciousness. To use a phrase due to Lewis (1990)[86], consciousness carries phenomenal *information."* (Chalmers D. J., 1996, p. 124) He further proposes that there is as yet some unknown new features of the world to be discovered and these will allow consciousness to supervene[87] naturally as opposed to logically. From this he arrives at what he terms 'Naturalistic Dualism'. It "is not a dualism such as Descartes, with a separate realm of mental substance that exerts its own influence on physical processes......... (It is) instead a kind of *property* dualism: conscious experience involves properties of an individual that are not entailed by the physical properties of that individual, although they may depend lawfully on those properties. Consciousness is a *feature* of the world over and above the physical features of the world. This is not to say it is a separate 'substance'..." (Chalmers D. J., 1996, pp. 124-125) So, what I believe Chalmers is saying is that his 'Naturalistic Dualism' is like 'Property Dualism'[88] which

---

84 David J Chalmers is Distinguished Professor of Philosophy and Director of the centre for Consciousness at the Australian National University and visiting Professor of Philosophy at New York University.

85 Nagel, T. 1974. What Is It like To Be a Bat? *Philosophical Review* 4: 435-50.

86 1990. What experience teaches. In W. Lycan, ed., *Mind and Cognition.* Oxford: Blackwell.

87 "The notion of supervenience formalizes the intuitive idea that one set of facts can fully determine another set of facts" (Chalmers D. J., 1996, p. 32)

88 'Property dualists claim that mental phenomena are non-physical properties of physical phenomena, but not properties of non-physical substances. Property dualists are not committed to the existence of non-physical substances, but are committed to the irreducibility of mental phenomena to physical

claims 'that mental phenomena are non-physical properties of physical phenomena, but not properties of non-physical substances'. And as noted above he proposes that there is as yet some unknown new features of the world to be discovered and as a result these will allow consciousness to occur naturally to an existing situation.

These, as yet unknown, new features of the world have a ring to them, not unlike the 'hidden variables' interpretation of quantum mechanics. Indeed, consciousness and quantum mechanics have been linked, not alone in this regard but for several other reasons, not the least being the mystery attached to both along with the role the conscious observer appears to play in collapsing the wave function. There has therefore developed, from eminent scholars, numerous interpretations of consciousness based on quantum processes. This is in spite of the fact that many physicists and scientists frown on such an idea not the least being Koch himself, "the specialists that study the structure of cells at the level of proteins and bilipid membranes, by and large see no evidence that quantum fluctuations play a critical role in the life of a neuron. Nervous systems, like anything else, obey the laws of quantum mechanics; yet the collective effect of all these molecules frenetically moving about is to smooth out any quantum indeterminacy, an effect called *decoherence.* Decoherence implies that the molecules of life can be treated using thoroughly classical, deterministic laws rather than quantum mechanical ones..." (Koch C., 2012, pp. 100-101) In addition, Stephen Manly advises, "the decoherence time for quantum processes in the brain has been shown by Tegmark[89] to be on the order of $10^{-13}$ to $10^{-20}$seconds.That's vastly shorter than even the most fickle individual can have a flighty thought. Said more academically, it is substantially shorter than the relevant timescale over which brain processes occur.[90]" (Manly, 2011, p. 88)

Others scholars however, are convinced that quantum phenomena will eventually be shown to play a part in consciousness. Indeed, to give Chalmers credit he presents a comprehensive analysis of the notion of quantum consciousness and one gets the feeling he would like to endorse it, but just cannot make himself. In *The Conscious Mind* we see this, "One cannot rule out the possibility that fundamental physical theories such as quantum mechanics will play a key role in a theory of

---

phenomena'. Source: Dualism and Mind: by Scott Calef, *The Internet Encyclopedia of Philosophy,* ISSN 2161-0002, http://www.iep.utm.edu/, 29/1/16.

89 Max Tegmark is author or co-author of more than 200 technical papers, twelve of which have been cited more than 500 times. He has featured in dozens of science documentaries, and his work with the SDSS collaboration on galaxy clustering shared the first prize in *Science* magazine's 'Breakthrough of the Year: 2003'. He holds a PhD from the University of California, Berkeley, and is a physics professor at MIT. (Aldersey-Williams, 2012) See Bio (Tegmark, 2014)

90 Tegmark, Max (2000). "The importance of Quantum Decoherence in Brain Processes." *Physical Review* E61 (2000): 4194.

consciousness." (Chalmers D. J., 1996, p. 120) Koch also, in spite of the quote above, may be hedging his bets as he thinks there may be a place for quantum playing some role "Yet we cannot rule out the possibility that quantum indeterminacy likewise leads to behavioural indeterminacy. And such randomness may play a functional role." (Koch C., 2012, p. 101) Paul Davies also contributes, "it seems likely that any attempt to bring consciousness within the scope of physics will need to be formulated within the context of quantum mechanics." (Davies, 2007, p. 260) In addition, some of the eminent scholars that have endorsed a form of quantum consciousness are cited by Chalmers in *The Consciousness Mind* 1996, these are; Winger 1961; Bohm 1980; Hodgson 1988; Lockwood 1989; Penrose 1989; Squires 1990; Stapp 1993: Of course there are many others, but I will add an additional four; Zohar 1990; Jibu & Yasue 1995; McFadden 2000.

I will briefly look at just four of the above namely; Penrose, Bohm, McFadden and Stapp.

First: Sir Roger Penrose[91] together with his collaborator Stuart Hameroff[92], proposed that consciousness had something to do with both gravity and quantum effects in the tubules within the dendrites of neurons. Their theory however, met with much opposition and condemnation. The final nail in its coffin seems to have been Max Tegmark's brain decoherence times noted above. Of course, Penrose himself being one of Britain's eminent mathematicians, knew well 'the undecidability of mathematical propositions' a la Kurt Godel. Philosopher David Papineau explains how, "Godel's theorem about the incompleteness of arithmetic also plays a role in Penrose's theory. Godel's theorem shows that no axiom system is powerful enough to generate all the truths of arithmetic. According to Penrose, this shows that the human mind must somehow have 'non-algorithmic' powers that go beyond axioms and rules." (Papineau & Selina, 2012, p. 128) Indeed, Tegmark also points out that Penrose and Hameroff did argue "there might be other quantum effects in the brain that weren't computations, which I never disagreed with in the first place." (Tegmark, 2014, p. 208)

Second: David Bohm, whom we encountered with the 'hidden variables' interpretation of quantum mechanics, conjectured that everything in the universe is given birth to from what he called an 'enfolded or implicate order' and what we see, feel, and are is the 'unfolded or explicate order'. This process of enfolding and unfolding is continuous, with particles enfolding and unfolding in interactions even changing their type. In addition Bohm proposed "that each moment of consciousness has a certain *explicit* content, which is a foreground, and an *implicit* content, which

---

91 Sir Roger Penrose is the Emeritus Rouse Ball Professor of Mathematics at the University of Oxford.

92 Stuart Hameroff is an anesthesiologist and Professor at the University of Arizona.

is a corresponding background........The distinction between the implicit and explicit in thought is thus being taken here to be essentially equivalent to the distinction between implicit and explicit in matter in general." (Bohm D., 1980, p. 259)

Third: Johnjoe McFadden, also makes the point for a quantum involvement in consciousness. "There is.... a perfectly good wave mechanical system in the brain: the electromagnetic field (em-field). All electrical phenomena involve the generation of electromagnetic fields...... displaying all the quantum-mechanical phenomena of interference,... superpositions, ....and uncertainty at any temperature. It is only matter, made up of atoms and molecules, which generally hides its *waviness* beneath a cloak of decoherence at normal temperatures." (Mc Fadden, 2000, p. 295) Consciousness, he believes is a product of our brain's em-field. He also points out that a quantum system can be manipulated by measurement via the quantum Zeno effect[93] and the inverse quantum Zeno effect.

Fourth: The American physicist Henry Stapp advises that consciousness cannot be explained by classical physics, "There is nothing in the principles of classical physics that requires, or even hints at, the existence of such things as thoughts, ideas, and feelings." (Stapp, 2007, p. 10) But he believes quantum physics is well placed for an explanation. Papineau advises, Stapp "argues that quantum waves collapse when intelligent brains select one among the alternative quantum possibilities as a basis for future action." (Papineau & Selina, 2012, p. 125) Yet, how is it possible for a warm brain, to stay in a quantum state long enough, in order to make the selection among the possibilities without decoherence happening? Stapp answers this with measurement manipulation to hold the quantum state via the 'quantum Zeno effect'. Vlatko Vedral article, 'Living in a Quantum World' in *Scientific American* June 2011 adds to the possibilities of quantum effects in warm living creatures, as noted in the article's 'In Brief' summary. "**The quintessential quantum effect, entanglement,** can occur in large systems as well as warm ones—including living organisms—even though molecular jiggling might be expected to disrupt entanglement." (Vedral V., 2011)

From the foregoing then, what is my own position with regard to the notions of consciousness? Well, as I stated above, 'information and specifically conscious information or awareness emanates from the quantum computer universe. This it does, by decoherence from the periphery, to programme the holographic classical world. So, it is my contention that quantum and consciousness are certainly

[93] "This 'holding-in-place' effect is called the quantum Zeno effect, an appellation that was picked by the physicists E.C.G. Sudarshan and R. Misra (1977) to highlight a similarity of this effect to the 'arrow' paradox discussed by fifth century B.C. Greek philosopher, Zeno the Eleatic......... The quantum Zeno effect can, in principle, hold an intention and its template in place in the face of strong mechanical forces that would tend to disturb it." (Stapp, 2007, p. 36)

linked and such linkage is an essential part of being human. In addition, I find myself, with regard to consciousness itself, to be in the 'dualist' rather than the 'materialist' camp, but as a 'naturalistic dualist' a la David Chalmers. Therefore I will designate a consciousness$_1$ of the duality as the non-physical element existing in the programming decoherence information periphery, while consciousness$_2$ of the duality I designate as the physical element existing in the brain. Such is illustrated later in fig: 9-3 Part 2. For now however, I have chosen to be a 'naturalistic dualist', a la David Chalmers criteria:

(1) 'The unknown new feature of the world to be discovered', regarding consciousness, is the 'holographic principle/holomovement', applied to the smallest spaces within the brain, and all that emanates therefrom, allows consciousness to supervene (occur to an existing situation) naturally.
(2) That 'consciousness is a *feature* of the world over and above the physical features of the world. This is not to say it is a separate 'substance'. But 'mental phenomena are non-physical properties of physical phenomena.' Consciousness processes of physical humans occur in the quantum realm, of the super position of states, which can be said to be beyond the classical physicality of humans in the world.
(3) 'Consciousness carries phenomenal *information*'. Information is carried continuously between the non-physical consciousness$_1$ and the physical consciousness$_2$ for decoherence adjusted or not.

A final note then for Part 1, with regard to our belief in 'free will' and our choices, I find the Stapp notion of 'when intelligent brains select one among the alternative quantum possibilities as a basis for future action' most attractive, and from it, in part 2 of, I will launch my 'consciousness mechanism' proposal.

## Part 2 A Symphony of Strings:

A schematic of human memory is seen below in Fig: 9-1.

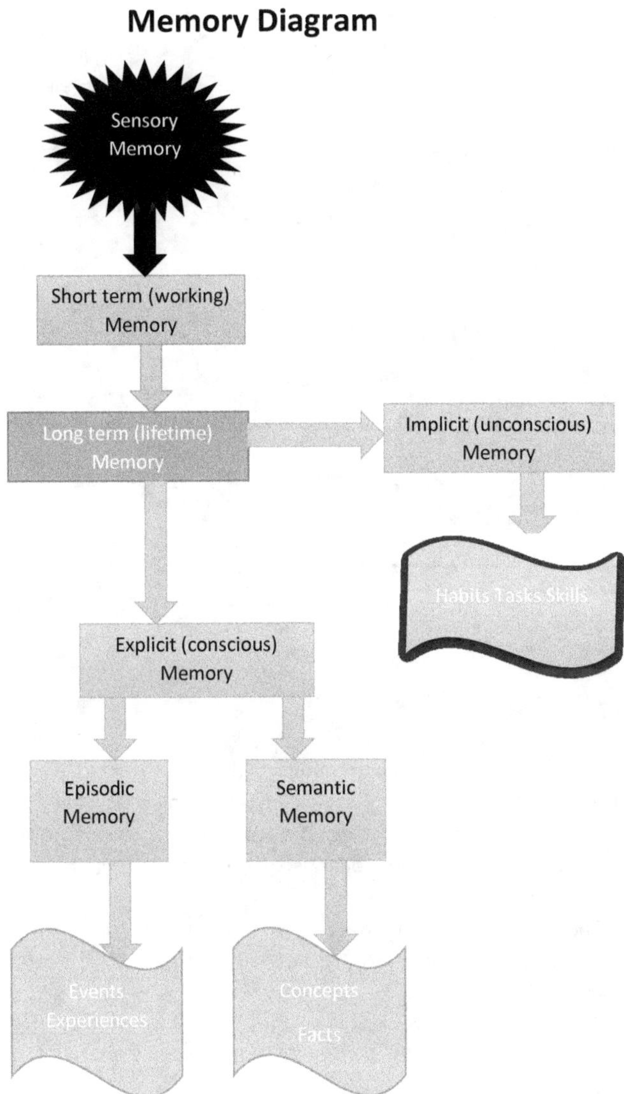


**Fig: 9-1**

Brain research thus far has told us that different brain functions are to be found in different brain areas. See Fig: 9-2 below for some of these functions.

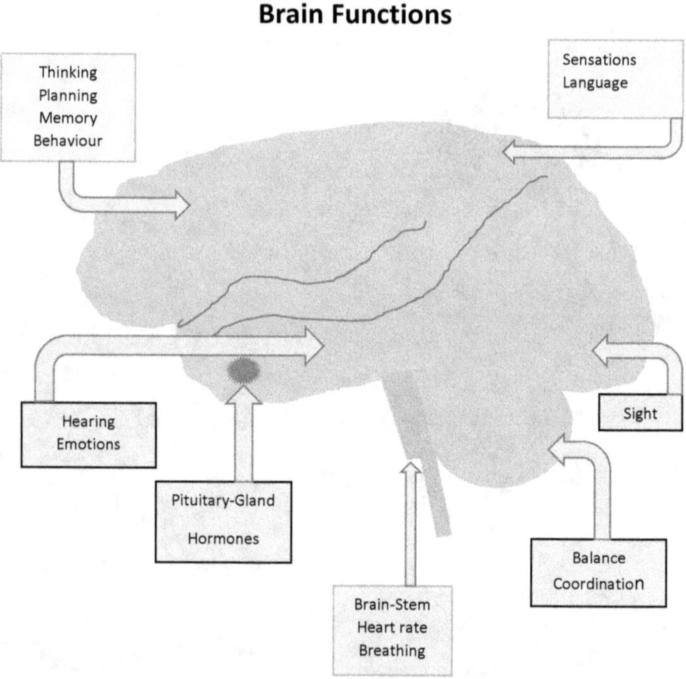


**Fig: 9-2**

So, we may now say that while different areas of the brain were shown to be specific for different functions including memory, memory also appears to be spread throughout as was noted above in Part 1 with the Rita Carter quote, 'The brain has 100 trillion connections joining billions of neurons and each junction has the potential to be part of a memory'.

The information contained in figures 9-1 and 9-2 above, was pioneered by psychologist Karl Lashley (1880-1956), together with brain surgeon Wilder Penfield (1891-1976). And indeed another prominent enthusiast in the field, scientist Karl Pribram[94] (1919-2015), building on their work and the work of others, together with

[94] Karl H. Pribram (1919-2015) the eminent brain scientist, psychologist and philosopher was born in Vienna. He was a professor at Georgetown and Stanford universities in the US.

his belief in the non-locality[95] of memory, finalised his own 'Holonomic' brain theory in 1991. Put simply the theory is, that memory is generated holographically. It was not an easy road for Pribram as the scientific community appeared at odds to his ideas from the start. There is no doubt that from the time it was first muted in 1965 and many years thereafter the theory appeared to go against prevailing views of memory processes. However, in light of the 'Holographic Principle' now accepted by most scientists, Pribram's theory may just be finding some credibility. Jibu & Yasue note "It is perhaps not too much to say that the phenomenon discovered by Lashley and Pribram in the experiments performed on the brain to find the trace of memory, is, indeed, characteristic of the hologram. The phenomenon was nonlocality. That is there appeared to be no specific loss of memory or function when part of the cerebral cortex was destroyed, but the greater the destruction the more globally degraded the memory or function became. No indication of the alleged localization of either memory or brain functions was found." (Jibu & Yasue, 1995, p. 134) We have seen previously that when a piece of holographic film is cut into pieces, each piece contains the information to produce the whole image. Of course the smaller the piece of film the less clear the projected image. The 'Holonomic' brain theory is further enhanced when we remember that the Holographic principle applies to the universe as a whole and to any other specific area in space. David Bohm was one among the limited number of scientists who embraced Pribram's notion as it fit nicely into his 'Holomovement' and 'Implicate/enfolded----Explicate/unfolded order. The part is the whole.

So, what are we to conclude from all this difficult information and different propositions on consciousness? Well, as stated in 'Part 1' above, I believe quantum mechanics has a definite role-playing part in consciousness, not least because everything else in our classical world originates therefrom, but also because I hope to show it will assist us to circumvent the 'free will' dilemma. In addition, this marriage of quantum and consciousness will enable us to demonstrate the primacy for change within capitalism.

So, to commence this process we need to understand that numerous studies, it seems, indicate that long-term memory is stored throughout the brain in the areas that acquired it and it is now also thought that when it is retrieved it is not like pulling a book from a bookshelf, rather the various neuronal activity that put it together have to be reworked for reproduction. Long term memory I believe may be equated with experience, and experience equated with information inherited and acquired. This 'experience information' then is held throughout the brain in long-term memory areas.

---

[95] This means that memories were spread throughout the brain rather than having a specific location.

Now, remembering that in black holes fundamental information is stored on compressed subatomic quantum strings and the more information there is, the more strings compress onto the surface of the 'fuzz ball' of existing strings and merge with the other strings. Clark advises that we should "Think of it as layers of paint, but instead of each successive layer overwriting the last one, they run together....the black hole simply expands to accommodate the new information." (Clark, 2010, p. 86) And most importantly as with all special areas of space, 'memory/experience' information, I believe, is held likewise in compressed quantum strings that are run together. Such strings of information are constantly being added and compressed to our memory functional areas or if you like our memory banks. Short-term memories are also quantum strings held in their own special area believed to be in the Pre-frontal cortex.

Thus, this unique and dynamic conscious self is built up over time from birth. It is this self, it is believed, calls on experience of long-term memory alone, or together with immediate/short-term memory, held in quantum strings, to make decisions/ choices. Yet, the brain is a classical organ and is decohered (or, its information is decohered) as a functional working classical model. All its activities as a warm sparking jiggling body confirm this. But we know that quantum states 'can occur in large systems as well as warm ones'. In addition, classical states, we have discovered fit our environments including ourselves and they hide quantum reality. So, behind all the classical appearance in the brain, quantum rules.

We also know that everything in our classical world is deterministic and automatic. We think we make up our minds to do something consciously but the process to do it has already begun before we make the decision, re the Benjamin Libet and other experiments. And we know that information decoherence time is 'vastly shorter than even the most fickle individual can have a flighty thought'. Therefore whether we think we have made a decision to do something and actually do it, or search our memory to weigh up the pros and cons, all this has already happened unconsciously at the quantum level because we cannot consciously access the quantum realm. In addition even if we make a decision to do something, but just before we actually do it we stop and cancel the action in our minds, it matters not! Why? Simply because the action to do or not to do is already underway before we think we make the decision. Indeed, we already know there is an automatic part of us in operation, be we conscious or unconscious, e.g. our hearts beating, our intake and output of air etc. Much of these automatic happenings in our body is inherited. We are born with the heart pumping blood around the body and we instinctively know as babies that we need nourishment and protection to survive as we cry if these needs are not fulfilled. Another example is our almost instantaneous reaction when we are exposed to danger e.g. moving quickly out of the way before a potential accident, or reacting automatically, without prior thought, in a contact sport. But other things we have to learn and then they may well become automatic. Things such as, riding a bicycle, driving a car or learning to play a musical instrument, these things we become capable of doing automatically, as while we are engaged in them our thoughts may be miles away.

So it appears that we are pretty much instant unconscious automatons yet have the classical ability to decide to do something in the longer term to change 'natural automatic' decoherence to 'adjusted automatic' decoherence. 'Natural automatic' decoherence disseminates the information holographically to project e.g. a heartbeat, an inhalation/exhalation of air, a tide ebbing and flowing, an electrical storm developing etc. Whereas, 'adjusted automatic' decoherence disseminates the information holographically to project car driving ability, business skills, medical/surgical ability, bicycle riding balance etc.

The 'dual naturalistic consciousness model' Fig: 9-3 below illustrates how, not only consciousness itself but all environments in the classical world are fed by the Programming decoherence centre. In addition, the Programming decoherence centre itself receives information, for adjustment or not, from the classical environments.

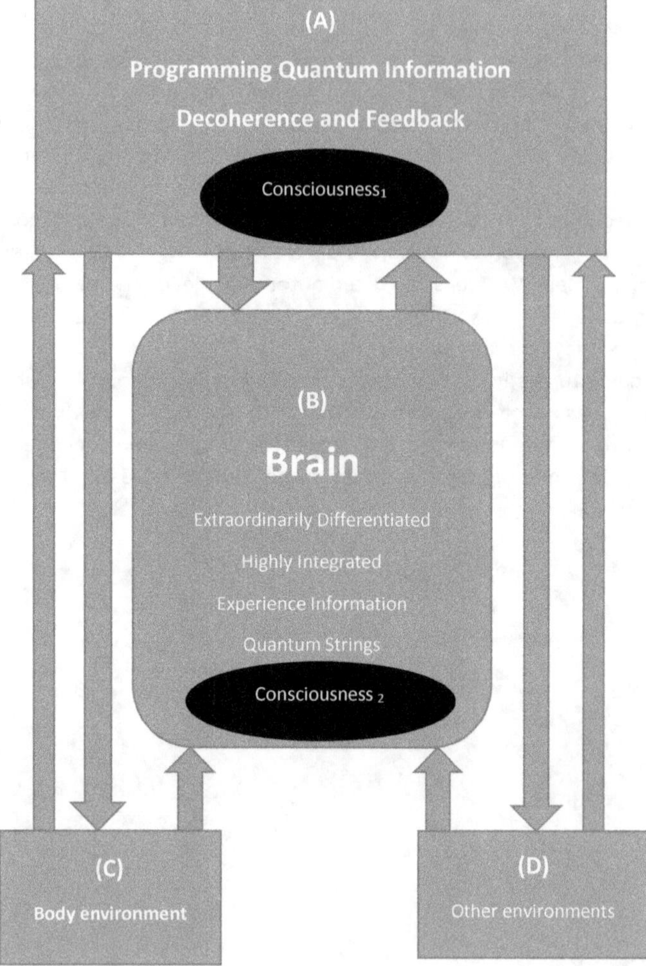


**Fig: 9-3**

In the above model, the top section (A) represents the programming decoherence centre for the holographic universe. The programming itself takes the form of 'natural' information decoherence based on environmental feedbacks as I will detail below. Just as all information originally emerged and continues to emerge from this area, so it was and is the case with consciousness. This 'consciousness$_1$'

represents the non-physical part of the 'naturalistic duality'. Thus, consciousness is decohered from the quantum into the classical physical world where Teilhard de Chardin believed, and Tononi postulated 'that consciousness is a fundamental of the universe and therefore not only 'matter' itself, but its constituent parts atoms and their ingredients all have a modicum of $\phi$'. So it was that up to the creation of life, a 'natural automatic' decoherence applied for the conventional classical world, as the feedback was simply from a non-living environment. Once life arrived however, based on its needs/desires, feedback was extended, (this feedback mechanism is explained and illustrated below) resulting in 'natural adjusted automatic' information decoherence.

Section (B) above, the brain, is the workhorse for directing and conveying messages to and from different bodily parts and functions, being a hive of nonstop activity. Also within, it houses the physical part of the 'naturalistic duality' termed 'consciousness$_2$' by way of its 'extraordinarily differentiated and highly integrated' processes a la Tononi. It is with the coordinated effort of the workhorse materialist consciousness$_2$ that we are tricked into believing we are directly steering the ship. In addition, 'information experience' is processed for housing in quantum strings within this classically warm organ (like Damasio's belief that 'conscious minds arise when a self-process is added onto a basic mind process.'). These conscioiusness$_2$ strings then, communicate on-going updated feedback to the non-physical consciousness$_1$ for, adjusted or not, 'automatic' decohered information.

Section (C): The environment of the human body, gives and receives feedback directly with section A and also with section (B) the brain for bodily processes and experience information storage.

Section (D): All other environments give and receive feedback directly with section (A) and also with section (B) the brain for other relevant worldly environmental processes and experience information storage.

In light of all this then each time we change from 'natural automatic' to 'adjusted automatic' decoherence, we are changing the environment for our personal desires or one might say our personal world. I say our personal world because as stated from the first chapter of this book it is my contention we all inhabit our own personal world within the overall classical world. Indeed, one might say that each time we change from 'natural automatic' to 'adjusted automatic' decoherence, it is a branching of the 'many worlds/minds' for our exclusive world/mind within the overall one holographic classical world. But our personal world, to a lesser or greater degree, infringes positively or negatively, on all other co-existing worlds/minds as indeed the co-existing do on ours. In addition, the higher the concentration of 'adjusted automatic' decoherence the greater will be the change to particular environments. This may be enacted either by a greater numbers of people with the same behavioural desires or indeed individuals with a particular behavioural desire and greater power.

Let me propose a scenario for the workings of this process:

1) The process of decoherence will only download its information into a suitable classical conventional environment, and this environment is known via entanglement communication. We know that everything was entangled in the beginning of the universe in the original 'dot', therefore instantaneous knowledge/communication between all particles/parts is pervasive.
2) It can therefore be anticipated what an environment requires (e.g. a heartbeat) with the appropriate information selected out automatically for decoherence of such.
3) The body and brain are specific environments.
4) The brain houses memories/experiences in quantum strings.
5) The brain is in constant sparking mode of communicating messages around the body, at speeds up to 120 m/s (432 Km/h).
6) The body gives feedback to the brain. John Coates advises on the research of Bruce McEwen, a renowned professor at Rockefeller, together with his colleagues found, "the hypothalamus sends a message to a gland instructing it to produce a hormone; the hormone fans out across the body, having its physical effects, but it also returns to the brain, changing the very way we think and behave." (Coates, 2012, p. 23) The way we think and behave changes the body environment and also is recorded in our stringed memory banks, thus changing the brain environment with new memories/ experience.
7) Environments however, via appropriate decoherence, are constantly being updated but at speeds far quicker than brain thought processes, on the order of $10^{-13}$ to $10^{-20}$seconds according to physicist Max Tegmark. This gives credence to the Libet experiment that an action is already begun before our thought processes believe we set it in motion. Therefore 'free will', as it was thought of, is not possible via the process of deciding/choosing in our mind to take an action and taking that action.
8) All particles in the classical world, we have seen, can cause 'natural automatic' decoherence/collapse.
9) It is my contention that human conscious beings can change 'natural automatic' decoherence to 'adjusted automatic' decoherence as e.g. in the process of going from ignorance of driving a car (natural automatic) to learning the skills to drive a car (adjusted automatic). So, while we do not have a free will as such, we still have the ability, via our conscious learning

desires, to change environments, via appropriate decoherence, to satisfy our desires.

10) This occurs I believe as follows: Our conscious desires are fed-back by the whole body to the brain where they are registered in the strings of our memory banks. 'Natural automatic' decoherence is a constant process taking place. In fact one can say it is a constant flow into our holographic classical world being programmed by the universal quantum computer. This is enabled by continuous instant entanglement communication between the quantum strings memory banks in the brain and the programming information on the periphery of the quantum computer universe (See Fig: 9-3 above). Also as we have seen David Bohm recognised this process even before the 'holographic principle' was established, in his proposal of what he called the 'Holomovement'. In addition, Physicist Brian Greene, an expert on string theory, tells us how the Argentinian physicist, Juan Maldacena, 'found a concrete, albeit hypothetical, realization of holography within string theory." (Greene B., 2005, p. 484)

So, while our conscious thoughts cannot penetrate the quantum downloading for choices, of our desires registered in our quantum string memory banks, it can do this unconsciously. This is enacted firstly, via entanglement communication which can be faster than the speed of light, and secondly, because the automatic process will have already begun, we know that 'the delayed choice' mechanism can be initiated to undo the past. Different choices may be selected from the myriad of choices available within the quantum (See the Henry Stapp notion above). Of course our conscious brain is telling us we are doing this at a conscious level like an on-going play but in fact we are influencing the process, by environmental feedback, for our desired behavioural choices. That is, our behavioural desires, in pursuit of growth, are fed back into the brain and constantly re-adjust the brain quantum string memory banks.

The behaviour we enact is automatic but we are under the belief that we cause it by consciously thinking to do it and then doing it. But in reality due to a build-up of 'extraordinarily differentiated and highly integrated' desires for a behaviour lodged in the quantum strings in 'consciousness$_2$' within the brain, such is communicated back up to 'consciousness$_1$' in the programming periphery for decoherence. Here this new information adjusts decoherence for the amended behavioural desire and so changes the environment to fit the behaviour. Shortly after this process begins, which occurs in the quantum realm and therefore unconsciously, our 'extraordinarily differentiated and highly integrated' brain surreptitiously tells us the behaviour we instigated via our behavioural desires are imminent. This prompts our consciousness$_2$

into believing we then choose and carry out the behaviour. This means of course we are still accountable and responsible for such instigation. This kind of conscious brain manipulation to make us believe something is happening one way when in fact it is happening another way, happens in other things as well, as noted in the previous chapter i.e. believing we see things like a movie when in fact it is a series of snap shots put together by the brain.

While we human beings are conscious then, our unconscious self is working at the same time. We have seen that many of our functions do not occur at a conscious level, e.g. the electrical activity in the brain or the beating of our hearts does not stop when we are asleep etc. So, as indicated above, these are the result of 'natural automatic' decoherence. But other things can also become 'natural automatic' once we have learned how to do them, examples are riding a bicycle or driving a car. Before we mastered the skills involved in these activities we had to somehow change our 'natural automatic' ignorance of the skill into achieving the skill. This is achieved by registering our need/desire for the skill, together with its learning, in our memory banks and this being communicated via entanglement with or without the 'delayed choice' mechanism to change the history of ignorance or doing nothing to accommodate the needed/desired something to become 'adjusted natural automatic' decoherence. In addition, this 'adjusted automatic' decoherence, when it occurs, will fit conventionally into the classical environment. This process follows a loop, based on a scientific 'positive feedback'[96] mechanism. This positive feedback then, to environments, may directly or indirectly result in progressive or regressive entropy and so have positive or negative consequences for complexity. Fig: 9-4 below illustrates the process.

[96] An example of 'scientific positive feedback' is when prices are bullish on the stock-market people buy, in the expectation of further price rises, and this in turn pushes the prices up further, so people buy more and this positive feedback continues.

## Quantum Consciousness Choices Model

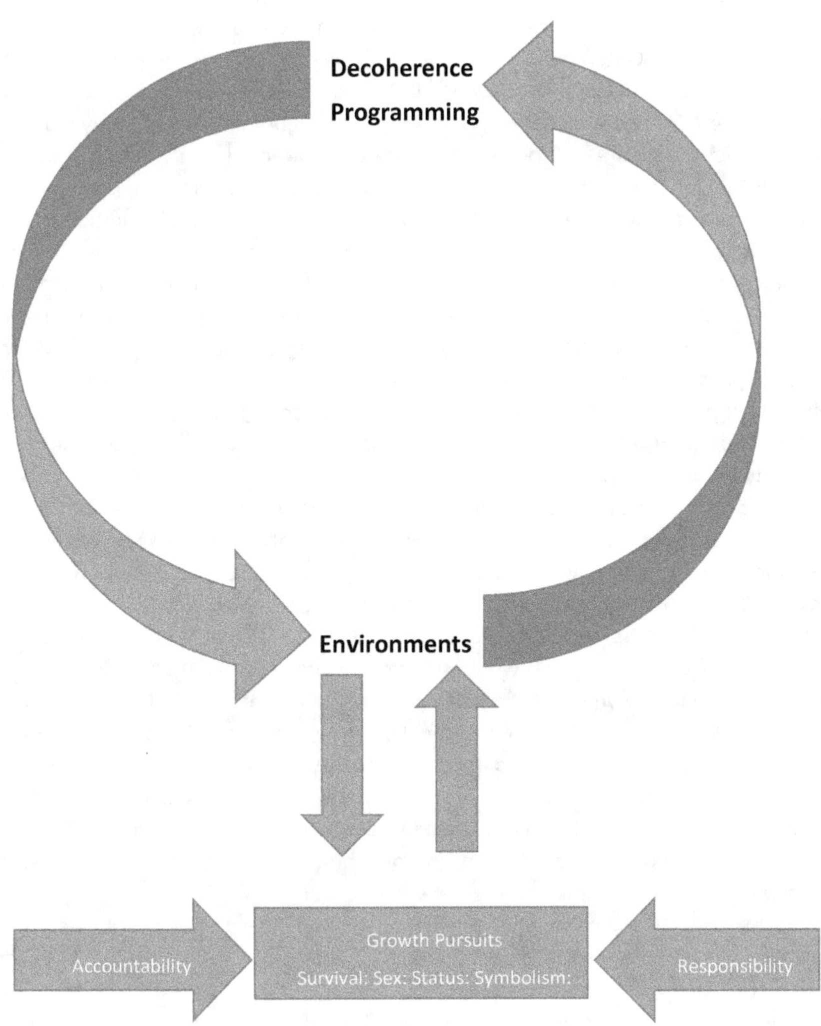


**Fig: 9-4**

Natural classical growth pursuits of survival, sex, status, and symbolism for our personal, familial and societal environments, loop up into the quantum via entangled communication and/or the 'delayed choice mechanism' to adjust decoherence for the loop back to accommodate these desires in the conventionally classical environments. From this process it can be seen that we, by way of causal desires generate 'Selected Outcomes' rather than use 'free will' to enact them. In so doing we are both accountable and responsible for all adjusted environmental change. The level of environmental change itself will of course be dependent firstly, on each unit's[97] (person's) degree of 'power force' for a feedback desire, and secondly, on the total 'power force' of the number of units (people) contributing to the same feedback desire. Now it seems that we as individuals, classically conditioned and positioned, believe changing our environmental world is of little consequence unless of course we wield massive power. This however is not the case, as individual changes are cumulative and enduring. These changes are not unlike, were it possible, to travel back in time to change some historical event big or small and therefore affect the present significantly. Whereas, with individual environmental change for our behavioural desires in the present we are constantly changing this present to affect the future, quite significantly, whether we like it or not. Of course such changes may be positive as well as negative.

This personal informational adjustment of environments sits at the core of the *Brilliantbranes'* proposition, and to gain appreciation of its significance let me visit the notion mentioned above of travelling back in time. As a thought experiment just suppose that, following leaks and numerous rumours, it was finally confirmed on January 1st 2015 by the international community that on January 1st 2016 one single unknown individual from somewhere on the earth would automatically jump back in time and place to the year 1940 in London. The announcement also revealed it had been scientifically established, due to the 'Uncertainty principle', the individual was unable to be identified, but it was ascertained that they were a responsible, caring and discerning person. In addition, the individual concerned was aware of their role in the January 1st 2016 ground-breaking event. As the identity/sex of the time traveller was unknown it was not long before the name 'Terry' (the time traveller) was established with the media.

To be sure, this ground-breaking event of time travel itself would generate even more media and societal coverage and speculation than e.g. the landing of Neil Armstrong on the moon in 1969. However, speculation with regard to the consequences of such an event would, I believe, be even greater. Indeed, governments

---

[97] I use the word 'unit' as a generic for a lifeform as, apart from people, other living things have the ability to change environments via the loopback mechanism.

would be hard pressed to control panic in communities terrified that Terry would do the smallest thing that set off a chain reaction culminating in some people not even being born[98] with others subjected to living in extreme ill health, slavery, and poverty under ideologies and economies that are dictatorial and repressive, etc. etc. It stands to reason then that should the identity of Terry be known her/his life would be worth little. Undoubtedly, there would be numerous international conferences to discuss and give advice to Terry as well as advice from religions and international organizations on what and what not she/he should do with regard to changing history. Indeed, some advice would probably be for Terry to avoid such a jump in time, do the right thing, and commit suicide, even if, as could equally apply, Terry's interference might change things for the better!

So, it is by belief then that such would be the reaction to one responsible, caring and discerning person going back in time seven and a half decades. But how would it be if Terry was not responsible, caring and discerning, and in fact, with the sophistication of 2016 knowledge, desired to change things to accommodate her/his selfish, greedy and megalomaniac aspirations? Well, I believe the answer is that the environmentally changing negative effects would be major. And indeed were thousands of such selfish and greedy megalomaniacs to make the time jump the environmentally changing effects would be momentous.

Returning to the present though, the pursuit of our growth needs/desires as individuals or groups is no less negatively or positively environmentally changing. It is just hidden, like the quantum, beneath the surface of our natural classical busy lives. Unlike the quantum however, we can access our consequential footprint but mostly, due to our selfish genes, we practice a wilful blindness in this regard.

We have seen already that our growth pursuits come at the price of the extraction of low entropy/high information from other environments as well as our personal environments, thus initiating regressive entropy/increased disorder. Excessive regressive entropy can readily be seen as individuals/groups/organisations extract surplus progressive entropy that may not be invested for general complexity but may be greed fuelled and/or wasteful. A schematic flow chart of extracted progressive entropy and its uses was presented in Fig: 7-1. It is obvious from this to conclude that a balance is required between the drives for progressive entropy and their potential regressive entropy consequences. Indeed, it is incumbent upon us as individuals to ensure our own extraction of progressive entropy is balanced by it being used for our own needs or societal use with no waste. It is also equally

[98] 'The grandmother paradox' in time travel proposes that should someone go back in time and somehow cause the death of their grandmother before she gave birth to your father or mother then you would never have been born and cease to exist. Of course a time traveller could also do something simple (for the want of a nail) and cause the deaths of hundreds of thousands thus causing millions to cease to exist.

in our remit to ensure any regressive entropy generated by others is neutralised and/or steered towards the progressive. Such is the environmental accountability and responsibility for ourselves, family, group, planet and universe. This is not an easy task, as our input, based on our growth pursuits, is somewhat handicapped as follows:

1) We believe our choices/decisions are made from the neck up (rationally) but are in fact a whole body programme.
2) Our growth pursuits have a tendency to be excessive due to their pleasurable feedback.
3) For most of us we believe our choices have little or no effects on others or environments but even classically, chaos theory dispels this myth.
4) We believe that by using our free will, we enact an 'outside-in' approach to pursue our desires from given environments. This, many of us believe we do as an individual right within societal regulations, to achieve growth for ourselves and others without limit.

So, yes we are handicapped in our beliefs, due to our selfish genes and wilful blindness however, the reality is that we are reprogramming environments from the inside-out to facilitate the procurement of our desires. In doing this environments will be changed not only for ourselves but also for the benefit or detriment of others. Our pursuit of growth then as we have seen generates a feedback mechanism of 'adjusted automatic' decoherence into our classical world environments. These environments being, ourselves, our planet, our climate, our culture, our economy etc.

With regard to market economies, firstly, the adjusted automatic information decohered for the cost saving aspect of businesses has skewed/changed the environment to erode the general business customer base. Secondly, information decohered for banking, because their pursuit of self-interest, has skewed/changed the financial environment for the whole economy. And thirdly, information decohered for capital investment has skewed/changed the environment of value distribution towards inequality. These three environmental changes are stark examples of regressive entropy, generated by the pursuit of growth, and as such are required to be neutralised and adjusted for progressive entropy. Regarding employment erosion, it is not enough to attempt to generate employment by state initiatives, capital investments, business growth and the likes. To be sure, all these processes are important but the root cause of the erosion needs to be tackled. In addition, it is not enough to introduce temporary regulations on banks that are later rescinded or watered down for political expediency or vested interest. Instead, the root cause of self-interest vs public interest has to be addressed. Finally, it is not enough to attempt to achieve a fair distribution of value by taxes that stifle growth. Rather, an environmental progressive change needs to be enacted.

In conclusion the most important lesson, by far, to be taken from this chapter is that our behaviour in the pursuance of our conscious choices, based on our needs and desires are not processed as we believe nor are they insignificant. On the contrary, their mechanism, due to our classical positioning, is counter intuitive and they carry with them consequences that, on the one hand we may recognise or on the other hand ignore or suppress. Whatever the case, we shoulder 'accountability' and 'responsibility' for these consequences, be they positive or negative, with regard to ourselves, families, future generations, society at large and the planet itself.

## CHAPTER 10
# Behaviour

Growth is a natural process. Firstly, we want ourselves to grow to participate in society in a positive way. Secondly, should we be blessed with children, we want them to grow perhaps even better than ourselves if possible. To this end we nurture and educate them to the best of our abilities. Indeed, we look for growth in everything from our food, energy supplies, to our organisations. We want our salaries/wages to grow. We want our businesses to grow. We also want our state economy to grow, so there is growth in jobs, and greater government revenue for less taxes and more amenities and services. Of course all our growth desires will be dependent on our own behaviour and on the behaviour of others.

We will in this chapter therefore concentrate on our behaviour in general, together with specific aspects of it in the pursuance of our needs and desires. In this, our examination will be firmly anchored in the classical world, yet, not forgetting that the quantum is still there but hidden. In addition and most importantly, even crucial, is knowing that all our individual environmental adjustments, to accommodate our desires, infringe on all other environments, to a major or minor degree, positively or negatively. Our behaviour, it is said, may or may not reflect our attitudes, but it can be a good indication of what our attitudes might be. For example, we might not like to hear a particular type of joke as we find such uncomfortable so our attitude to them is that they are abhorrent, but in certain social settings our behaviour is to laugh at them. We have therefore hidden our true attitude with behaviour that indicates a different attitude.

There are numerous definitions of behaviour but for our purposes the following will suffice: *Behaviour is the way individuals act or don't act, with or without stimulus, under different conditions.* So, to be clear, inaction as well as action forms part of our behaviour.

From the information gleaned in previous chapters it is probably fair to say that people's behaviour, throughout their lives, will be based on their inherited traits and learned information. This learned information will also allow us to anticipate some of the effects of a particular behaviour on ourselves or other living and non-livings environments. Therefore one's behaviour will have some impact on not just their world but also, however small or seemingly insignificant, on the planet as a whole and indeed the entire universe. Remember chaos theory how the smallest thing, changes everything.

In general people behave the way they do to gain an 'effect' for themselves and/or others. Some examples of why people behave the way they do is:

1) Personal needs/desires
2) Civil conventions
3) Moral standards
4) Religious beliefs
5) Group rules and regulations
6) To impress or annoy/harm others
7) To gain pleasure/feel good
8) To help others
9) To appear to be what they are not

It may be said then that an individual's behaviour is shaped by, 'Biological', 'Environmental', and 'Cultural' influences. These influences also determine, to a certain extent, an individual's 'personality'. I say to a certain extent because we have the ability, if not to change our personality, to exhibit a different personality type if required. We see actors do this all the time. Nonetheless, we have developed our individual personality, as the most comfortable for us, to enact our behaviour. With behaviour itself manifested through the previously mentioned natural human 'S' drives, of 'Survival', 'Sex', 'Status', and 'Symbolism'.

With the brief introduction above it will now be appropriate to take a tour through the behavioural influences, personality types, and finish with the 'S' drives together with their effects on our contribution to regressive/progressive entropy.

Biological influence:

Our inherited genes, first and foremost, represent the initial biological influence on our behaviour. These genes will provide survival instincts together with our sex, our race, colour, size and other features e.g. mannerisms. How we deal with our gene inheritance will add to the mix of all influences, for example, should we be born of very short stature, our behaviour in seeking a life partner will probably entail seeking someone of a similar size. In addition to the genetic influences we will develop further influences through the learning process (information) both formal and informal. Then, when we combine inherited and informational influences, this will help set us up for intuitive processes and emotional development.

Jonathan Haidt advises "*Intuition* is the best word to describe the dozens or hundreds of rapid, effortless moral judgements and decisions that we all make every day. Only a few of these intuitions come to us embedded in full-blown emotions....." (Haidt, 2012, p. 45). Intuitive rapid judgements however, are often based on primitive instinctual processes and may in fact be incorrect. We also make intuitive/instinctual decisions because firstly, as we have seen, we act automatically, and secondly because we cannot be bothered to take the time for 'rational' analysis and believe we just know instinctively what is best. How often for example, do we purchase something without actually reading the full terms and conditions of the sale? Physicist Leonard Mlodinow gives us an example of how we just intuitively feel we are correct in our decision making when in fact we are not. "Marilyn vos Savant, famous for being listed for years in the *Guinness World Records* Hall of fame as the person with the world's highest recorded IQ (228)...the following question appeared in her column one Sunday in September (Wording altered slightly): *Suppose the persons on a game show are given the choice of three doors: Behind one door is a car; behind the others are goats. After a contestant picks a door, the host, who knows what's behind all doors, opens one of the unchosen doors, which reveals a goat. He then says to the contestant. Do you want to switch to the other unopened door? Is it in the contestant's advantage to make the switch?*

The question was inspired by the workings of the television game show *Let's Make a Deal*, which ran from 1963 to 1976 and in several incarnations from 1980 to 1991.............it appears to be a pretty silly question. Two doors are available—open one and you win; open the other and you lose—so it seems self-evident that whether you change your choice or not, your chances of winning are 50/50...(But) Marilyn said in her column that it is better to switch.

10,000 letters 92% said she was wrong. 1,000 PHD's including many math professors, who seemed to be particularly irate. But first choice is a 3/1 the second choice is a 2/1 better chance." (Mlodinow, 2008, p. 50)

Regarding full blown emotions on the other hand, Antonio Damasio gives insight into the universal emotions of fear, anger, sadness, happiness, disgust, and surprise. "Emotions work when images processed in the brain call into action a number of emotion-triggering regions...Once any of these trigger regions is activated, certain consequences ensue---chemical molecules are secreted by endocrine glands and by subcortical nuclei and delivered to both the brain and the body..." (Damasio, 2010,

p. 110) Steroid hormones secreted by the endocrine system, John Coates tells us have particularly potent effects on our behaviour. "This group includes testosterone, oestrogen, and cortisol the main hormone of the stress response. Steroids exert particularly widespread effects because they have receptors in almost every cell in our body and brain." (Coates, 2012, pp. 22-23). We have also seen from the previous chapter that 'the hypothalamus sends a message to a gland instructing it to produce a hormone; the hormone fans out across the body, having its physical effects, but it also returns to the brain, changing the very way we think and behave'.

Probably the most commonly known hormone is adrenalin, as we often hear of the adrenalin 'rush' that speeds up physical reactions. The stress hormone cortisol, mentioned above, stimulates dopamine which itself is a hormone and also a neurotransmitter[99]. A Dopamine 'rush' gives us pleasure and indeed dopamine neuronal activity is increased with addictive drugs. Anything then that produces dopamine, we tend to pursue for the pleasure of it. "When we receive some valuable piece of information, or perform some act that promotes our health and survival, such as eating, drinking, having sex or making large amounts of money, dopamine is released along what are called the pleasure pathways of the brain, providing us with a rewarding, even euphoric, experience. In fact our brain seems to value the dopamine more than the food or drink or sex itself. Give an animal the choice between on the one hand eating and drinking, and on the other self-stimulating with dopamine, and it will self-stimulate until it starves." (Coates, 2012, p. 136)

At Rockefeller University Coates came across a model of testosterone-fuelled behaviour that offered a tantalising explanation of trader behaviour called 'the winner effect'. "In this model, two males enter a fight for turf or a contest for a mate and, in anticipation of the competition, experience a surge in testosterone, a chemical bracer that increases the blood's capacity to carry oxygen and, in time, their lean muscle mass. Testosterone also affects the brain, where it increases the animal's confidence and appetite for risk. After the battle has been decided the winner emerges with even higher levels of testosterone, the loser with lower levels. The winner, if he proceeds to the next level of competition, does so with already elevated testosterone, and this androgenic priming gives him an edge, helping him win yet again." (Coates, 2012, p. 25)

Coates further makes the point that women have only about 10% to 20% the level of testosterone to men which probably accounts for the fact that women don't start too many wars. And just to elaborate further on this, a report in 'The Times' 13/11/14 that pulls all the macho strings, talks of an up-coming G20 summit. The Australian

---

[99] Neurotransmitter: 'A chemical that mediates the transmission of a nerve impulse across a synapse or a neuromuscular junction.' Oxford Dictionary of Biology

Prime Minister Tony Abbott, claims to have evidence that "a Russian-supplied missile launcher was responsible for the crash of Malaysian Airlines Flight MH 17 over eastern Ukraine in July.....Mr Abbott, a former amateur boxer, had previously threatened to 'shirt front' – or 'knock down' – Mr Putin, a martial arts expert, over the shooting down of the aircraft, which was carrying 36 Australians." (Lagan, 2014) Now, while not downgrading the seriousness of the Malaysian Airline tragedy or that full responsibility and transparency of this horrific event is required, this report however, written by a man, presents us with two opposing individuals, both trained fighters, squaring up to each other physically, with their nation's defences hovering in the background!!! I mean seriously, is this not school-yard stuff?

An important point to remember, regarding all biological influences on our behaviour, is that they relate not just to our brains but to the whole body.

## Environmental influence:

It is probably obvious that environments play a major role in influencing our behaviour, and as such, the following questions may be asked:

- What type of climate do I live in, hot, cold, temperate?
- Do I live in a developed or developing country?
- What is the political set up in my country?
- What sort of economy does my country have?
- What are the education services, health services, social services?
- What are the employment/unemployment rates?
- Is there religious, race, sex, age, colour or ideological dominance/ discrimination in my country?
- Is my country rich/poor in natural resources?
- If rich in natural resources who controls/owns them?
- What are my country's laws on the environment?
- Have I been born into a wealthy or poor family?

Indeed, I may ask numerous other such questions, but one question probably sums up the lot namely, 'What, advantages/disadvantages, in general, has my environment given for me'? The answer, be it positive or negative, will certainly influence my behaviour and in many cases dictate it.

Apart from what I will call natural environment, such as climate, resources or geography, there is also a historically endowed environment, based on developmental or disastrous events. Scientist Jared Diamond's excellent publication

*Guns, Germs and Steel* (Diamond, 2005) illustrates this superbly. In it we see how those states/people who developed the most superior arms for war/defence will be advantaged over those who don't. Likewise, those who have resources (e.g. steel) will be advantaged over those who don't. And finally, those peoples who have been virtually wiped out by plagues or subject to inferior healthcare will be disadvantaged to those who have avoided such plagues and have superior health/healthcare. In addition those advantaged will develop superior educational facilities and methods.

A further example of environments affecting our behaviour is given by psychologist Bruce Hood. "WHEN IT COMES to making choices, most of us feel confident that we evaluate the evidence objectively, weigh the pros and cons, and act according to reason. Otherwise, we would have to concede that our decisions are unreasonable, and few individuals are willing to acknowledge this." (Hood, Supersense, 2009, p. 36) Hood then illustrates this point by relating how he demonstrates the psychological impression created by objects. At his lectures he hands out a 1930s fountain pen, telling the audience it belonged to Albert Einstein. He invites them to hold and touch it and many do with great reverence, somehow similar to how medieval society would probably have revered relics of the saints. By feeling and touching the pen there is somehow a 'feeling' that something of the original owner will be transferred to the holder.

Following the pen he then presents to the audience a gentleman's old cardigan that is a bit 'the worse for wear' and asks if anyone would like to slip it on. About one third of those present are willing, and additional numbers volunteer when he incentivizes further with a prize. Before the try-on however, he tells the audience the story of Fred West, British serial killer, whose photograph then appears on the power point screen. Once the audience is told the cardigan belonged to Fred West most hands drop down amid nervous laughter. Some, of course are still willing to show their inner strength and give it a go. Neither pen nor cardigan belonged to the Einstein or West respectively, but Hood's point is clearly demonstrated. We may believe we are rational reasonable folk but behind all of us lurks some primitive processes.

## Cultural influence:

Culture is social. That is, it is about doing things that are acceptable, praiseworthy, or contributory to and/or with other individuals, specific groups, or society at large. Haidt tells us that "other people influence us constantly just by revealing they like or dislike somebody." (Haidt, 2012, p. 47) If we lived alone without any other living things, we could do anything we liked to satisfy our needs or desires. But we live with other living things so our behaviour is related to them, particularly to other human beings and what we want our behaviour to convey to them. Also, by observing their behaviour, not alone their likes or dislikes but any behaviour will, when measured against our own attitudes or standards, probably affect our own behaviour to a certain degree. The result of this is that behaviour in most cultural endeavours is to a certain extent standardized and replicated.

The Meme of course, as we saw earlier is our cultural replicator? It may be individually or group initiated and then replicated to be applied as 'collective pressuring' and/or 'personally actionable'. Memes come in all shapes, sizes and colours. For example, the use of social media, the economic management of a country, and even the dominant religion in a country, as well as sports, jokes, songs, stories etc. may all be classified as memes that are replicated again and again. Indeed, some such memes not alone influence behaviour but in many cases dictate/ enforce behaviour. Cognitive scientist Daniel Dennett advises "Memes now spread around the world at the speed of light, and replicate at rates that make even fruit flies and yeast cells look glacial in comparison." (Dennett, 1993, p. 205) Societal culture of course is made up of 'Memes' and these fall roughly into three groups namely, *morals, utilitarian, and popular*.

With regard to *morals* Haidt advises, "Moral systems are interlocking sets of values, virtues, norms, practices, identities, institutions, technologies, and evolved psychological mechanisms that work together to suppress or regulate self-interest and make cooperative societies possible." (Haidt, 2012, p. 270) Morals then produce, e.g. religions, political ideologies and even economic practices. But of course, not all societies have the same morals. Nonetheless, there is in all of us a sense of what we perceive is right or wrong. So, it can be said that we are moral by nature but our morality is also influenced by the nurturing of given values and belief systems. Indeed, different religions, and political/economic ideologies stand out as examples of the diversity such nurturing can create. We see every day, how the differences between these and indeed within them, causes war, inequality, poverty, pollution, sexism, racism and various forms of discrimination from 'ethnic cleansing' to 'female genital mutilation'. Yet as noted, morals are necessary to 'make cooperative societies possible', positively giving us 'standards' on how we should act personally, as well as when interacting with others. An example here would be 'The Golden Rule or ethic of reciprocity' that is found in most religions, e.g. Luke 6.31 *Do to others as you would have then do to you.*

*Utilitarian* memes are simply those rules and regulations that evolve by convention or are embodied in law and implemented for the smooth running of society. Examples are, 'The rules of the road', 'Company law', 'Criminal law', 'Air traffic control', 'Medical ethical processes' etc. etc. Then there are conventions such as 'table manners' and general courtesies. Of course some of us, perhaps even most of us, do not always conform to these rules, regulations and conventions, especially when we believe we cannot be seen breaking them. Nonetheless, the alternative to not having them would result in chaos or even anarchy.

*Popular* memes are for example, 'urban myths', 'jokes', 'songs', 'brand loyalty', 'sports' 'clubs', 'fashions' etc.

All of these meme groups, it can be seen, contribute significantly as cultural influences on behaviour in virtually all societal groups. 'Biological', 'Environmental', and 'Cultural' behavioural influence then will shape our 'personality', which may be described as our individual behavioural modus operandi.

It appears that each of us fits into one or other of a five-factor model of personality. Behavioural scientist Daniel Nettle explains, there is a set of concepts, "called the five-factor model of personality, or the big five. The five factor model has emerged from a welter of research over the last few decades and looks to be the most comprehensive, reliable and useful framework for discussing human personality that we have ever had. The idea of the model is that there are five major dimensions along which all human characters vary. Thus any individual can be given five scores that will tell us a great deal about the ways they are liable to behave through their lives." (Nettle, 2009, p. 9) Nettle lists these big five personality dimensions giving high scores and low scores in Table 10-1 as follows:

## Personality Dimensions

| **Dimension** | **High scores are...** | **Low scores are...** |
|---|---|---|
| Extraversion | Outgoing, enthusiastic | Aloof, quiet |
| Neuroticism | Prone to stress and worry | Emotionally stable |
| Conscientiousness | Organized, self-directed | Spontaneous, careless |
| Agreeableness | Trusting, empathetic | Uncooperative, hostile |
| Openness | Creative, imaginative, eccentric | Practical, conventional |

**Table: 10-1**

Just to recap then the influences, namely biological, environmental, and cultural all contribute to behavioural processes by way of a completely individual personality. We are unique as is physically evidenced by, for example, our fingerprints, but we are also unique in how we interpret things. Dorothy Rowe, writing in *New Scientist* advises "it is not what happens to us that determines our behaviour but how we interpret what happens to us.....Over the last 20 years or so, neuroscientists have...

found that our brains function in such a way that we cannot see 'reality' directly. All we can ever know are the guesses or interpretations our mind creates about what is going on. To create these guesses, we can only draw on basic human neuroanatomy and on our past experience, no two people ever interpret anything in exactly the same way." (Rowe, 2010)

We hear a lot about the human 'rights' of individuals in so-called free countries and such rights need to be extended to 'adult' individuals who will then be accountable and therefore responsible for themselves, society, and the environment at large. Such accountability and responsibility needs careful consideration when making behavioural decisions, manifested through our natural human drives. This notion will now be examined with regard to the human 'S' drives of 'Survival', 'Sex', 'Status', and 'Symbolism' and their mix and implementation will determine the contribution to an individual's goal for increased complexity, for themselves, their children and future generations. Increasing complexity is of course another way of generating 'growth'. In other words growth is enabled by the 'S' drives that produce progress, and so generates progressive entropy. But negative growth is also enabled by the 'S' drives and that impairs progress and so generates or speeds up regressive entropy. Remember that *each individual*, who changes their own environment, also changes the overall world environment, for positive or negative outcomes affecting the rest of society and indeed future generations. With this in mind it is now time to examine the drives themselves:

## Survival:

Survival is primary and is maintained with food, warmth and shelter. It is no doubt primitive in origin but then develops as we get more consciously sophisticated and complex. Survival is firstly for self, then for family and group. Our basic needs are attended to first, and then we move on to accumulation for the rainy day and ever more comforts, but this accumulation may have no bounds for some. Excess will be sought for the immediate family or group. Indeed, the notion of sufficient excess may be sought to enable family/group survival and comfort following one's own death. Individuals must be free to work and/or have the opportunity to work for these rewards. At some point however, the excess may far exceed survival requirements/comfort for the self, the family and posthumous contributions. With this excess however, individuals must stand personally accountable and societally and environmentally responsible, firstly for their behaviour in the accumulation of the excess and secondly in its investment towards general complexity. Put simply, this means that their behaviour, once their own/family/group needs are reached, does not damage the self/society/environment, either directly or indirectly. An example of direct damage to self would be overconsumption of food, drink or stimulants, whereas, an example of damage to society/environment would of course be the causing of pollution. An example of indirect damage would be, preventing survival means for others due to profit motivation, greed etc.

Remember the balance between regressive entropy and progressive entropy must at least be maintained with the goal to increase the progressive for the self/society/environment. Damage caused by the survival drive however, increases/accelerates the regressive directly for some and indirectly for the rest of us one way or another. Indeed, those individuals/groups that acquire major excesses in the survival drive pursuit have as stated major responsibilities to society and the environment. But let there be no doubt, many such individuals attend their responsibilities with gusto. Unfortunately, many more do not.

## Sex:

Sex is the primitive drive to replicate. The drive itself may be further enhanced by the other 'S' drives for greater chances of its accommodation. The drive itself is different in males and females. Each individual will pursue sex for their pleasure (whatever turns you on?) or procreation purposes, based on the selfish gene. An individual's behaviour in the pursuit, act, and aftermath of sex however, needs to be tempered by self-accountability and societal/environmental responsibility. In this regard sexual acts should entail consensual participants as defined by societal norms. Such acts should not demean, damage or exploit any participants, unless they consent to such without force, or for example, their pleasure. With regard to the copulation act itself, accountability and responsibility for birth control methodology or not, rests firmly with both participants. Should a pregnancy result, again both participants in the sexual act causing the pregnancy must stand accountable and responsible. Should both participants wish to have the pregnancy terminated, then both participants are accountable and responsible in this regard within of course the legal framework of their environment. Should the female alone wish to terminate the pregnancy, the question must be asked, does the pregnancy itself then belong solely to the female in the physical and mental world she uniquely inhabits? If one believes the answer is yes, then the decision for termination, together with its accountability and responsibility, is with the female. Others of course do not believe the pregnancy belongs solely to the female and in such cases, state and/or religious laws may inhibit the woman's choice! On the other hand, as stated above, once the pregnancy is brought to term and the child is born, full accountability and responsibility rests completely with both parents. Only when such is secured should the state/society, if required, be expected to contribute to the child's support. Sex is a most beautiful, wonderful and pleasurable thing, however, when there is no accountability or responsibility, at any point from start to finish, it affects us all by contributing to the acceleration of regressive entropy. From Presidents to priests, this drive knows no bounds in its societal/ environmental contribution and also unfortunately its fallout.

Another issue relating to the sex drive is population control. Since the Reverend Thomas Malthus' view (see chapter 3) on population getting out of hand, population growth concerns have been on-going. Some methodologies addressing these concerns have ended in disaster like the one-child scheme in China or the sterilization programmes in India. Then there is the imposition of religious rules that prevent artificial birth control a la the Catholic Church. Not alone did this add to population growth but also resulted in the spread of AIDs. In light of these calamities, state and/or religious interference on birth control needs to be thoroughly scrutinized for their possible adverse consequences. This is not to say that adequate birth-control education/information, together with affordable preventatives be available to all. On the contrary, proper precautions together with accountability and responsibility have a twofold effect, firstly, they prevent unwanted pregnancies and therefore abortions, and secondly, they are the first line of defence in combatting overpopulation. There are indications that the world birth-rate is declining, and the prediction is that this decline will continue, see Table 10-2 below. It is believed that this is due to greater education in general, and in particular greater education of women. With increased birth control, there are more funds available to invest in the educational needs of fewer children, not to mention funds for a more comfortable familial lifestyle.

It is also true that people are living longer, again due to education and of course, major developments in healthcare. This is a wonderful thing, however vast amounts of funds, from most healthcare budgets are spent on 'end of life' care, and this is a respectful, honourable and loving thing, certainly for the patient but also for their loved ones. There are however, many of these patients who, given the choice, would prefer to have a premature death, and so not prolong, pain, indignity, and/costs. In spite of all the above the world population continues to grow and greater individual accountability and responsibility both at the instigation of the life process as well as at the end is the key to population management. Such management requires the assistance and educated understanding of society at large.

## World historical and predicated crude birth rates (1950-2050) Crude birth rate (births per 1,000) population

UN medium variant of World Population Prospects: The 2015 Revision.

| Years | CBR | Years | CBR |
|---|---|---|---|
| 1950-1955 | 36.9 | 2000-2005 | 20.8 |
| 1955-1960 | 35.5 | 2005-2010 | 20.2 |
| 1960-1965 | 35.4 | 2010-2015 | 19.6 |
| 1965-1970 | 34.1 | 2015-2020 | 18.6 |
| 1970-1975 | 31.6 | 2020-2025 | 17.5 |
| 1975-1980 | 28.6 | 2025-2030 | 16.6 |
| 1980-1985 | 27.8 | 2030-2035 | 16.1 |
| 1985-1990 | 27.5 | 2035-2040 | 15.7 |
| 1990-1995 | 24.5 | 2040-2045 | 15.3 |
| 1995-2000 | 21.9 | 2045-2050 | 14.9 |

Source: United Nations, Department of Economic and Social Affairs, Population Division (2015). World Population Prospects: The 2015 Revision, custom data acquired via website. (Retrieved 01/02/2016)

**Table: 10-2**

## Status:

The status drive fundamentally relates to our place in society. What I mean by this is not just status as it is generally understood, for example, leadership status, wealth status, religious hierarchical status etc. I mean we all have what I will designate as an 'occupational' status. Occupational status examples are, employer, employee, carer, professional, home-keeper, teacher, prisoner, independent heir/heiress, state dependent person, beggar, unemployed-person, voluntary worker, student and retiree etc. Whatever role we occupy is our fundamental status, and above all else we must be satisfied, as far as possible, with this. This is not to say we must love work, Monday mornings, or our very annoying boss! It is to say that we feel, on balance, we occupy a satisfactory place in society. This satisfaction or other of course will depend, to some extent, on how society sees our occupational status and this in turn will have effects on our behaviour. Let me make it clear however, that some state-dependent people such as, the unemployed and beggars are not to be perceived in the same way as prisoners. Unfortunately, some people do just that, in an attitude of 'blaming the victim'. Nonetheless, state benefits and helping beggars may be perceived by some as an incentive not to look for work. This perception is, in general, held mostly by those who are 'well-heeled' and/or in secure comfortable employment. To be sure state benefits can be exploited and in some few cases they do create a moral hazard[100]. The vast majority of people though would, if possible, seek a satisfactory occupational status for themselves within society. This may be a job, voluntary work, etc.

Status then is firstly for our individual selves and within the family group. It also drives us in regard to our position within society in that one has a useful role as a contributing member. Such contribution may afford you high status in the group/society as solid citizen, or even a leader. The more you contribute the more important you are for the group and you may then, due to this high contribution, be afforded or earned a higher status than others. Contributions need not be just monetary e.g. taxes, they may also be a skill contribution to industry, the arts, sport, politics, economics etc.

To be unable to contribute to the group (e.g. limited/no income or incarcerated) means a drop in status that can affect not just the individual but also their family and group. The behavioural drive for continued superior status is a natural process and a producer of progressive entropy however, over-drive simply for self-aggrandizement or infringing on the status of others breeds regressive entropy. Each individual will pursue a process for a status they are content with, or desire, driven by the selfish gene. Again such processes, be they demeaning, damaging, exploitative or hindering of others' opportunities for simple dignified status, will revert from progressive to regressive entropy. The point to be made here is that these excesses whether through outright greed or even religious or other ideological beliefs, not to mention ignorance and wilful blindness, once they are detrimental to others, due to their sexual orientation, their sex, race, nationality, beliefs etc. then result in regressive entropy. Your status at whatever level requires you to be accountable for your actions (behaviour) and responsible to society and the environment.

---

100 Moral hazard is an economic term basically means lack of incentive to guard against risk where one is protected from its consequences,

## Symbolism:

A symbol (according to AZ Collins English e-dictionary), 'is something that represents or stands for something else, usually by convention or association, esp a material object used to represent something abstract.' Symbols take the form of words, sounds, gestures, or visual images and are used to convey ideas and beliefs.' Major familiar symbols are, the cross representing Christianity, the swastika representing Nazi Germany, various national flags, badges, medals and honours of all kinds. Whatever our colour, or creed we all embrace symbolism directly or indirectly, from presidents wearing flag badges on their lapels to the local football team togged out in their colours. Symbolism can be, and is a great tool to bring like-minded people together, be it at a national or local level. When the national team wins a sporting event, the national colours are displayed with pride and people throughout the state feel, through the shared symbolism, part of the victory. Symbols can also be used to convey achievements, like a silver cup for winning a football tournament, a gold medal for winning the Olympic marathon, a university degree certificate, a Knight or Dame Medal, Sceptre, Crown etc. Winning and honours of course are synonymous of excellence and therefore growth resulting in progressive entropy.

Symbolism however also has a dark side in that, ideological and religious differences can and do create major disputes and even full scale wars. Wars are usually driven by greed, jealousy, envy, hate, and injustice, actual or perceived. Each side in disputes will have their own symbols and as a measure of hatred for the other side the enemy's symbol is often degraded and destroyed, while their own symbols are revered and respected almost in some cases, to the level of deification. Symbolism in this regard accelerates regressive entropy via waste, destruction and loss of life.

Our general behaviour then manifested through the 'S' drives has the promise of great and magnificent contributions to complexity. Unfortunately, excessive desires by some reduce the simple needs of the many.

So, to sum up this chapter the behaviour an individual exhibits, by action or inaction, is arrived at with the following three inputs: (1) Inherited and learned traits/information, (2) biological, environmental, and cultural influences, and (3) 'S' drive pursuits. These three processes form 'attitudes' that are not necessarily fixed, as well as a personality that is changeable. In addition, it is mostly believed that behaviour exhibited by a person/persons is indicative of their attitudes but it may be a false behaviour to hide true attitudes. Indeed, personality presented in a behaviour may also be false in order to convey a different message.

Whatever the case, accountability and responsibility remain attached to all behaviour exhibited. See Behaviour Model Fig: 10-1 below:

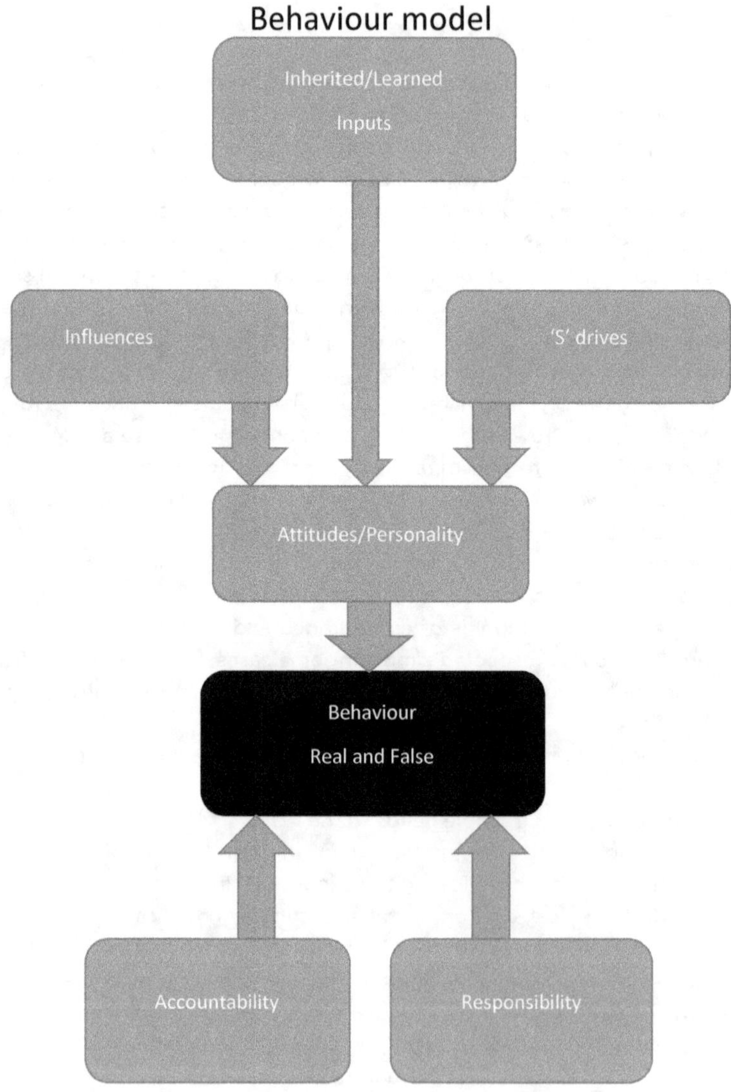


**Fig: 10-1**

Behaviour then can be a wondrous wand or a woeful weapon depending on how it is enacted. Indeed, a well-accepted woeful result of our behaviour is 'Climate Change'. This may nonetheless, be changed for the better with different behaviour. In general however, our behaviour not only affects the climatic environment but all environments be they biological, cultural, political economic etc. Indeed, we have also seen from our definition at the beginning of this chapter our behaviour is sometimes manifested by no action at all. In all aspects of our behaviour though, we are accountable/responsible for regressive and progressive entropy. With this in mind some questions need to be asked: On the one hand, do we wish for ourselves, our children and future generations to be exploited, deprived, or disadvantaged, due to the behaviour of others? I believe the answer will be a big 'No'. This being the case, we will then expose such individuals and **not** support them personally, in their organisations, in their businesses or in the businesses they invest in? Regressive for one is regressive for all.

On the other hand, do we wish for ourselves, our children and future generations, to have health, education, and opportunity for growth, due to the behaviour of others? I believe the answer will be a big 'Yes'. This then being the case, we **will** support and indeed promote such individuals, personally, in their organisations, in their businesses or in the businesses within which they invest. Progressive for one should assist in progressive for all.

I have no doubt that we wish wholeheartedly to support the behaviour that continues our complexity goal via progressive entropy together with retarding behaviour assisting regressive entropy. In this regard let me give the final inspiring words in this chapter to Richard Dawkins. "Let us try to *teach* generosity and altruism, because we are born selfish. Let us understand what our own selfish genes are up to, because we may then at least have a chance to upset their designs, something that no other species has ever aspired to. (Dawkins, 2006, p. 3)

# CHAPTER 11
# Technology

These days when we hear the term 'technology' the first thing we usually think of is 'information technology' or as it is commonly referred to 'IT'. But technology is extremely old, in fact it was one of the first things humans invented and used. But an important fact, we tend to forget, about technology is that it is 'energy intensive' both in its production and its use. This energy relationship I have broken into three categories designated as; Category (A) Technology based on biological renewable energy, Category (B) Technology based on non-biological renewable energy, and Category (C) Technology based on non-biological non-renewable energy. Specific elements of (A) will be adopted into (B), and elements of (A) and (B) adopted into (C).

Before I examine these three categories an important point to remember is that technology is a double-edged sword. It can assist us greatly in our journey through life, with sophisticated healthcare, technological education facilities, computer innovation, comfortable domestic living, international travel, and efficient working environments. All these are extremely positive outcomes, provided, of course, we have access to them and/or can afford them. Unfortunately though, technology can be the cause of great damage to societies, via warring weaponry, and polluting the environment with its misuse, intended or not. It has also accounted for major unemployment, wiping out some industries almost completely e.g. the printing industry. In addition we see the effects of climate change in the wake of the burning of fossil fuels.

Some of these positives and negatives will now examined within the three category development stages:

## (A) Technology based on biological renewable energy:

When the first stone axes were fashioned, by our cave dwelling ancestors, it probably marked the beginning of what we now refer to as technology. Indeed, the process of fashioning these crude axes probably caused the first 'spark' to literally ignite a fire, giving us heat to shield us from the cold and eventually cook food. Or perhaps it was the cracking of the stones to get a spark that broke one stone into a crude axe? Whichever came first, our use of technology had commenced. These technical wonders ranged from the stone axes, to Spears, Slings, Catapults, Bows/arrows, Wheels, Wheelbarrows, Pulleys, Tools to make tools, to make dwellings, transport vehicles for land and sea. The development and use of all this technology was assisted mostly by biological energy alone, firstly human and then in some cases by the energy of animals. It requires noting however, that those who had this technology were in a superior 'survival' position than those who did not. In addition those who did not have the technology were in danger of those who did. Such is evidenced, in different states to this day, not just in superior weaponry, but in healthcare, education etc.

## (B) Technology based on non-biological renewable energy:

Some of our non-biological renewable energy resources are, for example, (a) Wind; for windmills, sailing boats, energy generators, (b) Water; for mills, tidal energy, hydroelectric energy, (c) Sun; for water heating, dwelling heating and cooling, (d) Wood; for heating, energy generating, (e) Nuclear; for defence, naval vessels, energy generating. All these renewables are in sufficient supply on the planet with the exception of wood that is designated as a renewable, as it can, if managed correctly, be restocked/grown. While water may be in poor supply for consumption, due to contamination or drought, there is ample supply on the planet to use for energy if or when we have an efficient/economic technology to tap it, no pun intended. All of these resources contribute to just a small part of our energy needs.

To be sure, science is working extremely hard to improve supply from these renewables, firstly, as non-renewables by their nature are limited, secondly, because renewables are more ecologically/environmentally friendly, and thirdly, to develop a renewable with unlimited supply, at low cost, would be extremely economically advantageous for the developer/supplier. In this regard, apart from the current nuclear reactors that produce energy, there is a process that is termed 'thermonuclear fusion'. Research into this process is on-going, in its controlled development, for civil energy purposes. It is sufficient here to say that it is the fusing of two atomic nuclei that produces the energy. "But!" I hear you loudly say, "Surely we have such a resource with current nuclear energy?" And the answer is, we do, so let us confront this hot topic now!

Regarding nuclear reactors, the lobby against these has been extremely successful what with their link to nuclear weapons, as well as accidents occurring at numerous nuclear plants, such as Three Mile Island and Chernobyl. However, others point out that technology has progressed since these accidents and indeed has developed positively in efficiency and safety. In addition many who regard nuclear power as an essential part of our future energy needs also believe it is just part and should be combined with other clean alternatives. The pro-nuclear group also believe the lobby against nuclear energy development have misrepresented the facts either through ignorance or deceit.

"Science does not support critics of nuclear power" is the heading for a John Gibbons'[101] article in the Irish Times 6/6/13. Gibbons talks of a "documentary film, *Pandora's Promise*, which charts the almost Pauline conversion of five well-known environmentalists from bitterly opposing to strongly advocating nuclear power." He further points out that many of the deaths claimed to have occurred from nuclear accidents are in fact false. In addition he advises that, "Prof David McKay of the UK's department of energy and climate change recently endorsed a novel solution for dealing with its problematic 100 tonnes of plutonium and 35,000 tonnes of depleted uranium wastes. Rather than being buried, this waste material could fuel a new generation of 'fast breeder' reactors and provide enough zero-carbon energy to power Britain for up to 500 years"

More alarmingly, in an interview with Jeremy Taylor in the Sunday Times Magazine 19/1/14, Dame Sue Ion, one of the UK's top nuclear experts states, "I believe our future energy can only be served by combining nuclear power, renewables like offshore wind farms, and fossil fuels with carbon capture—which is shorthand for limiting the emissions that come from power stations. But we only have 5 to 10 years to make the change, or the lights in Britain will go out, literally. She advocates the development of "small modular versions of nuclear reactors. Large reactors can cost £8bn and are difficult to finance. Small ones cost about £1bn and can be built on a factory production line...They're more affordable to an investor and five or six can then be linked on one site."

As confirmation of the above Tim Webb reported in 'The Times', "Britain faces its biggest supply crunch threat in the winter of 2015-16 as old coal and gas plants close and because too few new plants are being built." (Webb, 2014)

---

[101] John Gibbons is an environmental writer and commentator. He is on Twitter@think_or_swim

## (C) Technology based on non-biological non-renewable energy:

The major example of non-biological non-renewable energy resources are, the fossil fuels e.g. coal, gas, and oil to burn for transportation and heat and to produce electricity to drive our industrialised world. The technology associated with this form of energy drove, with the help of steel production, the industrial revolution. A revolution that has grown today to give us our modern transportation vehicles, trains, ships, trucks, cars, aeroplanes and even space transporters. It also has given us modern comfortable dwellings (thermostatically controlled), washing machines, dishwashers, TVs, computers etc. In fact, all the devices too that are used in the work place like fork-lift trucks, photocopiers, communication systems. In addition there is the specialised equipment in hospital/healthcare, sports and sports facilities, etc. etc. The list is endless. Most of the energy required in all of the above is driven by non-biological non-renewable energy. Of course the energy of category (A) and (B) as already stated above, may also be used e.g. a biological human to turn on a machine and/or drive/control it.

As our thirst for a more 'energy driven' industrialization continues on a global basis, so also has the burning of fossil fuels, a relatively cheap energy source. Unfortunately, this escalating use of fossil fuels has resulted in an increasing global climatic change of major negative proportions. Indeed, governments around the planet are working together to try to reverse the approach of this on-coming crisis, while at the same time, not slow down economic growth, also a fundamental drive. For a long time many prominent scientists denied that climate change was taking place at all. But thankfully or regretfully there now seems little doubt as evidenced by the changing weather patterns and temperatures in different parts of the world. There has been a great shift in most societies to look for clean renewable sources of energy but will the investment in such be adequate, before a worldwide disaster strikes, or is some world paradigm shift required in this regard? Certainly, we can restrict, by law, the excessive use of this energy based technology and we can even curb our own individual use of it, but are we to stop progress? Vested interests of people and states have driven this energy supply and consumption thus far, but it appears that this now requires the following actions;

1) Positively modify the use of fossil fuels by way of carbon capture.
2) Invest more into current research for existing and acceptably safe renewables, e.g. wind, sun, and water sources.
3) Invest further into 'thermonuclear fusion energy' as it seems this will not create long-lived radioactive waste.

4) The current nuclear-energy reactors' safety, needs to be satisfactorily established for society in general and then used as an interim, in a mix of other renewables, until such time as, a plentiful and economic supply of renewable safe energy is found.

Let us now turn to that extremely sophisticated realm of technical development, namely 'information technology' (IT). I believe a simple definition of IT is, it is about the manipulation and dissemination of information via computation and communication. This technology has advanced rapidly via the process of 'digitalization'. Digital technology, uses 1's and 0's in its processes as already explained in chapter 7 'Information'.

The technology itself is enabled by devices known as transistors.

A simple explanation of a transistor is as follows:

1) A metal conducts electricity.
2) An insulator does not altogether conduct electricity e.g. insulating tape around electrical wire prevents electricity shocks.
3) A semi-conductor semi-conducts electricity.
4) Silicon is the semi-conductor used in most IT processes.
5) A transistor is a semi-conductor that can switch and amplify electrical signals.

Dr Anna Scaife, lecturer in radio astronomy, physics and astronomy at the University of Southampton, is quoted, on the subject in an article in The Irish Times. "Transistors are a type of amplifier ubiquitous in all modern electronics. The principle behind them is based on the fact that electrons in an atom have discrete energy levels and therefore move in different orbits around the nucleus depending on that energy level. The conductivity of a material depends on the electron orbits, and this understanding of conductivity allowed the transistor to be designed." (Holand, 2012) Think of a transistor as the IT equivalent of a brain neuron, and such transistors are, if you like, the brain cells of computers. Digital computers as units themselves, or part of other units or devices, now dominate, information sources, communication, news, business, entertainment and more and more into the realms of education. Their capacity and capability increases every year. In fact it tends to follow Moore's Law[102] as 'every two years approximately computers tend to double in their speed and memory'. Their pinnacle will supposedly be when quantum computers are

[102] "In the late 1950's the then chairman and co-founder of Intel: Gordon Moore, noticed a very interesting and remarkable trend: every two years or so computers tend to double in their speed and memory. Moore noted this trend in one of his reports and this has since become known as Moore's Law." (Vedral, 2010, p. 135)

developed to their full potential! And this potential will be extraordinary in its ability to assist us in our growth goals.

From a personal point of view I find it all exciting, informative and progressive. Others however, believe much of the scientific innovation in new technology is having a negative effect on human ethical development not alone with sophisticated weaponry etc. but with e.g. stem cell research, genetically modified crops and the likes. But has this not always been the case with progressive innovation? Something new and different is embraced by some immediately, while others take much convincing over time to appreciate its significance.

One of the most significant technological innovations of the 20$^{th}$ century is of course the digital computer, and when, in the 1960's, the process of interlinking them began, it marked the dawn of what we now know as the 'Internet'. The internet is simply a network of networks where millions of computers are interconnected. It took some decades to be firmly established. However, an innovation within the internet, 'the world wide web', was taken on relatively quickly. It is amazing that just 25 years ago a scientist at 'CERN', Sir Tim-Berners-Lee wanted a method for scientists around the world to communicate swapping information quickly, and he came up with the 'world wide web' WWW. Indeed, it is difficult to comprehend how the modern world could operate today without, computers, the internet, and the 'world wide web'.

Information communication is what permeates the digital world, be it in entertainment, news, politics, business and social interaction. In the entertainment arena, through the many digital media, of digitally enhanced movies, box sets, Netflix, documentaries, games etc., such are also becoming interactive so one may comment on them and even change them. News itself is now received through digital media. In addition, newspapers are available on the net as well as regular blogs from numerous groups, associations and organizations. 'Search engines' such as Google and Yahoo are used extensively for research and to get news and information on every subject and happening imaginable. As stated above it is difficult to imagine a modern society operating without such facilities.

More and more politicians and their parties use digital media to present policies and to comment on political issues. An example of the power of the digital process in politics need go no further than to look at President Obama's campaign funding. Using emails, the website, mobile phones, and social media for his 2008 campaign it is widely reported he raised circa $400ml and for 2012 he raised circa $500ml. Then there is the case of political spooks as revealed by Edward Snowden, "a former CIA technical assistant who was working at NSA as an employee of defence contractor Booz Allen Hamilton..."The *Guardian* published revelations this week that US security services monitored data about phone calls from Verizon and internet data from large companies such as Google and Facebook." (Reuters, 2013) Another example of the political power that can be tapped in this regard is that of the 'Arab Spring' which was fuelled in no small way by social media. In fact some countries' government leaders are reported to have pressured social network providers to switch off their network at particular times in order to stop communication in the disenchanted groups!

Then there is business. What business today in a modern society can exist without a website? Apart from detailing the business profile such websites are used to market and actually sell products and services. In fact, more and more, we are buying and selling on such sites. Indeed, it seems no industry uses communication technology more so than the financial, particularly in their world of stocks, shares, bonds etc. Businesses also use digital processes for recruitment of and references for candidates. Indeed, many candidates often have their own profile on the net in order to brand themselves.

Apart from the political and business arenas, individual citizens also use the digital communication network to great effect with their own, social network accounts, blogs, websites, YouTube, etc. where they may publish books, songs, photographs, and any other information they want to get 'out there'. To give a flavour of what can be achieved with this technology, it was reported in the Irish Independent 21/7/12: "An online campaign that aimed to raise $5,000 ( 4,000) to send a bullied, New York bus monitor on a holiday has ended—after raising $683,000. A spokeswoman for the fundraising site Indiegogo said more than 30,000 people had contributed to 68-year-old Karen Klein, with donations coming in from 84 countries and all 50 states." In yet another case in November 2014 when a dog was lost in the 'Lake district' in the UK and eventually found. The incident prompted 250,000 social media subscribers to swap information on the event.

Social media however, has certainly emerged as one of the enormous successes of the digital world. In this regard, Facebook, with circa 1.5 plus billion[103] users would represent one of the three largest populated countries in the world. The other two being China and India. Twitter, on the other hand, with a membership of circa 100 million[104] puts their membership, as a population, greater than such countries as, Germany, UK, France and Italy. An important thing to note of both the above social media networks is that their members are all computer literate, whereas, the populations of China and India would have major numbers of people who are not. In addition, members of each social media group have the facility for fast easy

103 This is an approximation as it is a moving target sometimes it is reported as less and sometimes it reported as more.

104 As above

communication with other individual members or indeed, groups of members. Therefore it can be seen that the potential to gain an interest and/or agreement on some societal issue with either or both of these groups could have world changing outcomes! Something 'going viral' could fall into this category especially when social networking is teamed up with the many other digital communicators.

A computer virus however has a history of something very negative e.g. something that can assist with the loss of much of your data. Indeed, such viruses are still about and one must be forever on guard against them. However, Tom Chatfield, in his excellent book[105] on digital ideas notes that, "the idea of viral spread itself has increasingly been applied to a more positive, active cultural process, where striking or amusing cultural nuggets are noticed and distributed online by a rapidly growing number of people." (Chatfield, 2011, p. 183) Chatfield goes on to say that such a process has much in common with the notion of 'memes' the cultural replicator proposed by Richard Dawkins and discussed in earlier chapters. Such a 'meme' once it is of a positive nature and in particular if it is beneficial would indeed be spread/replicated at a never-before-seen rate. Indeed, positive technological 'memes' no doubt operated in world markets up to the global financial crisis of 2008. And of course the crisis itself was aided and abetted by e.g. day-traders, having reduced costs in computerized trading, transferring funds from buyers to sellers and from country to country. To get some idea of what is happening in this regard Author Michael Lewis' book *Flash Boys*[106] as reported in the Irish Times[107], "highlights a persuasive system on Wall Street that has allowed certain professional investors to pay hundreds of millions of dollars to locate their computer servers close to stock exchanges so they can make trades milliseconds ahead of everyone else."

In summary, technical progress on the one hand, that benefits our species without infringing detrimentally on us or our environment, is an essential on-going part of our journey towards greater complexity. It will also assist in holding off the inevitable regressive entropy equilibrium. On the other hand, technical progress that has overall negative effects on some people and the environment, exacerbates the inevitable regressive entropy equilibrium.

Apart from the obvious need to manage technology use, regarding wars and pollution, management and research is also necessary for controversial areas, such as nuclear energy, GM[108] crops, stem cell research, etc. where their implementation raises not only ethical questions but also fear. In this regard the establishment

---

105 Chatfield, Tom "50 ideas you really need to know digital @" 2012 London Quercus.

106 Flash Boys: 'A Wall Street Revolt', is a non-fiction work by the American writer Michael Lewis, published by W. W. Norton & Company on March 31, 2014.

107 Irish Times 2/4/14 Business News 3 (New York Times service)

108 GM = genetically modified

of transparency with a free flow of information, will assist in removing this fear. Technical progress and its benefits are an asset on the road to complexity, however its implementation and use carries with it considerable accountability and responsibility.

## CHAPTER 12
# Business

Business is simply trade, a process of selling and buying. The basic differentiation in a business trade is in the product/service traded! Whatever business you are in, or deal with, one side sells to make a profit/gain from the other side. It matters not if you are selling horses, cars, dental care, holidays, or money, business is business. To be sure, investment packages for sale by a bank, a surgeon's operating techniques, or the inner-workings of a digital computer are all extremely complicated products/services to those not versed in them, but they individually all represent a product/service in the business process. From this point on I will refer to both products and services simply as 'products'.

One of the major differences between human beings and other animals is that we have language, and this, no doubt, advanced cooperation among early humans in the hunt and search for food as well as protection from danger. The same cooperation further advanced humans to trade with each other as different individuals acquired particular skills. Trading within groups soon developed into trading with other groups, and so evolved into the business process we know today. There are a lot of add-ons in today's 'Classical business' process but the duality of selling and buying is still a trade consisting of a mutually acceptable exchange between two parties. Indeed, selling and buying is all pervasive and its actors are found in individuals or groups of individuals from children swapping items in the school yard to firms/companies/corporations (businesses), political parties, religions, sporting bodies etc. exchanging their products in their own 'market' arena. It needs to be stressed however, that each party in the exchange is both a seller and a buyer, albeit to a greater or lesser degree. Some examples of such exchanges are as follows:

Little Bobby *sells* little Polly a comic for a yoyo.

Little Bobby *buys* a yoyo from little Polly for a comic.
Little Polly *sells* little Bobby a yoyo for a comic.
Little Polly *buys* a comic from little Bobby for a yoyo.

A business sells a product to a customer for cash.
A business buys cash from a customer for a product.
A customer sells cash to a business for a product.
A customer buys a product from a business for cash.

A politician sells policies to a voter for a vote.
A politician buys a vote from a voter for policies.
A voter sells a vote to a politician for policies.
A voter buys policies from a Politician for a vote.

And so on...

It can be seen then that each party in the exchange is both a seller and a buyer. Businesses however, are run to make a profit and profits are derived from maximizing sales and minimizing expenses. But let there be no mistake, business today, yesterday and tomorrow involves exchange and each party in the exchange is both a seller and a buyer.

Marketing philosophy is traditionally supposed to concern itself with satisfying customer needs, but inside most classical businesses there is a raw drive to sell, sell, and sell. In most 'business trades' it is the seller who brings the product to market for sale and for this reason it is the seller who needs to firstly have the buyer base, and secondly make sure there are buyers for future business. Certainly, sales should be driven but driven in a way that produces the highest positive return for both sides of the exchange. In market economies, profit is the driving force of business. Yet this same force, by its nature, is destroying the hand that feeds it. The evidence for this destruction is quite clear and is presented below. However, even apart from those to whom it is obvious, I believe it is fair to say there are many who practice a 'wilful blindness' regarding this cancer.

So, what is this self-destructive disease? I will outline this under five *self-inflicted nails (SINS)* hammered into business' coffin. But first a little necessary understanding of the business process.

Business as we know it today has many processes, however, every business requires three basic ingredients, investment, a product, and buyers. For our purposes we will use the term 'buyer' for both buyer and customer (customers being repeat buyers). These three business ingredients may be explained as follows:

**Investment:** In a one person business, the investment is in their skills, tools, transport, office etc. In a company/corporate business, sufficient capital is invested to produce, market, and sell their product.

Investment is mostly fuelled by the capitalist and/or through the financial industry. Investment in industry is on-going provided there is economic stability but when there is not, as occurred with the GFC of 2008, it results in investment drying up. Whatever investment there might be available then will cautiously go to secure businesses for adequate returns. Investment in any business, no matter what the size, is only worthwhile if it yields a profitable return.

**Product:** Products are purchased for many reasons but usually for their 'use value' e.g. food to eat or car to drive, or their 'investment value' e.g. a retail outlet will purchase goods at a wholesale price, as an investment, to sell at a retail price, or people will buy stock in a company or buy a 'work of art' as an investment to generate dividends and/or capital gains. Entrepreneurs within capitalist market economies will only seek a product to serve a given or created market.

**Buyers:** These are people who, on their own behalf, or on behalf of some entity e.g. another business or organization, purchase a product. The 'buyer' is by far the most important of the three business ingredients as without buyers, 'investment' and 'product' are redundant! Potential buyers are those with a need or desire and the wherewithal to make a purchase. They may also be people, with the wherewithal, who can be convinced they have a need/desire to make a purchase. Such, do not become buyers until they actually buy. Potential buyers with the wherewithal purchasing funds, acquire such funds by way of an income either as a 'recompense' or a 'benefit'. Recompense Incomes are: wage/salary for employees, contract price for contractors, fees for agents, or dividends/capital gains for investors. Benefit Incomes are: gifts, prizes, inheritances, or social welfare payments. Income of course may be acquired from any combination of these.

Business is happy to sell to buyers with income from any of the sources above, provided it is within their trading rules and/or code of ethics. But there is no doubt that the majority of businesses rely on buyers with 'recompensed Income', as those 'benefit income' buyers associated with gift, prize, or inheritance are limited, while those on welfare benefits have little to spend. Without the 'recompensed Income' buyers, most businesses would grind to a halt. Such is brought home to us all too well when unemployment soars.

In overall terms, due to its nature, business is happy to have buyers without knowing the reason (need or desire) for their purchase.[109] Individual buyers will purchase with their individual purchasing funds. Buyers on behalf of other entities will purchase with the funds of such entities. So, the vast majority of buyers are buyers with sufficient funds. These buyers in turn are the most important driving force for profit, as without such buyers all other business processes are a waste of time, money, and effort.

In times of recession we often hear the cry for more business development, as businesses create jobs. But **businesses do not create jobs they create profit,** and jobs are a mechanism to this end, albeit a good mechanism for the employee and other businesses, but a costly expense for the business/employer. So, all businesses seek to keep this cost down, to as little as possible, both in heads and remuneration.

The following simple 'Profit and Loss' five year forecast illustrates the process for a one product business (ABC).

| | Five Year forecast P and L (ABC) Product | | | | |
|---|---|---|---|---|---|
| | Year 1 | Year 2 | Year 3 | Year 4 | Year 5 |
| Selling price per unit | € 9.50 | € 9.50 | € 10.00 | € 10.00 | € 10.50 |
| Cost price per unit | € 3.50 | € 3.50 | € 3.50 | € 3.00 | € 3.00 |
| Sales Units | 20,000 | 25,000 | 35,000 | 50,000 | 100,000 |
| Sales Value | € 190,000 | € 237,500 | € 350,000 | € 500,000 | € 1,050,000 |
| Cost of goods | € 70,000 | € 87,500 | € 122,500 | € 150,000 | € 300,000 |
| Gross profit | € 120,000 | € 150,000 | € 227,500 | € 350,000 | € 750,000 |
| Less Expenses | € 150,000 | € 150,000 | € 150,000 | € 170,000 | € 170,000 |
| Net Profit/Loss | -€ 30,000 | € 0 | € 77,500 | € 180,000 | € 580,000 |

**Table 12-1**

109 In general businesses do know why their product is purchased. If it is purchased for some other reason of course the business would like to know, so it can pitch to such a market, but provided the product's use is within the legal framework of the sale then it is happy to accept all such purchases.

## Table Observations:

There is an increase in the selling price forecast in Year 3 and Year 5.

There is a reduction in the cost price forecast in Year 4 (probably due to increased unit purchases.)

The sales unit forecast each year is important in order to have sufficient product to sell.

Sales value is simply units multiplied by selling price.

Cost of goods is simply units multiplied by cost price.

Gross profit is the sales value less cost of goods or otherwise stated as, return on sales before expenses.

Expenses represents costs incurred in selling the product such as for example, advertising, wages/salaries, rent etc.

Year 1 shows a loss of €30,000. Year 2 is breakeven. Year 3, 4 and 5 return a profit for product ABC.

Mark up: This is the percentage of the cost price added to the cost price to arrive at the selling price. Taking Year 5, the cost price is €3.00 add 250% €7.50 = selling price €10.50.

Margin: The margin on the other hand is based on the selling price and what percentage of the selling price is profit. Again taking Year 5, €7.50 being the profit per unit as a percent of selling price €10.50 = 71.4%. In this case then the Gross profit/Margin percent will be 71.4%.

Business makes a profit by increasing sales and reducing costs. So, while business needs as many buyers as possible, it also needs as few employees as possible, and those, at a remuneration as low as possible. Employee wages and salaries plus their on-costs are all part of expenses line in Table 12-1 above. But the most important line in the table is 'the bottom line' profit, and the higher the expenses line value the lower will be the profit line value. It is important here to remember that our world requires growth towards complexity and business is not only part of the equation, but a vital part of it. Therefore, while some might argue that capitalist profit accumulation is for accumulation sake alone, and as such is a blight on humanity, I would argue that profit accumulation/growth is one of the most natural processes evolved in humans for humans. Therefore, such enterprise requires facilitation and encouragement, while at the same time it requires management and direction for increased progressive entropy.

Recessions are a well-known feature of capitalist market economies, as its boom/bust history is a study requirement for all first year economic students. In spite of this, very few economic graduates seem to agree when a bust is imminent. Many neo-classical economists claim that the boom/bust scenario is a 'normal' process within market economies, however, it is only 'normal' within badly managed market economies. A recession itself is caused by a 'scientific', rather than 'marketing', positive feedback' mechanism. We have encountered such a feedback mechanism in chapter 9 but it will help to distinguish between both types of feedback. On the one hand then, an example of 'scientific positive feedback' is when prices are bullish on the stock-market people buy in the expectation of further price rises, and this in turn pushes the prices up further, so people buy more and this positive feedback continues until the market completely overheats and crashes. So here we have a positive to increase prices that is eventually bad.[110] This process is exacerbated when, due to a bullish economy more money is made available on credit without sufficient collateral for all kinds of purchases. For example, the deregulation of the financial system, together with the financial services sector's self-serving manipulations, resulted in the global financial crisis of 2008. Marketing positive feedback, on the other hand, is when a business receives positive feedback on a product by way of customer satisfaction on product features.

We are now in a position to look at the five *self-inflicted nails (SINS)* hammered into business' coffin.

**Nail 1** Business wants as few employees as possible in order to reduce expenses for better profit. An example of this is a 'budget airline' that has the buyer do the work that numerous booking clerks, handlers, etc. originally performed. Indeed, one feels it is only a matter of time before pilotless flights, without any cabin crew, are the norm. But this is in keeping with the nature of business for greater profit, and therefore is to be commended, in its cost cutting initiatives. However, this nail in the coffin, caused by business, for all other businesses is that there are less potential buyers out there with the wherewithal to buy.

**Nail 2** Business wants to pay as little tax as possible for greater profit. This results in less revenue going into the public purse and therefore less public servants as buyers for business' goods and services. Then there are yet other businesses using the 'black economy'[111] to avoid paying tax that are literally robbing those that do meet their obligations. Such businesses are usually smaller in size, but due to the large numbers of them involved, the amount of tax avoided is quite significant. Furthermore, those buyers who actively seek cheaper prices using the

---

110 An example of 'Scientific negative feedback, is when a thermostat on the central heating or air conditioning unit in your home records a certain temperature has been reached the thermostat clicks off . The negative feedback gives a good outcome.

111 This is when dishonest buyers pay for a product/service with cash in the knowledge that they are receiving the product/service at a discount, because the product/service provider will not have to pay tax on the transaction. There being no record of the transaction, this allows a dishonest product/service provider the opportunity to avoid taxation.

black economy themselves are aiding and abetting the robbers! On the other hand, businesses (usually larger) with international affiliations, usually meet their national tax requirements. However, due to such businesses' ability to steer costs and revenues through different tax zones, overall tax obligations at the fair contribution level is avoided. Gavin Daly reports on just one such case in The Sunday Times 16/11/14. "Eaton boss earns four times what it paid in tax: Eaton Corporation, a US group that shifted its headquarters to Ireland in 2012, paid its chief executive four times more than it paid in corporation tax last year, according to figures filed in the Companies Office...Eaton paid just $6m (£4.8m) tax on profits of almost $1.9bn last year, an effective tax rate of only 0.3%.

The group which had revenues of $22bn last year and employs 103,000 people worldwide, said the low tax bill was a result of 'greater levels of income in lower tax jurisdictions' and the use of foreign tax credits. In 2012, the company paid $26m tax on profits of $1.2bn, a 2.1% tax rate." (Daly, 2014)

A business simply must pay their due taxes and not use, 'The black economy', 'Tax loopholes', 'Tax avoidance mechanisms', Transfer pricing[112], etc. to reduce their obligatory tax burdens. This is not to say that state sanctioned processes to reduce taxes should not be applied in business, rather it is the avoidance/reduction via, illegal processes, or international interplay and manipulation for example, 'the double Irish'[113], that requires stamping out. Indeed, international pressure did just that, when in the Irish 2014 budget, Minister for Finance Michael Noonan abolished the ability of companies to use the 'Double Irish'. He did this by having companies that are registered in the country, to be also tax resident.

---

112 **Transfer pricing:** price- setting for transactions within a business to avail of different tax regional benefits.

113 The Double Irish: explained by Peter Flanagan writing in The Irish Independent 27/5/13 'The scheme, which dozens of firms use to legally avoid billions of dollars in corporation tax, takes advantage of a quirk in Irish tax law that allows a company based abroad to be registered as an Irish company. For example, a company based in a tax haven such as Bermuda can be an "Irish" company.

Ireland also has generous laws on "transfer pricing", which allow a big company to move profits from one country to another, usually for tax purposes.

Those loopholes allow businesses to funnel profits through Ireland and on to tax havens in a completely legal manner. Google is one of the best known proponents of the Double Irish scheme.

In Google's case, an Irish subsidiary collects revenues from ads sold in countries like the UK and France. That Irish unit in turn pays royalties to another Irish subsidiary, whose legal residence for tax purposes is in Bermuda. The scheme involves two Irish companies, hence the Double Irish nickname.

Companies can lower their tax bill even further by moving their profits through Holland before sending them on to a tax haven. That method has also acquired a catchy nickname – the Dutch Sandwich.

Irish Independent'.

In addition in order that market economies can operate efficiently each business is subject to the 'competition law' within a state. Such law is known as anti-trust law in the US, and in Europe as the European Union competition law. There are also limited international laws regarding business' transparency for a fair distribution of tax value. But until these laws are robust enough and fully enacted many businesses including extremely large businesses will avoid their fair tax contribution. A business therefore, with international ability to avoid the full business tax, is in a competitive advantageous position to other businesses with no such international affiliation manipulation ability. Why should such a business, have the same access to a share of a buyer's disposable income, to a business that does? The answer is that they should not but their circumstance gives them a price advantage which of course they exploit and the additional profit is pocketed. Therefore businesses refusing to comply, to proportionally equal taxation should **not** be supported by a non-purchase of their products. While those businesses that do comply with regulation and obligatory fair taxation should be supported. In addition, tax compliant businesses should collectively campaign against non-compliant businesses as they are blatantly non-competitive and a threat to their own business.

**Nail 3** Business (Financial sector) supplies investment funds for business but due to its mismanagement regarding risk and credit, it contributed significantly to the GFC of 2008 resulting in massive unemployment. In addition, when financial institutions have to be bailed out, such bail-out funds have to be borne by the state citizenry under severe austerity measures. Such measures take the form of tax increases and restricted government spending, leaving less for overall spend in businesses. Indeed the repercussions of this continued in Ireland up to mid-2014, as reported in 'The Irish Independent' June 2014.

"Almost a quarter of Irish households are currently job-less—a level 'far above' the European norm in a situation described as 'not acceptable' by the Taoiseach.

The National Economic and Social Council warned that these households have a high risk of poverty, with the danger of passing on joblessness and poverty across generations.

Taoiseach Enda Kenny has now pledged to break the cycle and reiterated the Government's commitment to 'continue the plan to dismantle the passive welfare system' which had 'abandoned such large numbers of households to lifelong dependency on the state'." (Anderson, 2014)

These financial crises cause almost instant mass unemployment that have on-going and far reaching consequences. Thus the potential wherewithal buyers for business are simply obliterated by business itself!

**Nail 4** Business uses cutting edge technology and robots instead of people, so cutting out potential buyers. By the reduction of labour's services, required in various historical labour intensive industries, and substituting new technology, costs may be cut considerably, to create more profit. The Times Social affairs Correspondent Rosemary Bennett reported 11/11/14, "One in three jobs could be taken over by computers or a robot in the next 20 years, with lower paid workers the most vulnerable, a study has warned...

The report, from the accountants Deloitte and the University of Oxford, said that although new jobs would be created, they were more likely to be at the high-skilled end of the market, shrinking the pool of employment available for those with fewer qualifications." (Bennett, 2014)

Once again a further reduction in employees, with the wherewithal to buy, by business.

**Nail 5** Business, as is its nature, is required to pay existing employees as little as possible for increased profit. Janice Turner reports in The Times: "A Survey of Sainsbury employees by Unite last year found that 60 per cent relied upon government tax credits to top up their salaries. Even so, in the previous six months, a third had resorted to borrowing money to settle their bills...

Who could begrudge Sainsbury's new CEO Mike Coupe his £900,000 basic salary..., if only he paid all his 157,000 retail staff enough to live on without you and me chipping in? But he doesn't and bizarrely, no one is inclined to make him.....

Now 5.2 million people, a fifth of the workforce, are paid below a rate at which decent life is sustainable: £8.80 an hour in London and £7.65 for the rest of the UK. And since, without government support, families on minimum wage would barely be able to feed their children, in-work benefits cost taxpayers £28 billion a year." (Turner, 2014)

At the time of writing minimum wage in the US is federally $7.25 per hour. Some states have a higher rate, for example, Washington $9.32 per hour. There are of course literally millions who are paid just above the minimum rate everywhere, leaving little for only essential purchases. So, many potential buyers have the minimum wage and indeed many others with less than the minimum to spend with business in general.

Each of these five nails alone, and together are what I designate as, 'Systemic cancers rotting enterprising market economies' (SCREMEs).

To conclude however, it needs to be pointed out and understood that business more often than not is described in a positive light as a builder of, and contributor to society and this is in many respects an accurate description, for example, its investments assist in economic welfare. It also produces goods and services that we need and desire at affordable prices. In addition it generates employment for the good of society. It is in fact not just the backbone, but the whole skeleton upon which market economies exist. In addition, some businesses also, in order to help to improve their standing in society as well as help society in general, contribute to charities, communities, employee welfare, and other worthy causes. This practice is to be well praised as it has benefits for both the business and the recipients. We will discuss this philanthropic aspect of business further in a later chapter.

The 'Capitalist System' has served business well as it encourages risk in innovation and enterprise, and rewards the successful while at the same time assisting in the generation of income for the many. Unfortunately, on the other hand, business may also be seen negatively in that it may pollute the environment, exploit workers, overcharge for products and circumvent trading laws to increase profits. Business may also deprive certain sections of society of essential products, for example, how pharmaceuticals used to combat the AIDS virus were withheld from countries/people in most need. Such was due to these markets having limited or no profitability prospects. This of course is quite inhumane, but the reality is, it is simply the nature of the business beast.

Apart however, from the effects business has on society, it is, as stated above, the skeleton of market economies and therefore is required to be healthy and robust in the extreme. But as we have shown, with the nails in its coffin, its modus operandi also eradicates its customer base. To be sure, business will stimulate needs and desires in potential buyers but unless these have the wherewithal to buy it is pointless. The argument that business will of itself continue to produce customers is wishful thinking as buyers, we have seen, are a diminishing limited ingredient. To be sure, entrepreneurs can produce products for potential markets but such markets are restricted to a certain number of wherewithal customers. Business feeds on buyers who are there, basically from other businesses or Public servants, who have the wherewithal to buy. In other words business fishes for buyers from a limited pool of mostly 'recompensed income' buyers, without ensuring that there will always be enough. So, just like the limited fish in the sea unless it makes provision for the future the buyer base as we know it within current market economies will simply disappear.

This self-destructing mechanism within business i.e. employment erosion and therefore buyer/customer reduction/destruction is a blight on business itself and nothing less than, as stated above, a 'Systemic cancer rotting enterprising market economies' (SCREME). But! Is there a cure for this SCREME? I believe there is. However, business is addicted to the SCREME's causal behavioural aspect, and as we have discovered behaviour sets up the environment. Therefore the cure will require a new behaviour for a new environment. Cures for addiction are difficult and require self-commitment and incentive. Perhaps there is a motivation that is better than the alternative of complete self-destruction?

# CHAPTER 13
# Finance

We are all very much aware of our own finances, starting with our income and what we do with it. To be sure, some people have no income at all and their needs are supplied by others. However, the majority of people in market economies put their income to use in their preferred way. For example, they will spend part on basic needs like food clothes and housing and part may go on entertainment, savings, investments, and charity etc. In addition we may seek and secure loans, credit cards or overdrafts to help us manage our needs and desires. The receipt of our income from whatever source, e.g. wage/salary, inheritance, prize/gift or state social benefit, together with loans etc. will be facilitated in the most part by financial institutions, most often banks.

Non-profit associations such as clubs, cultural organizations etc. also attract income, and distribute it to promote its goals for member's benefits. All such associations are subject to their own and/or state rules and regulations. Once again the income and its distribution is facilitated by financial institutions. Indeed, some of these organizations are themselves financial institutions such as building societies.

Businesses (profit-seeking) of all kinds are by their nature risk entities, and their establishment requires, risk investment, usually facilitated through a bank. Their operation is subject to companies/businesses rules and regulations and while businesses run their own finances, on-going credit facilities and other financial processes are operated through banks. Indeed, banks from the outset of a business and for on-going credit facilities usually require financial forecasts and budgets such as those detailed in the previous chapter Table12-1. So, from their beginning and throughout their operation businesses are facilitated by financial institutions.

Financial institutions are of course businesses too, the most familiar being the banks and when referring to these institutions I will mostly use the term 'banks' as their generic. Banks then, as they are today, carry out two types of business which we may call 'traditional/retail' and 'investment'.

The following scenario will help explain the process:

1) Banks start off by taking in deposits from individuals or entities (e.g. Associations etc.) and paying them an interest rate e.g. 2% on their deposits.
2) The bank then lends out these funds to borrowers, individuals, businesses etc., at a higher rate e.g. 5% and makes a profit of 3% on the overall transactions.
3) Banks then begin to drift in their loans by extending credit (virtual funds), to borrowers, greater than the amount of funds they hold on deposit.
4) This drift has to be managed so that the banks always have enough funds to pay back depositors when required.
5) Central Banks act as the lending source of last resort for other banks in order to keep the financial system up and running. Deposits in, and loans out, of retail banks move at their own pace. For this reason Central banks are there to lend to retail banks to cover withdrawals if they don't have enough in the pot in deposits. Basically they are there to stop runs on banks.
6) Such is the case above for retail banks. However, investment banking then emerged from what used to be called merchant banking and it brought banking to a whole new level.
7) The banks moved on to extending their lending/speculation way beyond their capital deposit/loan ratio and indeed, borrowing themselves for additional speculation. Economist Andrew Smithers notes "Banks have changed. Their traditional activities of taking in deposits and lending the proceeds have lost their primacy. Banks have greatly increased their profitability and the increase has been driven by rises in the importance of their non-traditional activities, such as dealing, the sale of new and complicated financial products and fees for advice. Among these, dealing is probably the greatest contributor to profits." (Smithers, 2013, p. 90)
8) This extended activity in banking is great in a bull market because the value of traded units is always increasing together with the number of trades.
9) This situation is exacerbated if the regulation laws are relaxed or rescinded.
10) Eventually, when the inevitable crunch comes and the banks lose money and cannot pay depositors or bond holders they go to the wall or are bailed out by the state. So, on the one hand banks are carrying out their

traditional business of financially facilitating individuals, organisations and of course businesses, while on the other hand, they are carrying on an indigenous business which we will call investment banking.

Probably the best way to think of banks is, as a metaphor of the bodily cardio vascular system.

*The heart pumps blood around the body.*
The banks pump money around the capitalist market economy.

*The heart has its own blood supply system.*
The banks have their own investment banking system

*Cardiac health experts keep the heart in good working order.*
Financial regulators keep the banks in good working order.

*The heart can however be subject to disease when proper care is not taken.*
Banks can be subject to crises when proper care is not taken.

*When the heart's internal system is diseased (e.g. coronary artery disease*[114]*) the whole body is put in serious danger not alone of incapacitation but of death itself.*

When the bank's internal investment systems are in crisis the whole capitalist market economy is put in danger, not alone, of incapacitation but of complete disintegration.

In times of global financial crises the state has to give the banks a 'blood' money transfusion to keep the whole system from disintegrating. This bailing out of the system, by ordinary taxpayers, has been an on-going saga for a system that requires not just reforms but purification. In 2008 the great financial crisis came about for numerous reasons e.g. political, ideological, fear, greed, fraud and modern technology. Indeed, there are numerous publications detailing its birth, development, and the surgical patchwork of reforms to fix it. Unfortunately, without the stringent implementation of such reforms, things will quietly continue on with the boom/bust scenario. Only next time the whole system may completely collapse with devastating results. The 2008 crisis itself was not without casualties and indeed most of the casualties were innocent workers who lost their jobs, homes etc., not to mention their self-respect. A future complete collapse could very well change our notions of freedom in market economies and democratic self-management.

[114] In such a case a serious heart operation is required such as a 'triple bypass'.

With this in mind I will now briefly outline ten of the major viruses that fed the financial plague of 2008 and then look at our options.

## Virus 1 Insufficient regulation:

Regulation of the financial system was something that was considered extremely important in the past. This can be seen from the introduction by Franklin D Roosevelt in the early 1930's of the regulatory, 'Securities Act' for openness, and 'The Glass-Steagall Act' to deter 'retail banks' from acting like 'Investment banks'. However, in 1999 'The Glass-Steagall Act' was repealed and by then other forms of regulation in the financial system had been extremely diluted or in some cases even ignored. To be sure, more stringent regulation in the financial sector is currently being attempted to be implemented. However, such implementation is already under threat from politically strong financial lobby groups.

We do know that business can be regulated successfully regarding competition for example, antitrust and insider-trading laws, however there appears to be a political reluctance to sufficiently regulate businesses in the financial sector! Indeed, taking steps in reform and regulation in the financial industry is extremely difficult as can be seen from the report in the Irish Independent 11/4/12. "US Federal Reserve Chairman Ben Bernanke has said banks need to have more capital at hand in order to ensure the financial system is stable...Mr Bernanke said regulators were taking steps to force financial institutions to hold higher capital buffers, even if they allow for a long period of implementation to prevent any market disruptions.

Mr Bernanke made the comments the same day that the international bank lobby group, The Institute of International Finance (IIF), urged policymakers to pause in regulating the industry." (da Costa P. N., 2012)

## Virus 2 Insufficient capital reserves:

Andrew Smithers, details this succinctly "Many of the problems posed by banks have been well debated. These include a general agreement that banks need a great deal more equity capital both because their vestigial current ratios pose a major threat to the world economy and because taxpayer guarantees, which enable banks to operate with such low amounts of equity, distort the economy and are without a compensating economic justification." (Smithers, 2013, p. 94)

## Virus 3 Subprime lending:

Subprime lending is simply lending to people who have difficulty paying back the loan. The result is that most such borrowers, whom should not have been approved for the loan in the first place, eventually default.

Subprime lending occurs when:

- Pressure is put on bank lending officers to extend loan portfolio.
- Bonuses are paid to bank lending officers on loan numbers
- Loans are issued with minimum collateral checks.
- Loans are issued with little or no deposit from the borrower.
- Borrowers believe that interest rates will fall and/or their purchase (e.g. a home) will increase in value.

## Virus 4 Early low mortgage rates:

Early low interest mortgage rates with later higher rates were a bait for would-be real-estate buyers, based on a belief in an ever-increasing capital gain.

## Virus 5 Brokers and rating agencies:

Brokers and Rating agencies, who received payment for their services, were selected on the basis of those who best conformed to the goals of the banks.

## Virus 6 Securitization:

Securitization: This was when mortgages were bundled into packages, and then sold on by the bank to other speculators. Nobel economist Joseph Stiglitz advises in this regard it "provided a textbook example of the risks generated by the new innovations, for it meant that the relationship between lender and borrower was broken. Securitization had one big advantage, allowing risk to be spread; but it had a big disadvantage, creating new problems of imperfect information, and these swamped the benefits from increased diversification." (Stiglitz, 2010, p. 14)

## Virus 7 Moral Hazard:

'Moral Hazard'. Moral Hazard is an economic term, we have already encountered in this book, meaning e.g. If unemployment social payments are perceived to be too high or close to the state minimum wage then there is the possibility that people will not look for a job. Another example is when health services to GP's are fully paid or heavily subsidised by the state, there is the possibility that people will visit the GP for minor ailments and so burden the state with the cost. In both cases there is a hazard to the state's 'moral' payment. Moral hazards however, are not just a potential for poorer individuals, they also apply in the financial industry. Banks can take greater risks when they know that deposits are guaranteed by the state. In addition, should a bank become too 'big' to be allowed to fail, the officers of such an institution are indemnified to a certain extent against bad decisions and loss.

## Virus 8 Bank employee Incentives:

These incentives are quite substantial and can come in different forms of e.g. cash bonus, stock or options. Economist John Cassidy lists some of these incentives in major financial companies in 2006 in his book, *How Markets Fail.* (Cassidy, 2010, p. 289)

I have taken his information and put it into table form as follows:

## Financial CEO Payments

**Year 2006 ($ millions)**

| Company | CEO | Cash Bonus | Stock | Options | Total paid or earned | Overall stake in the company |
|---|---|---|---|---|---|---|
| Bear Stearns | James E Cayne | $17.1 | $14.8 | $1.7 | $33.85 | $1,000.1 |
| Lehman Brothers | Richard S Fuld, Jr. | $6.25 | | $10.9 | $40.5 | $930 |
| Goldman Sachs | Lloyd C. Blankfein | $27.2 | $15.7 | $10.5 | $54.72 | $581 |
| Merrill Lynch | Stanley O'Neil | $18.5 | $26.8 | | $48 | $270 |
| Morgan Stanley | John J. Mack | | $36.2 | $4 | $41.41 | $245 |
| Citicorp | Charles ("Chuck") Prince | $13.2 | $10.6 | | $25.98 | $140 |
| Bank of America | Kenneth Lewis | $6.5 | $11.7 | $5 | $27.87 | $230 |

**Table: 13-1**

Note: Regarding stock; Stanley O'Neil received a stock grant, Charles ("Chuck") Prince received a stock award, while the remaining five received restricted stock.

From the above remuneration packages, in an extremely competitive environment, it is easy to see why risk is pushed as far as possible especially when some of the debts have been sold on (securitization) together with the moral hazard indemnity of state back-up.

## Virus 9 Technology:

The use of modern technology and the internet played a significant new role leading up to the 2008 crisis. The speed with which deals, trades, transfers of funds, and almost instantaneous international communication were initiated, no doubt not only speeded up these activities but increased them exponentially. The result was that a 'positive feedback' of, never before seen speed, due to technology, appears to have contributed to the share of the upper decile in US national income peaking in 2007 just before the crisis hit. With regard to this, French economist Thomas Piketty asks, "Is it possible that the increase of inequality in the United States helped to trigger the financial crisis of 2008? Given the fact that the share of the upper decile in US national income peaked twice in the past century, once in 1928 (on the eve of the crash in 1929) and again in 2007 (on the eve of the crash of 2008), the question is difficult to avoid.....one consequence of increasing inequality was virtual stagnation of the purchasing power of the lower and middle classes in the United States, which inevitably made it more likely that modest households would take on debt, especially since unscrupulous banks and financial intermediaries, freed from regulation and eager to earn good yields on the enormous savings injected into the system by the well-to-do, offered credit on increasingly generous terms." (Piketty, 2014, p. 297)

## Virus 10 Non-transparency and deception manipulation:

The non-transparency, due to inadequate regulation together with limited buyer understanding of complicated financial packages, left buyers holding high-risk investments that finally crashed. There is also non-transparency for the general investor regarding specific information, but not for traders at the big banks. John Coates explains. "Traders at the big banks see the largest client trades, and therefore know before the rest of the financial community where the smart money, the big money—the central banks, the hedge funds, oil money, large pension funds, the sovereign wealth funds—is going. This enables them to get in first.......No one else in the world is privy to this fund of information, although the traders do share it with their big clients—especially the hedge funds they hope to work for one day—and so valuable is it that the big banks spend fortunes maintaining an extensive global sales force. (Coates, 2012, p. 135)

Regarding deceptive manipulation, perhaps an example of this is the manipulation of interest rates. Business journalist Philip Goggan advises, that of the instruments traded in the money markets "Much is in short-term bank deposits. Interest rates were quoted as the spread between the bid and offer rates. The bid rate is the rate which a bank is prepared to pay to borrow funds; the offer rate is the rate at which it is prepared to lend. The average of the offer rates, the London Interbank Offered Rate (LIBOR), is an important benchmark for other loans, although it came under some criticism for its accuracy during the credit crunch of 2008. LIBOR is used as a benchmark for loans to the corporate sector, with the interest rate being set every six months or so in line with the rates paid by banks." (Goggan, 2009, p. 56).

This LIBOR rate, it is now established, was manipulated to deceive, as reported in the 'Economist' December 2013: "The drumbeat of investigations, lawsuits and settlements in the widening scandal over the fixing of benchmark interest rates such as LIBOR has been so steady as to be almost soporific, reducing their ability to shock. The penalty of €1.7 billion ($2.3 billion) six financial institutions agreed to pay the European Commission this week for colluding to rig rates seems if anything a slowing of the tempo. Yet it could lead to a new crescendo of legal troubles for the banks involved.

In the agreement the banks admit not only to attempting to rig rates, but also to doing so in collusion with other banks". (Economist, 2013)

In addition reported in The Times 13/11/14: "Traders' online boasts about rigging markets and cheating clients led to fines of £2.7 billion for some of the world's biggest banks yesterday.

In what was billed as a more serious scandal than the manipulation of Libor interest rates that rocked London two years ago, six banks - including Royal Bank of Scotland, which is 80 per cent owned by UK taxpayers, and HSBC - were found to have tried to manipulate benchmark foreign currency prices.

The Financial Conduct Authority and regulators in the US and Switzerland fined the banks for attempts to manipulate the foreign exchange markets, which are at the heart of capitalism and international trade." (Hosking & Wilson, 2014)

And to add insult to injury, it seems the penalties for the individuals who committed such gross acts of fraud are almost nil. Hugo Rifkind reports; "Do you know how many people RBS[115] claims to have sacked over all of this? This sweeping pillaging of its own customers that may have gone on for years? No people, that's how many. None. Instead it has suspended three and is withholding bonuses." (Rifkind, 2014)

Prior to the bust resulting in the GFC, the financial boom was built up over a period, and gained momentum as more and more assisting behaviours contributed speedily to its growth e.g. political imprimatur, relaxed regulation, speed of communication, positive feedback mechanism, hidden manipulation etc. etc. Indeed, the behaviour of investors and traders in the financial markets played a major role in the development and bust. Their behaviour was of course influenced by their numerous bodily hormonal rushes of e.g. 'adrenal', dopamine', and particularly 'testosterone' manifested in the four 'S' drives all of which may be recognised in John Coates scenario thus, "as a bull market starts to validate an investors' beliefs, the profits they make translate into a lot more than mere greed: they bring on powerful feelings of euphoria and omnipotence. It is at this point that traders and investors feel the bonds of terrestrial life slip from their shoulders and they begin to flex their muscles like a newborn superhero. Assessment of risk is replaced by judgements of certainty—they just *know* what is going to happen: extreme sports seem like child's play, sex becomes a competitive activity. They even walk differently: more erect, more purposeful, their very bearing carrying a hint of danger: 'Don't mess with

115 RBS= Royal Bank of Scotland

me,' their bodies seem to say. 'I can handle anything.'" (Coates, 2012, p. 16) There then is 'Survival', 'Sex', and their perceived superior 'Status', as well as considering themselves a walking 'Symbol' of a successful elite.

In conclusion therefore there is no doubt that, not alone are individuals, companies, and banks caught up in the frenzy of a growing boom but so also are governments. In good times government revenue also booms and this in turn allows it to borrow more for public spending thus enhancing its chances of re-election. Unfortunately, when the bust comes revenue falls but the debt still has to be serviced. In addition, governments then will probably need to borrow more, at higher interest rates, just to pay for current services and indeed additional social services due to unemployment.

In Europe the 2008 financial crisis for countries like Ireland, Portugal, Italy Greece and Spain was further exacerbated due to these countries being part of the Euro zone. So, not having their own currency, they were unable to devalue in order to help trade out of the crisis. Instead, following the bail-outs of Ireland, Greece, Portugal and Spain by the 'Troika'[116], these countries were required to introduce austerity measures on their citizenry to repay these loans. Thomas Piketty observed. "The recession of 2008-2009 caused a sharp rise in the public debt of many countries that were heavily indebted before the crisis...and also led to a rapid deterioration of bank balance sheets, especially in countries affected by a collapsing real estate bubble." (Piketty, 2014, p. 553)

Banks and financial institutions need not just reforms but purification. Mere reforms are immediately challenged by vested interests and political expediencies. As we have seen above new attempted regulation is already being challenged, as well as the perpetrators of financial crime going, to all intent and purposes, unpunished. There is no doubt that the behaviour enacted in each of the ten viruses above together with little change or discipline in the modus operandi of the financial markets indicates that finance has a natural tendency to go feral, and as such can only be described as a 'Systemic cancer rotting enterprising market economies' (SCREME).

The system itself and its workings are, in general, an accepted economic process for the trading and distribution of goods and services facilitated by the financial systems/retail banks. Rules, regulations govern this whole process to a large degree. The problems arise firstly when banks begin to neglect or are allowed to neglect a workable deposit/loan ratio. The second problem is the state guarantee on bank deposits which can encourage higher risk taking. The third problem is the fact that banks also have their own investment business running together with its traditional

---

[116] (The European Commission, the European Central Bank and the International Monetary Fund).

retail business. Andrew Smithers, with regard to this third problem, points out it is "a problem that arises from the market-making[117] activities of banks, which are sometimes described as deal for their own account. This does not seem to me to have yet been properly debated or adequately understood. This is why we need to separate the dealing and market-making of banks from their more traditional activities." (Smithers, 2013, pp. 94-95)

The purification required to address the financial world's SCREME is awesome to say the least. Nonetheless, market economies form a vital part of our freedom to interact/exchange/trade and grow. So, it is necessary to eradicate the behaviour that is increasing regressive entropy. If not the system will eventually collapse and set us back years if not completely destroy us.

But fear not, we have the means to tackle this SCREME, it is just a matter of, will to implement it?

---

[117] Market Makers: In the Australian Stock Exchange. "Professional traders with trading and quote request obligations in the exchange traded options market." (Newton, 2003, p. 230)
Or, other dealers in securities who will buy or sell at specified prices and so facilitate trading.

## CHAPTER 14
# Economics

What is economics? What is it all about?

Well, it is certainly not just how choices are made in the distribution of scarce resources, as was the flavour of older definitions. To be sure, it will have elements of this but nowadays it is understood as much more. It encompasses how people, organisations and states deal with all resources, be they scarce or plentiful.

The original name for economics was 'political economy' which developed from moral philosophy. It studied production and trade and how state laws dealt with these activities, as well the distribution of their economics outcomes. I believe economics is all of these, but my own definition of contemporary economics, I believe, is simpler and encompasses all, *Economics is about the distribution of value.*

Whether it is influenced democratically/undemocratically, fair/unfair, appropriate/inappropriate it is still about value distribution. Value itself is personal, as what is valuable to one individual may have little or no value to another. Or what may be of value at a given time or circumstance, can change dramatically at another time or circumstance. Example, you are on a ship and all the cash you have in the world is in a briefcase. It amounts to $1ml dollars. So, you are, from a cash value point of view, pretty comfortable. Then the ship is wrecked and you manage to swim, with the briefcase in tow, to a deserted island. The only food on the island is coconuts. Suddenly, the value in the briefcase becomes far less to you than the coconuts. Another example, the parents of all children in Ireland are entitled to a social welfare 'children's allowance' payment every month. This payment is not 'means tested'. The value of this payment is different for different people. For a single parent living just above the poverty line, it is essential in order to make ends meet. For a middle class lady living in a good part of the suburbs it means she can have a lunch out with her lady friends every month on the state. For multi-millionaire and CEO of Ryanair Michael O'Leary, it is, according to him, a joke. The joke being that the state is paying him to have sex.

Values change all the time. Some things hold their value in stable societies but in unstable times values change. Values will change in society depending on political ideologies and the degree of ideological power influences, with the result even economists, the specialists in the discipline, do not agree on how best to run economies e.g. the famous economist and member of numerous US administrations John Kenneth Galbraith noted: 'In economics one should never be right too soon. The shrewd scholar always waits until the parade is passing his door and then steps bravely out in front of the band.' (Galbraith, 1977, p. 220) There are some important questions to be answered on the distribution of value, such as: *Who controls the process of distribution? And what are the influences on this distribution? Also for the recipients of value, do they have the correct information to get a fair share? Do they have the opportunity to get their fair share?*

Generally, economic activity will coincide with the prevailing political views of a state or organization of states. Political views themselves will be influenced by numerous contentious issues such as levels of social services, employment levels, stem-cell research, abortion laws, gay rights, and religious versus scientific programmes etc. etc. Nonetheless, a state's economy will certainly reflect much of the political power in situ. 'Political' power, being one of the three power forces acting within any economy. The other two are, 'Wealth' power, and 'Collective' power. Wealth power is wielded by individuals or groups of individuals with wealth or are in control of major sources of wealth within a society. Collective power is wielded firstly by democratic suffrage, secondly, by self-serving collective bargaining by business, religious or union organisations etc. Collective power may also be used for complete systemic change such as e.g. revolutions.

Political ideologies exist from the extreme left (Communism → Socialism →), to the extreme right (←Conservatism ← Fascism). In between, particularly in democracies, there are various compromises from both sides to maintain a civilised and harmonised society. There are of course numbers of people who occupy the centre position with beliefs emanating from the left and the right. Different countries have different names for their left and right wing political parties, e.g. In the UK, Labour is Left while the Conservatives are Right. In the US the Democrats would be on the Left while the Republicans are on the Right. For our purposes we will refer generically to the left as 'Liberals' and the right as 'Conservatives'.

Politics however, does accommodate various other ideologies with mixtures of the left and the right with their own specific agendas. Probably, the most prominent of these are the 'Libertarians'. The focus Libertarian ideology however, is on the freedom of the individual to act in their own or group's interest. Regulation of various kinds from government, they believe, is an infringement on their individual rights. Entrepreneurs, small business proprietors, and indeed Large Businesses and their industrial leaders, constantly exhibit various levels of libertarianism. This is a good thing, in many instances, as state bureaucracy can have a stifling effect on progressive enterprise. A vibrant economy though will have a mix of the Conservatism, Liberalism and Libertarianism plus various other inputs depending on historical and current societal beliefs and culture. Liberalism, conservatism, and libertarianism will be sufficient for our sojourn into economics. Of course the weight of the power force of each will exert different outcomes for different economies. In Jonathan Haidt's book *The Righteous Mind* there is an excellent analysis and insight into these three political ideologies which I abridge as follows:

Conservatives believe in proportionality (e.g. Payment in proportion to the work done). Conservatives are necessary as they conserve tried and workable methods and policies that help with stability. However, things should not be so wedged in the past as to prevent a better world, by way of innovation, for others.

Liberals seek overall equality and are essential for innovation, change and experimentation of new methods and approaches. Liberalism is good in that it encourages a more equitable world. It also promotes innovation and enterprise but this should not be to the detriment of others.

Libertarians demand freedom to implement their particular policies and pursuits, without interference from state or society in general.

Individual freedom to pursue unhindered your own trail is fine provided, I believe, you don't hinder other people in this pursuit or disenfranchise them in some way e.g. make it difficult for them to participate equally in the 'S' drives. This of course is not to say competition in business, sport or other cultural pursuits should be curtailed in any way, rather, such should be encouraged as an essential for growth. It is 'unfair' competition that requires eradication in order to allow real freedom to prevail. Different views are constantly jockeying for position (in so-called free societies at least). For example, Politicians wish to use their power to push the policies for their electorate, while those with wealth power, can influence the political sphere, not only by lobbying, but by direct investment into particular political/other projects. Likewise, major influences are brought to bear with the collective power of industries, unions, religions and groups, such as, farmers associations, gun lobby groups.

We are of course not all born equal into whichever society we arrive. We may arrive with the benefit or not of race, gender, wealth, poverty or indeed any combination of these attributes or others such as disabilities. Nonetheless, each of us is entitled to an equal opportunity to live out a dignified contributing life for the species. Indeed, we owe it to ourselves to ensure this is the case as we can never tell where or when an individual, such as Aristotle, Copernicus, Newton, Darwin, or Einstein will pop up to assist our progressive entropy.

There have been numerous economic commentators and thinkers over the last 250 years, however, I will just give the reader a flavour of a few who are pertinent to our present economic world.

The Scot, Adam Smith may be regarded as the man who first got people thinking about market economics and capitalism. He set out his views in his best known work published in 1776, *The Wealth of Nations.* In it he introduces the notion of the, "Invisible Hand" as referring to, 'The Law of Supply and Demand'. In other words if something is required it will be demanded by someone and so it will be produced. This law is, he believed, a 'natural law' and should not be tinkered with in any way by government. As everyone follows their own self-interest, he believed, competition will ensure self-interest, and no-one gains the upper hand. The more modern notion of Smith's doctrine is that of 'Laisse-faire' i.e. let do or leave alone.

A serious rival to Smith was Karl Marx (1818-1883). Indeed, even today, the mere mention of his name can raise the hackles on some people's necks. In his most famous work *Capital*, which took 18 years to complete, he set out the notion that the capitalist exploited the worker by acquiring the 'surplus value' of their labour as profit. This process led to an accumulation of capital for the capitalist. Thomas Piketty refers to it as, "the 'principle of infinite accumulation,' that is, the inexorable tendency for capital to accumulate and become concentrated in ever fewer hands, with no natural limit to the process." (Piketty, 2014, p. 9) He also advises that the study of accumulation of capital is as valid today as it was in the nineteenth century. Marx was greatly influenced by British political economy, French politics (e.g. the revolution) and German-Hegelian philosophy. Marx's philosophical notion, via Hegel, was of Societies going through a series of 'historical developments' ending in 'Communism'. Under Communism, property and 'the means of production' would be held in the hands of the workers thus eliminating their exploitation. Liberalism/ Socialism were not new ideologies but Mark brought them to a whole new level. The fact that communism was a godless creed did great damage to its chances of political implementation in the developed Christian/Judeo capitalist world. Revolutions would in these circumstances be required.

John Maynard Keynes (1883-1946) introduced the notion that governments had a duty to help the economy along when it got into depressions. They could do this by spending large amounts (even if it was borrowed) on social or defence goods. Examples are building, Hospitals, schools, roads and railway systems, navy ships, air-force aircraft, and military weapons. These would all stimulate employment which he believed was the backbone of the economy, as it would generate spending, which in turn would generate business creation and innovation resulting in a positive feedback loop. Keynes was also one of the designers of the 'World Bank' and 'The International Monetary Fund' set up after World War II. His doctrine was implemented with great success and kept the capitalist economy basically in line up to the 1970s.

Milton Friedman (1912-2006) on the other hand, put 'inflation' as the greatest threat to an economy and not unemployment a la Keynes. He believed that if inflation was kept in check and markets were left free, the economy would always find its natural level of supply and demand. Friedman was completely against government intervention in numerous aspects of economic life. Cassidy tells us, "Friedman conceded the need for some government activities, such as national defence and law enforcement....though he questioned the government's involvement in public projects, such as highway construction and the provision of public education, which he said the market could supply...he listed fourteen unnecessary government interventions, including tariffs on imported goods, price support programs for farmers, minimum wage rates, Social Security, public housing, the US mail's monopoly, limits on the ownership of radio and television stations, and regulation of the banking system." (Cassidy, 2010, p. 75) There is no doubt then that while Marx was, and still is the hate figure for the 'Right', Friedman, by a long shot, fits the bill as the hate figure for the 'Left'. Indeed, both these men can still raise the blood pressure of the many.

When we hear the term 'economics', particularly in the western world, we associate it with much coverage in the news. Indeed, economic coverage has somewhat dominated the news since the global financial crisis of 2008. Therefore, based on their political, educational/research, religious or other beliefs, economists of all persuasions have not been shy in giving their opinions on what is best for economies. The fact that they don't mostly agree with each other does not deter them in any way. These economists then, together with Politicians, Entrepreneurs, Religious figures, Union spokespeople, Employed/Unemployed, Charity heads, Health care/Social welfare bodies and Business association representatives all espouse their views and recommendations, coloured by their world view, into the economic debate. This debate encompasses numerous policies; e.g. Macro/ Microeconomic policies, Monetary/Fiscal policies, Interest rates/Taxes policies. We hear about such things as, Gross Domestic Product (GDP), Import Tariffs/Export subsidies, Balance of payments and the likes. In addition there are so-called economic laws and propositions, like, The Law of Supply and Demand, The Law of Diminishing Returns, and The Law of Diminishing Marginal Utility, Price elasticity, and so on. But some of the major issues in the economic debate are, unemployment, inflation, government fiscal/monetary policies, regulation/deregulation, and inequality. So let us take a further look at these major issues.

**Unemployment;** is a major social issue that confronts any economy. It is a vibrant economy, as Keynes was most aware, that boasts of near full employment and its follow-on benefits. Joseph Stiglitz sums up unemployment's recent manifestation, "In the great Recession that began in 2008, millions of people in America and all over the world lost their homes and jobs.......A crisis that began in America soon turned global, as tens of millions lost their jobs worldwide---20million in China alone---and tens of millions fell into poverty" (Stiglitz, 2010, p. xi) Employment of course, is a most important ingredient for 'survival' and therefore as a follow-on for the other 'S' drives. Indeed, the unemployed themselves may feel they are receiving unemployment benefits as a charity and by receiving such benefits they are a drain on state resources. Unemployment also affects the family members of the unemployed person both directly and indirectly. We have seen that much of the processes that cause unemployment detailed in the previous two chapters and therefore should deduce categorically that it is a major contributor to negative growth and all that that entails.

**Inflation;** occurs when the prices of goods and services continue to rise, making us pay more for each good, and so results in a reduction in the value of our money. The causes of inflation are basically two-fold; Cost-Push, and Demand-Pull. Cost-push is when the cost of making a product or developing a service increases, e.g. increase in rents, warehousing, wages and other expenses. These extra costs are passed on in an increased price to the buyer. Demand-pull is when there is an increase in demand for a product or service with the result businesses will raise prices to take advantage of higher margins. The increase in demand may be caused by cheaper available credit or a decrease in taxes. A small amount of inflation is acceptable in any economy and may even be encouraged for growth purposes. However, if not kept in check it can spiral out of control as occurred in Germany in the 1930s.

To boost the economy governments may;

1. Reduce taxes
2. Increase credit by reducing interest rates
3. Increase government spending
   -Too much and you get inflation

To constrict the economy governments may;

1. Increase taxes
2. Reduce credit by increasing interest rates
3. Reduce government spending
   -Too much and you stifle growth

**Regulation/deregulation:** In general the different policies emanating from the different economic theorists has resulted in an on-going boom and bust cycle. For example, rules are relaxed and the boom gathers momentum until it bursts. Or too much regulation stifles growth so rules are relaxed to encourage growth and the cycle begins again.

Adam Smith's 'invisible hand' supposedly guiding a 'laissez faire' free market worked for a time and increased the wealth of the capitalist but exploited the poor through a boom time from the beginning of the industrial revolution up to the extraordinary bust in 1929 and the Great Depression. The Great Depression, saw the introduction of greater regulation and transparency by government intervention, and this cooled world economies down. There was however a price to pay namely, untold unemployment and poverty.

Socialist and Communist movements had taken off in the 19th century fuelled by Marx's ideology and a desire for equality. Left wing parties began to thrive and gave opposition to the Conservative and Libertarian establishments. Communism as an ideology was quite successful in that it has been claimed that by the 1980's one third of the world's population lived in some form of communist state. As a political process however, it was a disaster due in the main to its stifling of entrepreneurial innovation and activity[118].

In most democratic market economies, following World War II, Keynesian policies were implemented, with a view to avert unemployment and increase employment. This resulted in steady growth, with, to be sure some hiccups, up to the 1970s and 1980s. It was then that Milton Friedman's doctrine of little or no regulation in the financial system together with monetary policy to curb inflation, took root. This doctrine was preached, practiced and purveyed by its main acolytes, Ronald Regan and Margaret Thatcher. Indeed, parts of it (de-regulation and mild monetary policy to check inflation) helped the bubble grow until it finally burst in 2008. Friedman's neoclassical economics, based on supply and demand and 'so-called' rational choices together with low interest rates and de-regulation, did of course boost the economy into a faster gear. But, left relatively unregulated it

[118] The fact that it was a godless greed also did not help, particularly in Christian western societies.

eventually burst in 2008 and so the inequality wedge between the rich and poor was further widened.

Why did this burst happen then? One reason John Coates believes, is that neo-classical economics is based on the assumption of a focus on the mind and the thoughts of a rational person. "According to this school of thought, we are walking computers who can calculate the rewards of each course of action open to us at any given moment, and weigh these rewards by the probability of their occurrence...

Consequently, neo-classical economics has largely ignored the body. It is economics from the neck up." (Coates, 2012, pp. 29-30)

Of course we know that the whole body is in a constant process of receiving, analysing, and sending messages around itself regarding its environment, and very often we believe we actually make decisions that later we attempt to justify. One of the reasons for this is that we believe we know, automatically, the best way to act or the best decisions to make, even when they may be wrong. Remember the 'game show' where the odds were 3 to 1 and then 2 to 1 to get a car or a goat!! Indeed, one of the reasons we believe we know best is because we think mostly in an empirical[119] way. Scientist and mathematician, Nassim Taleb's notion of naïve empiricism fits the bill for neo-classical economists together with traders and investors in a runaway market. With "naïve empiricism, we have a natural tendency to look for instances that confirm our story and our vision of the world—these instances are always easy to find, Alas, with tools, and fools, anything can be easy to find. You take past instances that corroborate your theories and you treat them as *evidence.* (Taleb, 2008, p. 55) In his enlightening publication *The Black Swan* he maintains such empiricism is naïve as it fooled generations into believing that only white swans existed until black swans were discovered in Australia, and then these beautiful creatures became a reality along with their white cousins. We cannot therefore rely on past evidence. To be sure we can use it, but we never know when a 'black swan' will appear. Taleb further believes that philosopher Karl Popper's notion of 'falsification' (to falsify is to prove wrong) would be a superior process to our 'natural' empirical process. However, falsification is a difficult process as it is natural for us to look for corroboration.

An example of how strong belief is in the notion that positive growth will continue, was demonstrated in 2007 by the then Irish Taoiseach Bertie Ahern who said that people who expressed doubt about the economy should commit suicide!!!! He did later apologise for this remark, nonetheless, it shows the level of feeling he

[119] Based on observation or experience.

had for the previous extraordinary growth the country experienced in the 'Celtic Tiger'[120] years and indeed its continuation.

So, what is the long-term societal consequence of this irrational, Laissez faire, greed induced, mostly masculine, empirically driven process operating within a capitalist market economy? The answer is simply 'inequality'.

Thomas Piketty's tour de force, ***Capital*** *in the twenty-first century*[121], addresses this issue of inequality like nothing else to date. The following table details his interpretation of various economic terms.

120 The term 'Celtic Tiger' refers to the boom experienced in the Irish economy in the latter half of the 1990s. This was fed by foreign investment and a property construction expansion.

121 "This book is based on fifteen years of research (1998-2013) devoted essentially to understanding the historical dynamics of wealth and income. Much of this research was done in collaboration with other scholars." (Piketty, 2014, p. vii)

| Economic Term | Value |
|---|---|
| **Gross domestic product (GDP)**: | Total amount of goods and services produced within a country within a given year |
| **National Income** | This is **GDP** less depreciation on capital (he estimates depreciation is around 10%) and he calls the approximate 90% that remains **domestic output** or **domestic producti**on |
| **National Income** | Domestic output plus net income from abroad. |
| **National Wealth** | Public wealth plus Private wealth |
| **Global Income**. | Global output |
| **National Income (contributors)** | **Capital Income** plus **Labor Income.** |
| **Capital** | The sum total of nonhuman assets that can be owned and exchanged on some markets. Capital includes all forms of real property (including residential real estate) as well as financial and professional capital (plants, infrastructure, machinery, patents, and so on) used by firms and government agencies. |
| **Capital Income** | Income derived from capital. |
| **Labor income** | Any form of remuneration an individual labourer, tradesperson, manager or professional etc. receives for the use of their skills/ability. |

**Table: 14-1**

Piketty tells us that the heart of his book, "is that the dynamics of wealth distribution reveal powerful mechanisms pushing alternatively toward convergence and divergence. Furthermore, there is no natural, spontaneous process to prevent destabilizing, inegalitarian forces from prevailing permanently." (Piketty, 2014, p. 21) With regard to convergence he advises, "Over a long period of time, the main force in favor of greater equality has been the diffusion of knowledge and skills." (Piketty, 2014, p. 22) On the other hand he tells us that the fundamental force for divergence is when the average rate of return on capital[122] is greater than the average rate of growth of the economy[123]. He points out that society and its wealthy have changed in recent times. "To a large extent we have gone from a society of rentiers to a society of managers, that is, from a society in which the top centile is dominated by rentiers (people who own enough capital to live on the annual income from their wealth) to a society in which the top income hierarchy, including the upper centile, consists mainly of highly paid individuals who live on income from labor....income from capital used to predominate in the top centile but today predominates only in the top thousandth." (Piketty, 2014, pp. 278-279) His research further highlights inequality specifics for Europe, the US, and globally with a strong comeback of private capital in the rich countries[124] since 1970.

We saw an example of the high remuneration levels received by some of these above society of managers in the Finance chapter Table 13-1. While a new Oxfam report shows "that the 62 richest billionaires own as much wealth as the poorer half of the world's population." As reported 18/1/16 by Larry Elliott Economics editor *theguardian.*[125]

One of the consequences of these observations is that, apart from the inequality on an individual basis, certain systemic processes could seriously damage state relationships. For example, "it is almost inevitable that the sovereign wealth funds of the petroleum exporting countries will continue to grow and that their share of global assets in 2030-2040 will be at least two to three times greater than it is today...

If this happens, it is likely that the Western countries would find it increasingly difficult to accept being owned in substantial part by the sovereign wealth funds of oil states, and sooner or later this would trigger political reactions..." (Piketty, 2014, pp. 459-460)

Such reactions, due to instability, tend to dry up capital as happened in the 'two world war' period 1913 to 1950 resulting in a major destruction of capital. When this occurs market economies of course greatly suffer. In his solution to the major issue of inequality within the system, he points out that certain actions are required to counteract its development. He notes that in the 1950s controlling capital together with new regulations and tax policies reduced capital's share of income to historically low levels. In addition as already mentioned above, the main

---

122 Including profits, dividends, interest, rents, and other income from capital.

123 Therefore (r > g) (r = rate of return on capital, > = greater than, g = growth of economy or if you like output and wages.

124 United States, Germany, Britain, Canada, Japan, France, Italy, and Australia

125 http://www.theguardian.com/business/2016/jan/18/richest-62-billionaires-wealthy-half-world-population-combined

force in favour of greater equality has been the diffusion of knowledge and skills. He therefore proposes greater transparency in the financial industry together with a progressive tax on capital to regain control over the dynamics of accumulation. He admits however, that the implementation of such a global tax is a 'utopian ideal'. Nonetheless, he points out the need for such a tax, giving an example relating to declared income for tax purposes on fortunes, being only a fraction of economic income. The bulk then of this economic income remains tax-less[126], as far as we know, growing at plus 5% in some trust or tax haven. This is nonetheless all quite legal but continues to feed the inequality spiral. However, with regard to the need of a wealth tax he believes it should be a progressive annual tax on individual wealth on the net value of assets each person controls. This tax rate, he suggests, might be 0% for assets below €1 million, 1% for assets between €1-5 million and 2% above €5 million.

There is no doubt that there is now a chance, albeit extremely small, of such a tax happening on a national basis when greater transparency of the financial industry appears to be on the cards with more robust tax laws such as the Foreign Account Tax Compliance Act (FATCA). This Act was "adopted in the United States in 2010 and scheduled to be phased in by stages in 2014 and 2015. It requires all foreign banks to inform the Treasury Department about bank accounts and investments held abroad by US taxpayers, along with any other sources of revenue from which they might benefit. This is a far more ambitious law than the 2003 EU directive on foreign savings, which concerns only interest-bearing deposit accounts...... Luxembourg and Switzerland (also) to abide by the provisions of FATCA, discussions in Europe resumed with the intention of incorporating some or all of these in a new EU directive." (Piketty, 2014, p. 522)

To be sure, the head-quarters of capitalism namely the United States will not take the Piketty analysis of its economic management on the chin, and/or immediately set about reforms for greater equality. To quote Galbraith again, "People have an enduring tendency to protect what they have, justify what they want to have. And their tendency to see as right the ideas that serve such purpose." (Galbraith, 1977, p. 11) But no doubt the data from Piketty's analysis will be questioned even though it all appears to be from indisputable statistical sources. His extrapolations into the future may be rejected on the basis that experience in historical data, will prevent such a future. But we must never forget that the 'black swan' is always at the ready to swim the unchartered waters. Indeed, it is difficult to see how one can be sceptical of Piketty's thorough research and analysis. However, Michael Shermer, in his monthly

126 There may be capital gains tax deducted depending the location or type of home the fortune resides in. However, with different countries and institutions competing for such capital, taxes are driven down to next or nothing.

article in Scientific American, *Skeptic (viewing the world with a rational eye)*[127] writes about 'The Myth of Income Inequality'. In fairness to Shermer he does not deny the existence inequality itself, however, in this article Shermer refers to specific studies/reports[128] and makes the point that not alone are the top income earners increasing their share of the national income but so also are the remainder of income earners. In addition there is evidence for social mobility as well as people overestimating the differences between the rich and the poor, "income inequality and social mobility, though not as ideal as we would like them to be in the land of equal opportunity, are not as large and immobile as most of us perceive them." (Shermer, 2014)

Shermer's article and the likes are essential for balance, however they do not negate the enormous disparity existing between the rich/superrich and the low income/extremely poor. Nor indeed, do they give us solace in that the gulf is steering us for the disaster of destroying market economies as we know them today. There is no dispute that while the rich have gotten richer and some of the rest of us have certainly moved on with regard to wages, working and living conditions. And I think most would agree that such progress, in most of the western world, has been the case. Certainly, we would not like to be back as a child working in a mill in England during the industrial revolution! In the nineteenth century the gulf between the rich and poor was enormous and what Piketty is saying is that he believes from his research is that we are once again heading for a similar gulf. "When the rate of return on capital exceeds the rate of growth of output and income, as it did in the nineteenth century and seems quite likely to do again in the twenty-first, capitalism automatically generates arbitrary and unsustainable inequalities that radically undermine the meritocratic values on which democratic societies are based." (Piketty, 2014, p. 1) "Today, in the second decade of the twenty-first century, inequalities of wealth that had supposedly disappeared are close to regaining or even surpassing their historical highs." (Piketty, 2014, p. 471)

Let us not forget however, that inequality itself, among human beings, is a most natural phenomenon. We all know that some people are born into this world at one extreme of poverty while others arrive with a silver spoon in their mouths. In addition, some arrive with natural abilities that may be developed into

---

[127] "Economics has an Achilles' heel. Until recently many practitioners attempted to ignore or dispute this shortcoming-but it can ultimately be held responsible for many of the glaring mistakes economists have made for hundreds of years. It is the erroneous assumption that human beings are rational." (Conway, 2009, p. 186)

[128] Brookings Institution: Gary Burtless analysing tax data from the Congressional Budget office for after tax trends from 1979 through 2010 (including government assistance).

A report by the Federal Reserve in early 2014.... noting the overall wealth of Americans.

A 2013 study published in *Psychological Science* entitled "Better Off Than We Know," St. Louis University psychologist John R. Chambers and his colleagues.

exceptional skills. Indeed, the application of such skills deserves recognition by way of compensation and/or increased status. So, inequality in itself is not a problem of regressive entropy. Rather, what needs to be addressed is firstly, 'inequality of opportunity', and secondly, inequality of proportionality[129] (payment for work done) and thirdly, inequality of value distribution.

In summary then under the economics banner there is little doubt that inequality of opportunity and proportionality may be addressed, to a certain extent, with 'a diffusion of knowledge and skills' i.e. education. The inequality of value distribution however, is a more toxic infection to cure. Indeed, its eradication or even part eradication thereof would significantly assist in addressing the inequalities of opportunity and proportionality. These inequalities, and in particular the inequality of value distribution with its process under existing capitalist market economies, are severely damaging. Indeed, damaging to the extent that this toxicity could not alone end up poisoning itself (the system) but also be the cause societal upheavals and national sovereignty disputes and reactions. Proportionality, opportunity, and equality are all wonderful ideals, as is the ability of the many to weave a path that embraces and integrates them. But one of the great uniting forces and activities in social endeavour is our participation in market economic processes and therefore such processes must be always protected, not only from other processes that have failed but also from itself, if needed.

Inequalities therefore, produced by the system may be described as 'Systemic cancer rotting enterprising market economies' (SCREMEs), and as such must be treated with a radical cure and a particularly delicate aftercare program. However, with the main perpetrator of inequality, within market economies, being 'the rate of return on capital being greater than the average rate of growth of the economy', does this mean we have to somehow increase the rate of growth of the economy and/or reduce the rate of return on capital? Well firstly, every country, business etc. is constantly endeavouring to increase its rate of growth, so that will continue as always with fervour. And indeed, to try to reduce the rate of return on capital would be ludicrous, as it is one of the drivers of market economies. Therefore, with the root cause of inequality in market economies being 'indigenous' to it, such a perpetrator needs to be addressed, and addressed in such a way that market economic processes remain in situ. In other words, when addressing the problems as such, a harmonious and functional neutralization solution needs to be implemented. In this regards part of the solution will undoubtedly be 'a diffusion of knowledge and skills'

[129] "Since the 1970s income inequality has increased significantly in the rich countries, especially the United States, where concentration of income in the first decade of the twenty-first century regained—indeed, slightly exceeded—the level attained in the second decade of the previous century." (Piketty, 2014, p. 15)

which as noted above causes a convergence to greater equality. But are Piketty's reforms, together with a tax on capital rather than just a tax income a solution? Perhaps? Perhaps not?

# CHAPTER 15
# E-Capitalism 1

To begin this chapter I believe a major recap will be of assistance as follows:

*Information emanates from the 'programming decoherence centre' at the periphery of the universal quantum computer that is the universe. This information programmes the universe via decoherence to form our holographic classical deterministic world.*

*Entropy we have discovered is about degrees or levels of information ranging from high information (ordered) to low information (disordered). Or one might say ranging from the educated to the ignorant or from the complex to the unravelled.*

*Progressive entropy is moving toward the ordered or complex, while, regressive entropy is moving toward the disordered or unravelled.*

*Our behaviour, is not initiated in the classical way we believe, such as making a decision to act or not, and then carrying out the action or inaction. Rather, our classical reactions, to ourselves and surroundings are constantly changing our environments. In turn this continuously adds changing information to our quantum string experience banks.*

*These experience banks are therefore continuously updating our environment for decoherence into the deterministic automatic classical world. However, our string memory banks are quantum, so they are not subject to classical determinism.*

*Therefore unconsciously, as consciously we cannot directly access the quantum world, we have the ability to change a pending 'natural' automatic decoherence to an 'adjusted' automatic decoherence based on our preferences, desires etc.. This is enacted then unconsciously, from the 'quantum string memory banks' within the classical brain, via entanglement and the 'delayed choice' process, to the 'programming decoherence centre' for the most up-to-date experience and then fed back (decohered) for the appropriate classical environmental fit.*

*As such then, we are still accountable and responsible for our behaviour which is driven by survival, sex, status and symbolism. It changes environments to be compatible with our desires, as stored in our memory banks, thus determining the decohered information which will result in progressive or regressive entropy.*

*Entropy in the classical world moves naturally and ultimately towards the 'regressive' end of its spectrum. Life moves in the opposite direction, temporarily.*

*Our classical environment will dictate what is decohered into our classical world. Therefore, our human (body) environment, our earth's environment, our climatic environment, our societal environment and even our economic environment etc. dictates, via classical human feedback desires, what is decohered into it, be it progressive or regressive.*

*By changing 'our individual world' environments we automatically change all other living or non-living world environments progressively or regressively from the immediate present into the future. This change is no less significant as, were it possible, to visit a different time in history and change the past, thus reconstructing the present.*

*Genes, Memes, SCREMEs:*

*Genes are biological replicators. Evolution has assisted in progressive entropy by natural selection. Some destructive genes however are not selected out and result in what we call genetic disorders, such as cystic fibrosis, and hence regressive entropy.*

*Memes are cultural replicators that may produce progressive or regressive entropy. A meme that produces progressive entropy for example, is the cultural process of bequeathing your body parts for transplant. Whereas, a meme that produces regressive entropy is the cultural habit of smoking cigarettes that cause lung cancer, heart disease etc.*

*Behaviour that was natural resulted in changing the climatic environment regressively. This entailed memes for an overuse of resources. Currently, this environmental change is affecting the whole planet, and if not managed will have even worse consequences for our children and children's children.*

*In spite of the world acceptance of this situation now, some so-called educated, informed, or vested interest individual or groups of greedy people pay little heed and continue to overuse the earth's resources with little regard for their children's children or indeed their fellow human beings. But thankfully, world governments have got together for on-going management by legislation, of this crisis! Of course individual accountability and responsibility is the real issue, in this regard.*

*Trade evolved, from the social interaction of our species to be an essential behavioural ingredient for survival and growth. This has now developed into what we call market economies, or the economic environments pervading the world.*

*SCREMEs (systemic cancers rotting enterprise market economies) are* ***behavioural destructive economic replicating memes.*** *They are therefore memes that produce regressive entropy.*

*In chapter 10 'Behaviour' we noted that; 'On the one hand, do we wish for ourselves, our children and future generations to be exploited, deprived, or disadvantaged, due to the behaviour of others? I believe the answer will be a big 'No'. This being the case, we will then expose such individuals and* ***not*** *support them personally, in their organisations, in their businesses or in the businesses they invest in? Regressive for one is regressive for all. On the other hand, do we wish for ourselves, our children and future generations, to have health, education, and opportunity for growth, due to the behaviour of others? I believe the answer will be a big 'Yes'. This then being the case, we* ***will*** *support and indeed promote such individuals, personally, in their organisations, in their businesses or in the businesses within which they invest? Progressive for one should assist in progressive for all.*

*Individuals engaged in, or condoning behavioural destructive economic replicating memes are assisting regressive entropy. Such individuals are infringing on everyone else currently, as well as future generations.*

We have discovered from the last three chapters that there are SCREMEs within market economic systems that have the mechanism to bring down capitalism itself. Firstly, there is the SCREME in business that seeks to reduce employees as well as their remuneration, thus constantly eroding its own and other business' buyer base. This can be referred to as self-inflicted (albeit natural) 'Employee Erosion'. Secondly, in the financial world where the non-transparency/deregulation SCREMEs allow for its mechanisms to literally go wild. This can be referred to as self-inflicted (albeit natural) 'Feral Finance'. Thirdly, with rates of return on capital constantly outperforming national growth rates, the SCREME of inequality is inevitable. This can be referred to as self-inflicted (albeit natural) 'Indigenous Inequality'.

Within the disciplines of business, finance and economics while there are numerous SCREMEs that need to be addressed, but for our purposes we will concentrate on the three major ones noted above namely, 'Employee Erosion', 'Feral Finance' and 'Indigenous Inequality'. If these SCREMEs are simply ignored by an apathetic society, or even if the many think it is 'just too hard' to engage for reforms with the powers that be, like politicians, business industries, financial institutions and the super-rich, then severe consequences are inevitable. Consequences that will not just affect our way of life but put our way of life in serious jeopardy. Now, you the reader may feel that firstly, the powers that be will not allow such a thing to occur again, or secondly, your own circumstances will keep you immune from the consequences. But what about your children and grand-children or other future generations around the world? Are you happy to be 'ripped off' by the perpetrators of these SCREMEs? Are you the type of individual that just does not get involved and allows others do the work? Are you content to have your children's future put in danger by some people's greed, stupidity, inadequacy and selfishness? Are you content to know that, due to lack of opportunity, some of the greatest innovations for the human race may not materialise? Do you mind that you and your family are being used, so others might have excessively more than one person could ever need in this world. Do you **really** care that children the same age as your own are suffering from diseases, malnutrition, lack of education, lack of medicines? Do you care that due to slave labour, children are used to develop products for your comfortable convenience?

All of the above questions, and many more, are questions that relate to the identified SCREMEs which urgently and vitally need to be addressed. But it is important that they be addressed in such a way that market economic processes remain in situ (for growth) as noted above. How then, are we to remove these bad apples without upsetting the applecart?

Economists of all persuasions, financial and business leaders, together with religious heads, including the pope in Rome are all calling for economic reforms of this, that, and the other, to make it all 'fair' and 'right' for the particular society they envisage. Unfortunately, I believe, as most of us do deep down, that the Galbraith quote from the previous chapter represents reality. "People have an enduring tendency to protect what they have, justify what they want to have. And their tendency to see as right the ideas that serve such purpose." Mere reform in a patchwork fashion is of course better than nothing, but patching repairs are only temporary. What in fact is clearly required is a revolutionary process of purification, or if you like a paradigm shift to a 'new capitalist' system. Old capitalism has served us adequately, some well but others not so well. This old capitalism however, now needs to move on. Indeed, this required revolutionary movement will be facilitated, in a special way by current and future technologies, particularly communication technologies.

What I mean by this **'new capitalist system'** is that **the masses with access to communication technology will run market economies.** And the 'new capitalist' paradigm, I will call 'E-Capitalism 1'. The 'E' obviously stands for electronic and the 1 stands for 'version 1' as economies are dynamic and evolving and much of their problems arise from attempting to maintain or revert to vested interest processes, rather than embracing reformation and revolution. So, how will 'E-Capitalism 1' work? How will it differ from the existing model? How and where will it be implemented?

How will it be monitored? What will be its advantages? All of these questions cannot be fully answered in this publication, however a basic understanding of what is envisaged, together with a methodology to set the ball rolling, with particular emphasis on a process to reverse the foregoing SCREMEs will help us well on our way.

'E-Capitalism 1' then, needs to address the 'three SCREMEs, namely, (1) 'Employee Erosion' (2) Feral Finance, and (3) Indigenous Inequality. No longer will only existing 'Political', 'Wealth', or 'Self-serving collective' power brokers run the Capitalist system, instead, a 'Mass collective of people power' will exert and influence change to harmoniously create a metamorphosis to 'E-Capitalism 1'. The change itself will be via the implementation of 'Beneficial Economic Multiplying Entropies' (BEMEs) or economic replicators.

Remember:

A Gene is a biological replicator

A Meme is a cultural replicator

A BEME is a specific type of Meme that enables market economies to become more efficient and grow. It is therefore a meme that is **beneficial** with an **economic** specificity, replicating **multiplying** progressive information **entropy.** Information of course being the essence**.**

A BEME then is 'An Economic replicator'.

A BEME in addition, as an economic replicator, may be voluntarily or mandatorily initiated/implemented.

Table 15-1 below details the biological, cultural and economic replicators.

**Replicators:**

| **Replicator** | **Type** | **System** | **Methodological/Process** |
|---|---|---|---|
| Gene | Biological | Reproductive | Sex |
| Meme | Cultural | Societal | Human- copying/ imitating/emulating |
| BEME | Economic | Capitalist | Progressive entropy multiplier |

**Table: 15-1**

Examples of existing BEMES are, **cash discounts** given by business, **capped mortgages** given by banks, and **philanthropic donations** given by the wealthy.

Table 15-2 below details the emotionally charged issues emanating from the SCREMEs and the specific BEMEs to address these.

## SCREMEs/Issues/BEMEs

| SCREME | Issue | BEME |
|---|---|---|
| Employee Erosion | Unemployment | Regenerate employment |
| Feral Finance | Citizenry exploitation | Regulate banks |
| Indigenous Inequality | Escalating inequality | Redistribute value |

**Table: 15-2**

Like any other meme, a BEME needs to be established, protected and facilitated for replication. As we have seen a meme and therefore a BEME may be individually initiated and then replicated to be applied as a 'personally actionable' or 'collective pressuring' process. A BEME may be a 'protector' of existing progressive entropy or a 'generator' of progressive entropy. Indeed, some BEMES will have elements of both. A BEME may be a stand-alone or a contributor to a greater BEME.

A BEME requires the following processes: (1) Its formulation, (2) A launching pad, and (3) Continuous pressure for implementation and replication.

This book *Brilliantbranes* is itself a BEME. Its formulation is the writing down of its theory. Its launching pad will be its publication and its implementation and replication will hopefully be the execution of its revolutionary programme.

The SCREMEs of, 'Employee Erosion', 'Feral Finance', and 'Indigenous Inequality', have developed due to individual and/or group behaviours that are natural, but excessively self-motivated, resulting in the infringement of others and eventually, if unchecked, will be systemically destroying. Such SCREMEs alter the environment negatively, resulting in decoherence that adds to regressive entropy for all.

The BEMEs advocated within this chapter will address the issues emanating from these SCREMEs. The formulation of each of these BEMEs will be presented below. However, their launching pad for implementation/replication is dependent on **you! Yes,** you the readers or in this case the BEMERs provided, of course, you agree with the need for change. BEMERs, hopefully like you, are intelligent, sophisticated, and electronically communicative individuals who will exercise their rights to ensure progressive entropy for themselves, their children, and future generations. So, BEMERs are the ones who must **electronically** lobby, by way of a communication **'Sales pitch'** to have the BEME implemented. In this regard, a marketing/advertising methodology of 'Reach' 'Frequency' and 'Continuity' will be required to make the greatest impact. Just as St. Patrick taught the Irish about the 'Trinity', being three persons[130] in the one god, so also are there the three elements of reach, frequency, and continuity, the god of marketing.

As a BEMER, your BEME **reach** will be your target audience of friends, politicians, media/personalities commentators, businesses, employees of businesses, religious/church organisations, sporting/relevant organisations etc. Your target audience will be communicated to via social networks, emails, YouTube, websites, bloggs, etc. Lists of addresses for all reach targets are easily accessable/available on the net. Note well, that the wider and more targeted the reach the better the results will be.

Your BEME **frequency** will be the number of times you communicate the 'sales pitch' message for BEME implementation. In other words just one communication 'hit' has little effect. It needs to be carried out as frequently as possible. Just as we know advertisements on TV[131] keep hitting us with great frequency because marketers understand it takes many 'hits' to get a message across. We should aim for at least 10 'hits'.

Your BEME **continuity** will be the same message over and over and over again up to at least 10 times so it will sink in for reaction. It matters not that the message may be worded differently but it must be consistent in what it is saying. So now, let us take the three identified above BEMEs and set out the process for their implementation.

**(1) Regenerate employment:** This will be voluntarily initiated/implemented and may be termed a 'BEME-Back'.

BEME Rationale: It is my contention that the more, healthy, educated, and informed human beings are, they will make better choices for themselves, family, friends, groups and society at large. People cannot contribute to the positive progressive journey of complexity unless they have an income and better still a recompensed income, in order to satisfy their occupational status.

Everything we use for the purposes of growth on this earth is either naturally available in sufficient quantities or has to be replenished/replicated, and at a rate pertinent to its use, or it will eventually run out. But, while some resources will be sufficient, all things being equal, for perhaps thousands of years, other resources need to be managed efficiently. For example, fresh water resources together with replenishment of fish in the sea, and crops in the ground. However, if we continue to

---

130 The Father, the Son, and the Holy Spirit.

131 TV ads work on what are called *target audience rating points* or 'TARPS'. These work as follows: Should you wish to reach a target of teenagers aged 13-17 and are told that a specific TV show's audience for this target group is 60%. Then for our target audience this show has a TARP of 60.

take from the earth's bountiful pie, without sufficient management/replenishment, we will end up with no pie.

The same goes for the use of buyers in a business. We know for example, from Richard Dawkins that, a biological entity as a whole may not be selfish but its genes on the other hand are, due to the survival requirement of the whole. Business likewise as a whole is a necessary and worthy pursuit, however within it are selfish memes, such as the five *self-inflicted nails* 'SINS' discussed in chapter 12 'Business'. A BEME then to regenerate employed buyers must be enacted and indeed needs to be enacted specifically in the private sector of the economy as this sector represents circa 80% of a national economy's employment base[132]. This BEME may be developed and implemented as follows:

- It will take the form of a promotion strategy on the sale of the product to give an amount back to the buyer.
- It follows the notion of a turnover/value-added tax, but it is not compulsory so it is not a tax, rather it is a selling promotion expense that may be used or not at a Sellers discretion.
- It is somewhat like the notion of promotions of supermarkets giving coupons/stamps/vouchers for various amounts purchased. It might also for example, be included on the product bar-code.
- It also follows the custom of Irish cattle dealers giving a 'luck penny' back following payment of a purchase. The amount is at the discretion of the Seller, depending on the size of the purchase, it could be 1%, 5%, or 10% of purchase price whatever? It is to give a little bit of thankful luck to the purchaser for the purchase. So, the buyer gets a little gift back.
- This BEME-Back gift should not be a pre-net profit expense, rather it is paid from the selling price to the buyer.
- It may be given on all and every product/service sold.
- It can be calculated as a percentage of the purchase price, or a percentage of the profit margin if known. A profit margin may be revealed by the seller at their discretion. An example of a known profit margin is the interest rate a bank charges on the sale of a loan.
- A BEME-Back percentage of a purchase might commence at .25% of purchase price or 1% of profit margin and increase at the seller's discretion for greater promotion/sales.

132 Public employees in the UK represent 19% of total employees, therefore employees in the private sector will be 81%

- The buyer/receiver of the BEME-Back will not immediately have access to its value, rather it will be invested in enterprises to generate jobs/other buyers for business.
- A BEME institute facility[133] will be set up, preferably independent of the state, with an international affiliation[134]. Perhaps the facility would be a type of 'building society' but in this case a 'building society' to build jobs.
- Buyers may register with this facility and have their BEME values credited to their accounts. Current technology can easily accommodate this process
- The accumulated BEME values in the BEME institute facility will then represent funds available to create high employment businesses.
- These businesses will be concentrated on sound ecological endeavours as well as, if possible, renewable energies and/or high human physical concentration on arts, crafts, skills, etc.
- Employees in these businesses will contribute towards the administration of the overall BEME employment strategy.
- The funds invested in these businesses will be procured from different accounts in the BEME facility and converted into issued shares in the created businesses.
- Investment of funds in specific enterprises will be at the discretion of the BEME facility's administration under its charter.
- Account holders will **not** have access to the funds until two years after they have been used to invest in a job generating business. Then they may keep or sell them. The sale may be at a profit or loss depending on the success or other of the enterprise.
- Account holders will also receive a small interest on their BEME funds, part of which will go the administration, and the remaining part added to their account fund.

Advantages:

- Apart from business' 'normal' generation of buyers[135] this type of BEME-Back ensures future buyers for growth and profit.

---

[133] A BEME institute facility needs to be established in each national market economy. This facility should preferably be independent of the state. It should be run by an internationally accepted independent body. Now, while organisations like the UN, The World Bank, IMF etc., might to some, appear to lack a certain amount of independence, such bodies would be ideal, as they already have representation in many countries. A BEME facility can only be set-up within an economy when enough 'collective pressuring' is brought on politicians for this to happen.

[134] E.G. the World Bank or the IMF.

[135] E.G. Creating a need for the product by promotion.

- This contributes to the *occupational status* of the many.
- This means that a self-destructive mechanism within market economies is neutralised without changing the mechanism.
- There is an advantage here also to the seller in using this BEME-Back, as an incentive to buy, thus giving them a competitive edge.
- Buyers have the advantage of receiving a gift in return for their purchase as well as an opportunity to make that gift work for them as an investment for profit and a positive contribution to the economy as a whole.

So, it is like Shakespeare advises in 'The Merchant of Venice' that some things are twice blessed, "it blesseth him that gives and him that takes." Or indeed to quote Jonathan Haidt, "Human life is a series of opportunities for mutually beneficial cooperation. If we play our cards right, we can work with others to enlarge the pie that we ultimately share." (Haidt, 2012, p. 136)

**(2) Regulate banks:** This will be voluntarily initiated by BEMERs and mandatorily implemented by the state and may be termed a 'Bank-BEME'.

Bank-BEME Rationale: Just as laws are passed to protect the environment in which we can live a healthy, safe and nutritional life, so laws are required to allow for a healthy, safe and progressive market economy.

Banks perform a necessary societal role in market economic states in addition to their private business enterprise. This dual operation is open to corruption as observed in the GFC of 2008. In order to fully appreciate this internal conflict let us take a different organisation e.g. 'The police force' that has a societal role of protecting citizens. Now suppose this organisation is privatised and run as a business, doing its ordinary traditional role of fighting crime while at the same time having the legal right to make additional earnings from operating a string of legalised brothels and gambling outlets. These additional earners prove to be very lucrative especially when the legalities are relaxed by way of non-transparency of operation, political imprimatur, and deceptive opportunities to fix the odds! Unfortunately, the private business earners infringe upon the traditional police work to the extent of causing a major policing crisis, such that without government intervention, anarchy would ensue. To be sure such a situation would/could not be allowed in a democratic society. As we may recall even the non-interventionist economist Milton Friedman 'conceded the need for some government activities, such as national defence and law enforcement'. But is this any different from the 'Banks'? Is it even more important for the facilitator of the economy's blood not to be operating with internal conflictual processes? I truly believe these conflictual processes require a regulatory Bank-BEME. Specifically, such a Bank-BEME may be developed and implemented as follows:

- The Introduction of laws and regulations such as, 'The Securities Act' for openness, and 'The Glass-Steagall Act' to deter 'retail banks' from acting like 'Investment banks', need to be re-established not just in the United States but in all democracies. What we want here is firstly, to ensure financial institutions are risk regulated, to protect the system, and then monitored so they do not deviate from such regulation. Secondly, there must be transparency regulation, to protect the system, and again monitored so there is a complete understanding of all their products and processes.
- There is no doubt that while governments once more attempt to enact and implement processes to address this issue, lobby groups with vested interest in de-regulation are already up and running! So, what is required is a 'collective pressuring' BEME targeting politicians, superseding de-regulation lobby groups, to implement sufficient regulation for a robust, safe, fair and transparent financial system.
- In addition the notion of regulation has to be sold to politicians. You the BEMER will be the salesperson with the politician the potential buyer. Therefore you must firstly, support the politicians who back the complete separation of banks into their traditional role and their investment role. Withdraw support from those who don't, and campaign for others to do likewise. And secondly, support banks that actually separate, or institutions that are one or the other. Withdraw your business from those banks that don't separate and campaign for others to do likewise.

**(3) Redistribute value:** This will be voluntarily initiated/implemented and may be termed a 'BEME-Aid'.

BEME-Aid rationale: This is probably best explained in 'parable' form as follows: *Following a tragedy at sea, twenty people find themselves on a desert island where the only food source is coconuts. One person, the only adult, let us call him Rich Leechman, is an able strong man capable of climbing coconut trees while the other nineteen are children, under the age of five, and cannot climb the trees. The man can climb the trees and get, not alone, plenty of coconuts for himself, but actually accumulates literally thousands into a stock pile that in his lifetime he will never get to eat, not even as much as 1% of them. At the same time he does not share any with most of the kids but gives one or two of them the smallest amount to just keep them alive in exchange for services he requires. The other children quickly die off.*

This parable demonstrates how inequality in the distribution of value in a world, can, with greed, results in over- abundance for some with the disenfranchisement and ultimate destruction of others. We saw in chapter 9 that one of the two major impacts on the level of environmental change will be the 'power force' for a feedback desire of a single unit (person). The above parable is an example of such an environmental change with Leechman being the catalyst.

What sort of man is this Rich Leechman? A man in such circumstances, who has been blessed with the ability or luck, to accumulate such wealth in his world and yet refuses to feed those who have not got the skills, ability or even understanding to fend for themselves! There are unfortunately millions of Rich Leechman, male/female in the world today and unfortunately many of us approve, admire and revere them, indeed many of us even aspire to be like them!!!!! In addition, many of the Leechmans of this world flaunt this overabundance with what Thorstein Veblen described as 'conspicuous consumption', thus rubbing salt into the wounds of the unfortunate and disadvantaged.

Entrepreneurship is the great driving force within market economies and is to be encouraged, nurtured, and protected. Entrepreneurs themselves, be they the generators of businesses from the ground up, or, innovatively skilled senior business managers, should be rewarded for their skills and abilities and of course results. In market economies such individuals control vast amounts of capital investments for profitable return. They also accumulate vast personal fortunes in the process, indeed, far more than they could ever expect to spend on themselves or their families. Such Individuals, in this wealth creation, are however, accountable and responsible for its efficient distribution on the complexity journey and in this regard the following questions need to be answered.

Are such individuals' skills/abilities subject to the laws of diminishing marginal utility[136]? In other words, they may have a superior skills in one enterprise and, due to their success therein, have investment funds to set up second enterprise where they have inferior skills, thereby retarding the growth of this second enterprise.

While the entrepreneur themselves may be skilled in productive capital investment and diversity for greater overall growth, will those to whom they bequeath their fortunes have the same abilities?

Will the amounts invested be in businesses that generates employment and its add-ons in community spending, taxes etc. or will it be to a certain extent a less productive, low tax capital investment in e.g. art, property, hedge funds or trusts

---

[136] This has to do with use value of e.g. owning a car its use value to you is 100%, but were you to buy an additional car the first car's use value drops to 50%. Add another and the first car's use value is reduced to one third.

etc.? See Charles Hugh Smith blog for an informative article on *Productive and Unproductive Capital*[137].

So, what is the solution to the excess accumulated? Specifically, a BEME-Aid to redistribute value must be developed and implemented as follows:

- We need to initially generate a BEME-Aid by the 'collective pressuring' of governments to initiate a programme to secure donations from the superrich/rich to go directly to overall healthcare and education. People cannot participate in full education unless they are healthy. "Over a long period of time, the main force in favour or greater equality has been the diffusion of knowledge and skills." (Piketty, 2014, p. 22)
- Piketty suggests a progressive tax on capital to solve value inequality. He does however note that this is a Utopian ideal. I, on the other hand believe there is a better chance with 'collective pressuring' to have the superrich/rich voluntarily make donations, via a BEME-Aid programme, according to their means (assets).
- What incentive is there for the rich to make such a donation and what form will this donation take? It is my proposal that the BEME institute facilities, apart from coordinating BEME-Back processes to regenerate buyers, would also have the power to confer 'degrees' of contribution somewhat like a university. That is depending on the higher the BEME-donation, then the higher the degree status. Indeed, the 'status' element 'S' drive would assist us by conferring this major honourable status on donators for their contribution to the human race.
- This contribution will be based on assets. So let me take 2 million euro as the starting point, as many people's homes are close to or exceed this value and so forms a large part of their assets.

137 http://www.oftwominds.com/blogdec08/capital12-08.html (Retrieved 7/10/2015)

A proposal then of assets value to contribution rate, relating to degree status, might flush out as in Table: 15-3 as follows:

| € Asset amount | % Rate PA | € Contribution PA | Degree status |
|---|---|---|---|
| 2 million | 1 | 20,000 | O-PE |
| 5 million | 1.5 | 75,000 | M-PE |
| 10 million | 2 | 200,000 | PHD-PE |
| 20 million | 2.5 | 500,000 | Knight/Dame-PE |
| 50 million | 3 | 1,500,000 | Baron/Baroness-PE |
| 100 million | 3.5 | 3,500,000 | Viscount/ Viscountess-PE |
| 500 million | 4 | 20,000,000 | Count/Countess-PE |
| 1 billion | 4.5 | 45,000,000 | Duke/Duchess-PE |
| 5 billion | 10 | 500,000,000 | Grand Duke/ Grand Duchess-PE |
| 10 billion | 15 | 1,500,000,000 | Prince/Princess-PE |
| 50 billion | 20 | 10,000,000,000 | King/Queen-PE |

**Table: 15-3**

Degree legend as follows: PE stands for 'progressive entropy' therefore O-PE is 'Order of progressive entropy, M-PE is Master, PHD-PE is Doctor. The remainder are self-explanatory. Knights, being male, may be referred to as 'Sir' and their designated partner, if female, referred to as 'Lady'. Or if a Knight's designated partner is male, they may be referred to as 'Gentleman'. The same will apply to the other male degree recipients. In other words it will only be 'Sir', 'Lady' or 'Gentleman', not e.g. 'Highness' or 'Majesty'. With regard to female degree recipients from Dames to Queens, their designated partners may be referred to as, 'Gentleman' or if female referred to as 'Lady'. Of course other titles could be used, for example, the 'honourable' with his/ her 'Excellency' etc. etc.

The donation will be a lump sum or an annual gift/aid and the degree will be conferred ceremonially at the BEME centre with great pomp and ceremony or should the donators prefer it may be conferred in absentia. Obviously, the numbers are suggestions only and the degree status may or may not be publicised or kept private according to the wishes of the donator. An amount entitling a degree will last from the time of its conferring. The amount of donation relating to the asset is not fixed. In other words someone with a higher asset base can donate to a lower degree level or someone with a lower asset base can donate to a higher degree level.

To be sure it can be said that in effect the rich are buying their status degrees! So what? Many of the honours bestowed are political anyway and involve political contributions. Indeed, many 'wealthy' and/or high profile people, already voluntarily, use their time and money to help fill the ever increasing void of inequality. Some come from the entertainment industry, like artists such as, Oprah Winfrey, Angelina Jolie, Bob Geldof, and Bono. Their contribution is admirable and has shown a great spirit of regard for the welfare of the species. Many others, with little or no profile as such, also give of themselves in this regard. In addition some of the 'extremely wealthy' have donated vast amounts for the needy of this world, with the provision of food, housing, healthcare, and education. Again this philanthropy is to be much admired. Detailed examples of such contribution are as follows:

Tim Montgomerie, writing in 'The Times' tells us that Bill Gates "Over the past two decades he has given away about $30 billion of his personal fortune.....the new era of billionaire philanthropists who, like Mr Gates, have signed the Giving Pledge: so far, 127 of 1,645 known billionaires have agreed to give away more than half their wealth. They will never give as much as welfare states to fighting poverty and some, including Mr Gates have questions to answer about the aggressive tax avoidance of the businesses that made them their wealth. Overall, however, the value of Michael Bloomberg's donations to urban renewal projects, or Mark Zuckerberg's to education, is that these great minds bring to the fields of social policy the same disruptive thinking that made them rich.

The aid sector needs disruptive thinking." (Montgomerie, 2014)

Niall O'Dowd in the (Irish) Sunday Business Post tells us that Denis O'Brien "sits comfortably in the current Forbes 400 list with wealth estimated around the $5 billion mark...

But accumulation of wealth which drives so many on the Forbes list is not O'Brien's only goal. His franchise is best described by the new buzzword, philanthrocapitalism - giving back in spades to help make his business better, and the world better too.

In Haiti where his company Digicel holds the main telecom licence, O'Brien has built 100 schools, and his philanthropy has been featured on the front page of the New York Times. In Papua New Guinea, he has given huge commitments to improve schools.

O'Brien saw what Bill Gates and others now see - that philanthrocapitalism was a far better way to achieve success and make a difference than just building up a bank account. 'We are not robber barons," he says." (O'Dowd, 2014)

Chuck Feeney is an Irish-American philanthropist who "believes fervently that people who have been fortunate to amass great wealth should use their wealth for a greater good. He established The Atlantic Philanthropies in 1982, which have since made grants totaling more than $7 billion—focused on promoting education, health, peace, reconciliation and human dignity—primarily in Australia, Bermuda, Northern Ireland, the Republic of Ireland, South Africa, the United States and Viet Nam. In the mid-1980s, Chuck quietly transferred virtually all of his assets to The Atlantic Philanthropies; for the first half of Atlantic's history, its grantmaking was done anonymously..... Chuck Feeney's philosophy of Giving While Living was an inspiration behind the Giving Pledge, an initiative created by Warren Buffett and Bill and Melinda Gates to persuade many of the world's wealthiest people to give the majority of their wealth to philanthropy." (See: http://www.atlanticphilanthropies.org/history-and-founder).

Alex Morrell of FORBES reports regarding Warren Buffett: "In what has become an annual summer tradition, Warren Buffett has once again donated a breathtaking sum of money to charity. This year: more than $2.8 billion.

Buffett announced the gift of 20.64 million Berkshire Hathaway BRK.B +% class b shares on the company's website Monday. Berkshire Hathaway's class b stock closed at $137.39 per share Thursday, making the gift worth $2.84 billion. He gave away about $2.8 billion last summer, and $2.6 billion the year before that.

The major recipients are, as has been the tradition now for 10 years, the Bill and Melinda Gates Foundation as well as the foundations of Buffett's family members — the Susan Thompson Buffett, Sherwood, Howard G. Buffett and NoVo Foundations.....Buffett is, along with Gates, the creator of the Giving Pledge, which encourages the world's wealthiest to donate a substantial portion of their fortunes to charity. Buffett has pledged to give away 99% of his wealth. His lifetime giving now tops $25.5 billion" See: http://www.forbes.com/sites/alexmorrell/2015/07/06/warren-buffett-unleashes-another-2-8-billion-donation/#44bfd243e2ae

The philanthropy of Bill Gates on the other hand, is reported in 'The Telegraph' 18/1/13 by Neil Tweedie under the heading: Bill Gates interview: **I have no use for money. This is God's work.** Tweedie advises that "Having already given away $28bn, Bill Gates intends to eradicate polio, with the same drive he brought to Microsoft." (See:http://www.telegraph.co.uk/technology/bill-gates/9812672/Bill-Gates-interview-I-have-no-use-for-money.-This-is-Gods-work.html

The contributions of these mega wealthy are brought home when we see what wealth can buy regarding human welfare. In this regard, Michael Shermer writing in

Scientific American August 2014, advises on the findings of Bjorn Lomborg[138] on how to solve major world problems and these in turned ranked in their order of perceived importance. The rankings were based, "on a cost-benefit analysis. For example, an investment of $300 million 'would prevent the deaths of 300,000 children, if it were used to strengthen the Global Fund's malaria-financing mechanism.' (Shermer, 2014)

Some might say that people of such wealth have no need for the honours above and many prefer to donate without public scrutiny. This of course I accept. However, no matter who they are or what they have achieved they all have to live in this world with the rest of us. Indeed, their businesses depend on us. We have the option to support them or not. In addition such vastly wealthy are also subject to our approval for their status. Many, of course would project an indifference to our approval or not, but the human condition makes us all want to be loved rather than hated.

I accept that many of those with vast wealth have quite excellent skills and ability in their wealth accumulation process but they need to take some time to really understand just how much of their wealth was actually down to them?? For example, did they come into the world with these skills and ability? Or, did they arrive into an already wealthy family? How much of their wealth is based on luck? Just even one lucky moment? Have they acquired their wealth in the entertainment industry? If so, do they really believe that they are something special that deserve such major sums as against the millions of other actors, singers, musicians who are equally as good but just did not get the right opportunity?

Again the same applies not just to the superrich but also to the super-managers of major banks and corporations. Do they really believe that it is their special ability that entitles them to such huge remuneration? Would they never think that given a few hits and misses regarding background, education, and opportunity, the person cleaning the wash rooms in their office block might even do a better job than them? Indeed, I'm inclined to think that following the GFC of 2008 the cleaners would probably have made better job heading up the banks than the so-called experts. Others again with vast wealth were simply born into it and contributed nothing to its accumulation! However, while all these people are entitled to their wealth, under present capitalist ideology and indeed under my proposed E-capitalism 1, as it gives everyone the incentive to go for the same. They are all however, obligated (accountability and responsibility) not to prevent progressive entropic processes by deprivation to others. It is also important for us not forget that these people are not special just because they have wealth. And to be sure, many of them

---

[138] In the second edition (2014) of his book *How to spend $75 Billion to Make the World a Better Place* Bjorn Lomborg reports the findings of a study sponsored by his Copenhagen Consensus Center 2012 in which more than 50 economists evaluated 39 proposals on how best to solve such problems as armed conflicts, natural disasters, hunger, disease, education and climate change.

have a talent that is certainly worth praise. However, circumstances of history and opportunity played a role in their success and indeed many freely admit to this. Others unfortunately believe they are something really special and deserve all the praise, adoration and money they get.

What would make them really special however, would be for them to give the (underprivileged) the opportunity to have a go themselves. They can do this by donating via the above BEME-Aid donation of redistribution of value for the purposes of health and education in the world. Then they will be special in our eyes and then we will honour them as they should be honoured. Not alone will such contributors and their businesses be honoured but the 'massive people collective' will support them and their businesses in return. Indeed, such support will favour them against those who have the means but not the heart.

By addressing inequality as such the overall major advantage is that it increases growth. Rosemary Bennett (Social Affairs Correspondent) reports in The Times. "Closing the gap between the rich and the poor boots economic growth, according to new analysis from a global think-tank.

'This compelling evidence proves that addressing high and growing inequality is critical to promote strong and sustained growth and needs to be at the centre of the policy debate,' said Angel Gurria, the OECD secretary-general. 'Countries that promote equal opportunity for all from an early age are those that will grow and prosper.'" (Bennett, 2014)

Of course unless sufficient numbers join the revolution there is every chance of grim and regressive developments. However, I have set out in the 'Appendix' a simple draft structure for a communication 'sales pitch' together with examples for each of the BEMEs considered above. Please consider, or better still create your own, for a progressive and prosperous future!

## CHAPTER 16
# Conclusion

In the 'introduction' I set out 10 elements required for a successful revolution within capitalism as follows:

1) The process or system to be revolted against has to be corrupt, inefficient, unfair or any combination of these.
2) The corruptions, inefficiencies and unfairness has to be completely exposed and transparent.
3) The revolutionary goals have to address the current issues and initiate a superior process or system.
4) The revolutionary goals have to be completely articulated, understood and transparent.
5) Information will be the arsenal, and technology the vehicle for the charging revolt.
6) Participants in the revolution must, (a) understand how and why the current system evolved, and (b) how and why the new system is progressive for the further evolution of human beings and their nature.
7) Sufficient numbers of people and organisations have to be recruited to ensure success.
8) Motivation/benefits to participate are essential.
9) A high profile of the revolution's anticipated positive outcomes will assist with general motivation for participation in a feel good exercise.
10) It will be a bloodless revolution within current market economic capitalism.

I feel confident I have addressed all of the above, however, participation of the communication-savvy populous will be essential for success. Our journey together has I hope informed you with new insights or considerations into our origins, development, and current status as human beings. In addition you should be better equipped to question 'reality' as well as your ability to change it. There is no doubt that the difficult areas of entropy, quantum, and consciousness have been but sampled, nonetheless, they make us what we are, therefore a greater examination of each is strongly recommended.

Regarding entropy: Is there any way its inevitable road, of complete disintegration and final equilibrium, can be avoided? Perhaps there is! Remember that this final disintegration is only in the classical world. It may well be that this is not a problem in the quantum world. We know we cannot directly access the quantum world but via our environmental and consciousness processes we may eventually be able to address the thermodynamic entropy issue. Also, it should be remembered that this issue is a symptom of our three space/one time dimensional world. However, should we be attached to another dimension or brane, we may well be able to overcome complete disorder. Indeed, other eminent scientists also believe this disorder is not inevitable. In their publication 'Order out of Chaos', chemists Ilya Prigogine (Nobel Prize winner), and Isabelle Stengers propose that the inevitable entropy slide to disintegration may not be the case. In the 'Foreword' to this book, futurist, Alvin Toffler tells us, "one of the key themes of this book is its striking reinterpretation of the Second Law of thermodynamics. For according to its authors, entropy is not merely a downward slide toward disorganization. Under certain conditions, entropy itself becomes the progenitor of order." (Toffler, 1990)

The management of entropy needs to be addressed where and when possible, as if not, the greedy will prevail, and that may have disastrous consequences for us all. There is a divide in how best to manage the balance between regressive and progressive entropy. On the one hand we wish to protect our environments, and on the other hand produce good science to enhance them. Such may have a tendency to separate those with the same ultimate goal. Unfortunately, ignorance, and politics, can hammer this wedge in further to the detriment of all. Example, from Ben Webster, Environment Editor 'The Times'. "The chief scientific adviser to the European Commission has been ousted after a lobbying campaign led by Greenpeace, which objected to her support for genetically modified crops.

Professor Anne Glover had said there was no evidence of adverse impacts of GM crops and that opposing them was 'a form of madness'...her post ceased to exist.

Greenpeace and eight other campaign groups wrote to Mr Juncker (the commission president) to abolish the post because it 'concentrates too much influence in one person'. The letter accused Professor Clover...of giving the media 'one-sided, partial opinions' on GM crops and wrongly claiming there was scientific consensus about their safety.

More than 20 scientific bodies...wrote to Mr Juncker days later urging him to ignore the demands of Greenpeace and other groups." (Webster B., 2014)

The second difficult area we covered was, quantum physics, and we saw that while we experience its activity in experiments and workings, we are not yet in any position to consciously experience it from within. Quantum computation though may finally assist in the unravelling of the quantum world itself, which is the reality behind the classical façade. We do however, I believe, have an indirect path into the quantum world and that is by feedback, of our likes and dislikes by our behaviour in our personal environment.

Consciousness, the third great enigma we tackled, I believe is tied to the quantum, but because of the classical façade we are fooled into believing our decision making processes are different from reality. That is, we believe we consciously decide to do something and then do it! In other words, we believe we have 'free conscious will'. Instead, we have what I might describe as a 'free unconscious will'. This happens because the behaviour we exhibit, while automatic, is actually instigated by our environmental behavioural desires firstly fed into to our experience quantum string banks and then communicated to consciousness$_1$ for adjusted decoherence programming of such desires. Our brain then facilitates our classical positioning to accommodate our free will action belief. Graham Lawton, writing in New Scientist tells us......According to Gregory Berns, a neuroscientist at Emory University in Atlanta, Georgia, the problem is that much of the decision making process happens at a sub-conscious level, and experiments reveal that people are generally not very good at explaining the thinking behind their choices. 'Sometimes they simply don't know why the choose things,' he says. They correct explanations after the fact, or make up explanations that are socially acceptable" (Lawton, 2010)

Then there is the notion of us living in a hologram, its make-up being projected from the periphery of the universe! I accept that initially this concept may have been difficult to swallow. I have nonetheless, given the findings and views of the experts, together with the notion of its high status standing in the scientific community. To be sure, we know that holograms, as we know them, are not made up of matter[139], but when you realise that all matter is mostly space anyway and the minutest amount that is left may be transposed into pure energy via the Einstein equation, we are left with no matter at all. In addition particles dragged through the 'Higgs' field, it is believed, take on mass.

[139] Simply an image created by 'light' manipulation.

I noted in chapter 2 that I believed us to be living in an incubator rather than a goldfish bowl. I hope it is now clear that within our incubator we are growing and moving from the Alpha toward the Omega. The energy/nutrients outside the incubator are dispensed into us from without. However with our ability to change our environment within we have the wherewithal to influence, so to speak, what will be dispensed into us. We are without doubt though accountable and responsible for the influences we initiate, as whatever they are, good or bad, they will affect everyone else and their environments.

The areas of business, finance, and economics are all part and parcel of the market economy. There is no 'invisible hand', a la Adam Smith, guiding market economies. Rather, if there are a little over 7 billion people in the world, there are a little over 14 billion hands grabbing for a piece of the action. These hands are driven by the selfish (survival) gene which in turn will change environments for a relevant fit of information, to automatically decohere programmes for our classical world.

All areas of study produce experts in their particular field/area, and I have used these throughout this publication. Some of these disciplines of study have experts that are more worthy of being called 'expert' than others. For example, one would prefer a qualified brain surgeon to operate on one's brain than perhaps a GP. And in general scientists, within their particular area, are expert in that area, due to generally accepted scientific practices. Such however, is not the case for experts in other disciplines! Examples are in the 'Law', 'Psychology' and 'Economics'. Different legal experts interpret different laws in different ways. Different psychological experts, based on their own emotions/prejudices/political ideology assess patients/clients differently. Economists we have seen come in various colours and with diverse beliefs, they cannot all be right! And indeed, quite often economic journalists are ahead of the so-called experts in this field. The reason for not-so-expert opinions in these areas is mainly, or at least in part, due to emotions.

"We find that emotions are really important,' says Mirja Hubert, a consumer researcher at Zeppelin University in Friedrichshafen, Germany. 'Even rational decisions are not possible without emotion.' Emotions are also key to the elusive concept of 'brand loyalty'—the often irrational preference for one version of a product over essentially identical competitors." (Lawton, 2010) Decisions or opinions believed to be arrived at rationally (from the neck up) are in fact arrived at by from the whole body and its history.

Three specific SCREME's (systemic cancers rotting enterprising market economies), have been identified namely, 'Employee Erosion', 'Feral Finance' and 'Indigenous Inequality'. There is no doubt that diseases have to be cured, and they can be cured, by the medicine of the BEME for each, namely, 'Regenerate employed', 'Regulate banks', and 'Redistribute value' respectively.

# CONCLUSION

The many experts and not so expert, have proposed reforms that might address some of these cancers, but they have not articulated a comprehensive in situ programme that looks like it will be anywhere near enough to succeed. Talking about reforms, proposing them and debating then, is to be sure, one way to approach these cancers. However, when one has cancer one would be more than happy to have a complete purification from the disease together with a structured aftercare programme. A BEME revolution carried by the masses for their own and their children's children health, based on E-Capitalism 1, is, I believe, a beginning. As there is no doubt that whatever the culture individuals find themselves in, (1) generation/regeneration of employment, (2) transparency/regulation of the financial system, and a fair distribution of value will enable growth in that culture together with a path to universal and harmonious human integration.

With E-Capitalism 1: we will have communication technology as the vehicle for the charging revolt. We have seen the power of electronic communication in President Obama's funding campaign, also in raising money to send the bullied, New York bus monitor on a holiday, and even when the dog was lost in the UK Lake's district, not to forget the power of social media in the revolts of 'The Arab Spring'. Indeed, there seems no end to the power and manipulation of electronic manipulation for good and bad. James Dean Technology Correspondent notes in, 'The Times' 28/11/14: "This year it emerged that Facebook had secretly conducted an experiment on 700,000 users in which it successfully manipulated their moods. In July OkCupid, a popular dating website, admitted that it had deliberately mismatched unsuspecting members as part of a psychology experiment. Both companies said that users had consented to their data being used in this way...

Ed Vaizey, the culture minister, told the committee it was laughable to expect that people should read and understand 150 pages of terms and conditions before signing up to online services." (Dean, 2014)

If Facebook can do it internally then the masses should be able to use all the systems externally and with transparency to spread the progressive message.

Do not allow the greedy, ignorant, incompetent and ruthless to decide yours or your children's future!

We need to be in control, not be controlled.

We need the revolution to go viral!!!!

Be a BEMER not a SCREMER

**Change the Hologram for a better future**

Only smart people can!

BRILLIANTBRANES

A poem by English poet Edgar Albert Guest.

*Somebody said that it couldn't be done*
*But he with a chuckle replied*
*That "maybe it couldn't," but he would be one*
*Who wouldn't say so till he'd tried*
*So he buckled right in with a trace of a grin*
*On his face. If he worried he hid it.*
*He started to sing as he tackled the thing*
*That couldn't be done, and he did it.*

*Somebody scoffed: "Oh, you'll never do that;*
*At least no one ever has done it,"*
*But he took off his coat and he took off his hat*
*And the first thing we knew he'd begun it.*
*With a lift of his chin and a bit of a grin,*
*Without any doubting or quiddit,*
*He started to sing as he tackled the thing*
*That couldn't be done, and he did it*

*There are thousands to tell you it cannot be done,*
*There are thousands to prophesy failure,*
*There are thousands to point out to you one by one*
*The dangers that wait to assail you.*
*But just buckle in with a bit of a grin*
*Just take off your coat and go to it;*
*Just start in to sing as you tackle the thing*
*That "cannot be done," and you'll do it*

# Appendix

The table below lists examples of Tweet and Text messages for the BEME *Brilliantbranes* (the book), as well as the BEMEs to 'Regenerate employment', 'Regulate banks', and 'Redistribute value'. Other social media communication messages, sent via e.g. Facebook, LinkedIn, Pinterest, Google Plus +, Tumblr and Instagram etc. together with ordinary emails may take their lead from the messages below.

| Tweet | SMS Text |
|---|---|
| Brilliantbranes: a BEME brain-stretching scientific exposé for growth, employment & equality, all within capitalism. brilliantbranes.com | Brilliantbranes: a brain-stretching scientific exposé for growth, employment, and greater equality, all within capitalism. Read and enjoy. brilliantbranes.com |
| Job creation via BEME-Back business promotion investment will increase jobs growth & savings. Please support. brilliantbranes.com | Job creation via BEME business promotion investment will increase jobs growth & personal savings. Please support. brilliantbranes.com |
| Citizens exploited due to inadequate financial regulation. Please support Bank-BEME to ensure level playing field. brilliantbranes.com | Citizens exploited due to inadequate financial regulation & transparency. Please support Bank-BEME to ensure a level playing field for all. brilliantbranes.com |
| Escalating inequality is the road to ruin. Please support 'Wealth' BEME-Aid initiative for stabilization & growth. brilliantbranes.com | Escalating inequality is the road to ruin and anarchy. Please support 'Wealth' BEME-Aid initiative for stabilization & growth. brilliantbranes.com |

**Table: A-1**

# Post Summary

(This summary is for recall only. A reading of the full body text of 'Brilliantbranes' is required for a comprehensive understanding of the book's theoretical proposition.)

Black holes, holograms, incredibly small strings, communication faster than the speed of light, changing history to accommodate the present, and modern electronics, are the fundamental ingredients necessary to understand the self-destructive mechanisms within capitalism, as well as its proposed evolution to a greater model namely, E-capitalism 1.

Cooperation from the earliest times between primitive humans, sharing and trading their skills together with the fruits of their labour, may be described as the beginning of economic interaction and activity. Such interaction and activity developed into what we now refer to as market economies. Contemporary economic activity plays a major role in the four human drives for growth, namely, 'Survival', 'Sex', 'Status', and 'Symbolism'. In today's world the majority of us require money to survive. We also need sufficient funds to commit to a sexual relationship and raise a family. Our status, or our role in society, whatever it may be, will usually be tied to a monetary value. And symbolism which relates to our group, ideology, religion, nationality etc. requires funding to operate.

Many economists believe economic crises are naturally cyclical and indeed students of economics learn, early on, that economies follow the cycle of boom to bust. Other economists however, believe these crises are caused by structures within the system. It is my contention that these crises are as such structural.

The general proposition presented in *Brilliantbranes* is that contemporary capitalism has within its component parts of business, finance, and economics, natural self-destructive mechanisms. Business, in its aspect of cost saving, finance in its self-serving role verses its economy serving role, and economics in its aspect of the distribution of value. The solutions I propose for each are respectively, regeneration of employment, regulation of finance, and redistribution of value. There is no doubt the three defective areas are well known and documented, together with numerous proposals for their solution. What I present however, is the genesis of the problems, together with their development and application as being natural processes, within the system. The forensic examination I conduct is of a reality that is hidden, either through ignorance or choice, but is, nonetheless, required to be exposed in order to create the motivation for permanent change. To date, patch-work fixes have been implemented to avert the inevitable but represent only temporary solutions. The permanent change I offer represents a new approach in implementation methodology. This new approach is based on the fact that while genes are biological replicators and memes are cultural replicators, economies also require in-built replicators for reproduction, protection and universal value distribution. Social media together with other digital communications will play a pivotal role with these economic replicators.

The late great physicist John Archibald Wheeler coined the term 'black hole' for those amazing, large and small, spatial phenomena scattered throughout the universe. Indeed, he also gave us the phrase 'it from bit' to denote the notion, now an increasing trend, "to regard the physical world as made of information, with energy and matter as incidentals." (Beckenstein, 2003) Throughout this book I will treat 'Information' as the most fundamental entity in the universe. I hope to convey that everything within the universe is made up of 'bits' of information (see Fig: 1-1 main text). Indeed, dissemination of and access to information together with its suppression, limiting and falsifying are all key factors in the operation of capitalist market economies. In addition, the whole perspective on information has changed relatively recently, by way of black hole scientific research, developing the 'holographic principle' which will be explored later on.

Business and finance, together with the distribution of value represent sociobiological endeavours. This simply means that the developers and practitioners of these endeavours arrived at their current practices through the evolutionary processes of natural selection. Firstly, there was inherited development and secondly there was development via the natural drives of 'survival', 'sex', 'status' and 'symbolism'[140] which in turn were and are influenced by different environments. Such environments are a country's people together with their history, politics, climate, geography, demography, wealth, culture, and religion etc. The result is that market capitalism as we know it today, while sold as a democratic process based on supply

140 Survival is the priority drive for food, clothes etc. Sex is the drive for pleasure, procreation, love, companionship, family. Status is the drive for your acceptable place in society. Symbolism is the drive to belong to a group, culture, religion, country club etc.

and demand together with reward for effort, unfortunately, due to its participants, has evolved with these idyllic features severely damaged. In fact, damaged to the extent of probable disintegration due to some natural systemic destructive aspects. These aspects I will now address.

Business: In order to achieve the highest profit, businesses are constantly trying to achieve the highest sales with the lowest expenses/costs. A major element of these expenses are employee costs and savings on such require the fewest in number at the lowest remuneration. Technology advances have assisted in this cost being consistently reduced. This is a natural process for the business itself but a major problem for other businesses who want employees from other businesses as buyers/customers. But let there be no doubt there is little appetite for one business to generate customers for other businesses.

Finance: The financial industry plays an essential role in the greater economy by providing loans, investment, advice, and facilitation. The industry's institutions e.g. banks are also businesses in their own right and naturally operate for the best profitable returns. This dual role, perhaps even conflict of interest has engendered, within many of its major institutions, procedures of non-transparency, subprime lending, and even fraudulent activity. For example, as reported in The Times 11/5/15, "Barclays faces fines and penalties of more than £2 billion this week as the big investment banks make final settlements with British and US authorities over their involvement in the rigging of global currency markets." (Wilson, 2015) In other words finance has a tendency to go feral. A patch-work of reforms and regulations are often instigated to address these financial issues but are quickly watered down and even repealed with lobbying from vested interests and/or for political expediency.

Economics: Economics is about the distribution of value by way of allotment, or 'who gets what?' Such allotment depends on the laws, rules, regulations, conventions and economic drivers operating within economies. One of these major drivers is 'return on capital'. Capitalists naturally seek the highest return possible on capital investment. To be sure, such investment can result in a low rate of return or even a loss. However, a high rate of return will add to the accumulation of capital for the capitalist. When such private wealth's average rate of return outperforms the average rate of growth of the economy, as appears to be the growing trend, the divergence generates inequalities within society together with the concentration of the private wealth in fewer hands. "When the rate of return on capital exceeds the rate of growth of output and income, as it did in the nineteenth century and seems quite likely to do again in the twenty-first, capitalism automatically generates arbitrary and unsustainable inequalities that radically undermine the meritocratic values on which democratic societies are based." (Piketty, 2014, p. 1) In addition, private wealth now dominates market economies as public wealth is neutralised by debt. The problem is that there seems to be no desire to heavily tax the super-rich, for a more diverse distribution of value, as we are told this would infringe upon the freedom of the individual and curb entrepreneurship.

In order to address these three self-destructive mechanisms within capitalism, a thorough analysis of the development of human pursuits for growth is imperative. Only then will the necessity of the solutions I advocate become manifest. The solutions themselves, regeneration of employment, regulation of finance, and the redistribution of value, will be detailed at the end of this summary. The analysis however, will be executed initially through a grounding in what may be called the 'classical world' which satisfies our logical beliefs. This will then be followed through a grounding in the 'quantum world' which will hopefully be shown to be closer to reality. Our place within the 'informational' universe will then emerge from both.

The classical world as we know it commenced, at the beginning of the universe, with what is termed a 'singularity' or for our purposes a small 'dot' much smaller than the tip of a pin. This 'dot', from within, inflated out, following the 'Big Bang'. It is important to understand that the 'Big Bang' was not an explosion as such of the dot in space bursting out in all directions, rather, it was like a balloon inflating from within and expanding. So, everything that is in the universe today was originally together in that one 'dot'. Indeed, one might say everything was entangled together in the 'dot'. Following the 'Big Bang' natural processes produced 'force' and 'matter' particles that formed into atoms, and eventually stars, planets, and ourselves. An amazing feature also of our classical universe, physicist Brian Greene tells us, and most scientists believe, is that "Symmetry underlies the laws of the universe"[141] (See Fig: 2-2 main text) Also, another seeming consistent phenomenon is that our universe appears to be mathematically fractal. Fractals delve into things and expose that a small part of it is like the whole. A Fractal is a repeating pattern (See Fig: 2-3 main text) each small section is the same as the larger sections and the whole. In addition, there is a consistent approximate temperature throughout our universe of circa -270.3° c. There is no doubt we feel comfortable within the classical world we inhabit, as it works conveniently for our logical thoughts. For example, if we throw a ball up in the air, depending on the force of the throw, at some point in time thereafter the force of gravity will pull it back down to earth. Prior to throwing the ball, our logical thoughts tell us that this scenario will occur. When the scenario does occur it fits in with our logical thoughts.

---

141 "...the symmetries of an object are the manipulations, real or imagined, to which it can be subjected with no effect on its appearance. The more kinds of manipulations an object can sustain with no discernible effect, the more symmetric it is." (Greene B., 2005, p. 220)

This universe itself is subject to two important laws, namely, the First, and the Second laws of thermodynamics. The First Law is the conservation of energy. This means that if some energy is used in one place it will appear again in another. We cannot create any more energy. What we have is all there is and it is conserved. Think about this energy also as 'bits' of information as referred to above. We cannot create any more energy/matter, what we have, is all there is and it is conserved. The energy/matter information in one place however, may be created into a different form with new bits of information, someplace else in the universe. A stark negative example of this law is the use of fossil fuel energy on earth changing global warming that results in devastating climate change. In fact, chaos theory tells us that even simple energy use of a butterfly flapping its wings in e.g. Japan can have consequences for weather patterns in the US. The use of energy in one area, of course, may also have positive consequences in other areas, e.g. using renewable energy, or personal and group energy for the increase of growth via education, health, and economics. The use of energy then is not just confined to changes in weather and the likes but to all aspects of life in the pursuit of needs and desires.

The Second Law called 'entropy' is commonly referred to as 'disorder' and it always increases. It means that everything in the universe will finally disintegrate, including the human body, into a state of complete disorder to eventually reach maximum equilibrium. In fact, the only one thing in the classical world that can avoid this entropy is life forms, but such avoidance is only temporary. Again entropy may be referred to as information. For example, I referred above to entropy as the breakdown of orderliness. In other words the higher the entropy the more loss of ordered information towards eventual destruction and death. Whereas, the lower the entropy the more gain of ordered information and therefore temporary suspension from disintegration.

Think of it as follows:

(A) High entropy/highly disordered/low information: An example is pollution and regressive disintegration of the self, the environment, and the economy.
(B) Low entropy/highly ordered/high information: An example is protection and progressive replication of the self, the environment, and the economy.

Human beings slow down the natural flow to 'high entropy' by extracting sufficient 'low entropy' (highly ordered/high information) from the environment. The result is that human beings wage a constant battle to enhance order for themselves for others and their environment against the inevitable slide into disorder. But they do this at a price. The key to understanding this is that life itself, halts temporarily, the ever increasing disorder of the Second Law of thermodynamics. This it does by extracting 'low entropy' e.g. protection, heat, nutrition, and order in general, from its surrounding environment. So, we are constantly changing/attempting to change our own environment to satisfy our needs and desires but at the same time using up 'Low entropy' in other areas e.g. food.

Self-replicating human beings over generations, have been assisted in their own orderliness, with the occasional 'positive' organic mutational variation. They require, (a) protection of the replication process for natural replication, and (b) positive enhancement for superior replication. The positive enhancement may come from positive mutational variation but it is also assisted by accumulated 'Low entropy/ highly ordered/high information'. This continued increase in orderliness is often referred to as a journey towards greater and greater complexity. This journey for complexity entails the quest for growth in body and mind and is evidenced in the progressive achievements, particularly for those in western societies, in science, economics and culture. These achievements in turn have been assisted with superior standards of health care, education and relative equal opportunity.

The journey toward greater complexity is however an extremely fragile one, as natural and/or people-made events can, and often do, suspend or revert it. Indeed, it is also possible that events such as, an unstoppable deathly virus, a nuclear holocaust, or a complete breakdown in society, could wipe out the human race completely. Thankfully, thus far, we have avoided such disasters (as far as we know). Individuals and groups nonetheless, can and do revert the journey towards greater complexity by indulging in an excess of the drives of human needs and desires. These drives being 'Survival', 'Sex', 'Status', and 'Symbolism'. Reversal of the journey to greater complexity, I have called 'Regressive entropy', while contributions to it I have called 'Progressive entropy'.

**(A) Regressive entropy** is decreasing or missing information producing disordered degeneration, and on-going increasing disintegration of the self and the environment toward complete equilibrium. Some practical examples of regressive entropy are, natural disintegration as stated, together with ignorance and/or prevention of information. Regarding ignorance, it is either through not attempting to gain information, or 'Wilful Blindness' to information that is available. Prevention has to do with the suppression or hiding of the general information flow specifically to some groups as well as to society at large. This may be enacted because of ideological beliefs, ignorance, selfishness, thoughtlessness, or simply laziness.

**(B) Progressive entropy** is increasing information to produce ordered generation, and on-going increasing integration of the self and the

> environment toward greater complexity. Evolutionary biologist Julian Huxley says of this, "It is an anti-entropic process, running counter to the second law of thermodynamics with its degradation of energy and its tendency to uniformity. With the aid of the sun's energy, biological evolution marches uphill, producing increased variety and higher degrees of organisation." (Huxley, 2008) Practical examples of progressive entropy are firstly, temporary prevention where possible, or otherwise management of regressive entropy. Secondly, informing oneself, together with a contribution to the flow of information to society at large for use toward on-going complexity (See Fig: 7-1 main text).

This classical world is of course subject to classical physics. Classical physics, is also known as 'Newtonian' physics named after Sir Isaac Newton. Classical physics is described as deterministic, and an example of this determinism was summed up by French mathematician Pierre-Simon Laplace who roughly said, 'Give me enough information about an object, and I can predict its future state, or how it arrived at its present state'. This determinism, it seems, applies to everything in the classical world including human beings. In other words everything we do is already determined! Yet we believe our free will allows us to make a decision/choice and then perform, or not, an action. But we now know this is not the case, as when we believe we decide to do something at a conscious level it has already begun, prior to our decision! This phenomenon will be examined further on.

We evolved into our classical world from the first Microbial cells to multicellular animals, then vertebrates e.g. fish, at which point some of these vertebrates made the move from water to land, becoming what we now know as Amphibians, Reptiles, Mammals, Primates, Apes and finally Humans or if you prefer, Homo sapiens. Human beings then along the way developed the highest consciousness of all living creatures. However, we also retained primitive and other developmental natural whole body functions. In other words, our actions and responses for our needs and desires are not only subject to so-called rational thinking from the neck up but are also visceral.

A recent proposition known as the 'Holographic Principle', which physicists mostly agree is true, has a major bearing on our place and indeed our activity in the universe. This principle was developed from studies of 'black holes'. A black hole being a star, the mass of which has collapsed in on itself. Nothing except what is called 'Hawking radiation' can escape from it. It is surrounded spherically by its 'event horizon'. It was originally believed that once anything e.g. matter and even light passes the event horizon it is pulled in and compressed smaller and smaller with infinite intensity to a single point, a 'singularity'. Indeed some say the same type of 'singularity', from which the 'Big Bang' commenced. Eventually black holes evaporate and disappear.

It is known that the Hawking radiation escaping black holes does not contain information, the reasons for this are due to quantum mechanics rather than classical mechanics. However if information does not escape a black hole before it disappears then there is a problem as information/energy cannot be destroyed. But thankfully, with further investigation, it was agreed that the information for a black hole was kept at the event horizon and therefore did not disappear. 'String theory', as described above, adds some clarification here with astrophysicist and science writer Stuart Clark advising, string theory suggests that black holes are a fuzzy ball of quantum strings that would store fundamental information about objects that had fallen into (it). "In this view, matter does not pass *through* the event horizon on its way to the singularity; instead it compresses itself onto the surface of the 'fuzz ball' and merges with the other strings." (Clark, 2010, p. 86) String theory therefore suggests that black holes do not have singularities but the quantum fuzziness of strings. As a consequence, prominent scientists were led to conclude an astounding hypothesis as follows:

We know, for example, that a square 10cm by 10cm is equal to 100 square cm. So, were we to have a box measuring 10cm wide X 10cm high X 10cm deep we know that its volume would be 1000 cubic cm. The volume then, i.e. the amount inside a container is based on its cubic capacity. Similarly, the volume of a sphere is its cubic capacity. With black holes however, the cubic capacity is the square of its outer surround. In other words to find out the amount of information deemed to be sucked into a black hole, you calculate the square of its event horizon. It was from this notion that the 'holographic principle' was born[142]. Now, if this is not mysterious enough, scientists have extrapolated this notion for any region in space, and indeed for the whole universe! In addition, it is my contention that with the laws of the universe being symmetrical, together with fractal mathematics exposing that 'a small part is like the whole', it will also apply to extremely small areas of space like e.g. areas in the brain that house memory information, similarly in fuzzy strings. String theory however, with its quantum fuzzy strings, is a subject of the quantum world rather than the classical.

---

142 Holography is an application of the wave theory of light. In fact it was first conceived as a theoretical possibility on that basis by the British scientist Dennis Gabor in 1947. His idea was to combine two sets of coherent beams of light, to record the interference pattern produced by their interaction in a photographic emulsion, and to do this in such a way that the plate would then contain such complete (or *holo-graphic*) information about a scene that with suitable illumination of the plate a realistic image of the scene could be reconstructed." (Kasper & Feller, The Complete Book of Holograms, 2001, p. 13)

## POST SUMMARY

So, what exactly is the quantum world? Well, it is often stated that the quantum world is the world of the extreme small, and the classical world is the world of the big. The world of the extreme small, on the one hand, is often thought of as the atomic and sub-atomic realm. A simple atom consists of electron particles orbiting a nucleus of proton and neutron particles. Regarding an atom's size, physicist Kenneth Ford tells us, "If you are a proton, an atom is very big about a hundred thousand times larger than you. If you are a person, very small, about 10 billion times smaller than you." (Ford K. W., 2011, p. 9) Electrons, protons, and neutrons, are commonly called 'matter' particles. In addition, there are 'force particles' one of which we will encounter below. All these particles cannot be observed in their quantum state from our classical observation positioning/conditioning. The world of the big, on the other hand, or our classical positioning/conditioning, is everything we can see, feel and sense. In spite of this it is now generally accepted by the scientific community that the universe and everything in it is 'quantum based' even though it appears to us as 'classically based'. Due to this enigma though, knowing where the boundary is, between both worlds it seems, is beyond our grasp.

The strangeness of the quantum world began with the investigation of light. It had been established early in the 19$^{th}$ century by scientist Thomas Young, that light travelled in waves. He did this by setting up what is known as a 'double-slit' experiment. The experiment consists of cutting two slits in a sheet of, say metal, and shining a light through these slits. Behind the sheet is a detection screen that records the pattern of how the light emerging from the two slits lands on the screen. The light in fact lands on the screen in dark and light bands, a result indicating an 'interference pattern' of light travelling in waves (See Fig: 5-1 main text).

However, German physicists Max Planck and Albert Einstein while both solving different problems concerning radiation changed the world of science forever. In 1900 Planck proposed to the world that light/radiation travelled in pieces, or bits, which he called quanta. In 1905 Einstein confirmed that light exists in quanta which are now known as photons. So, on the one hand, Young showed categorically that light presented itself in waves, while on the other hand, Planck and Einstein showed that light presented itself in particles. A photon being the 'force particle' carrying the energy for electromagnetic radiation (light). Light therefore, presented as both a wave and a particle. It was later revealed, with the 'double-slit' experiment, that not only photons of light, but other particles e.g. electrons, protons and even atoms and molecules could all be demonstrated, within this experiment, to travel as quantum waves. Indeed, it is now accepted that if the experiment could be conducted with even larger sets of molecules e.g. the size of elephants they too would present as quantum waves. So the notion of quantum being just for the small is not correct, it is for everything. It is just that our classical positioning does not allow us to directly access the quantum world, or if you like the world of the wave function.

In addition the double-slit experiment was to highlight what has come to be known as the 'measurement problem' of quantum mechanics. This simply means that if we try to see, register, or measure something within the quantum wave function it causes the wave to collapse to its classical state of a particle. As a quantum wave, it is in all possible states, but collapsed, it is in only one state. The wave function therefore is also known as the superposition of position states. The quantum world for us consciously then is not concrete, rather, it is a fuzzy mist of possibilities. Whereas, the classical world is concrete, precise, deterministic and measureable.

The double slit operation also enabled the 'delayed choice experiment', proposed by John Archibald Wheeler. This was to show that doing something in the present can have an effect on the past. In other words, the past or history accommodates present activities. In effect we can undo the past!

Another strange occurrence within the quantum realm is known as 'entanglement'. This occurs when two particles interact with each other and then separate with the result that each separate particle has an innate understanding and connection with the other. This situation prevails even if each are on either side of the universe. Albert Einstein was not at all happy with this notion and referred to it as 'spooky action at a distance'. Irish physicist John Bell also disliked this notion and devised a method to see if this was the case, as it raised the problem of information seeming to be transferred 'faster than the speed of light'. Several experiments have shown since, via the John Bell process, that it appears there is 'spooky action at a distance' with 'faster than the speed of light' possible within the quantum.

To delve even further into the world of quantum, a brief mention of 'string theory' is appropriate. String theory began life based on the idea that each particle is not a dot as such but an extremely small string, or to put it more precisely the vibration of an extremely small string. In other words, if you take the string on a violin and pluck it you will get a specific vibration, pluck it harder to get another vibration. Each vibration, according to string theory, represents a different particle, depending on its energy. To give an indication of their size, these vibrating strings are believed to be some hundred billion times smaller than a proton.

Quantum phenomena itself has been interpreted differently by numerous scientists, but I'll just relate a few of the more accepted ones, starting with the so-called 'standard' or Copenhagen interpretation, a la Niels Bohr (1888-1962). This, put simply, states that an object does not exist until it is registered i.e. observed/ measured. The observation brings it into existence. That is, it collapses the wave function or superpositions.

Another popular interpretation is that of the 'many worlds' or an extension therefrom called 'many minds'. This interpretation proposes that what we think of as a collapse of the wave function is simply a branching off into a particular universe from the myriad of universes that exist.

Then there was the 'hidden variables' interpretation which Einstein embraced. He and his friend, physicist David Bohm, preferred to believe that there was something in the process that was hidden and not yet apparent or discovered.

The interpretation that seems to be the most accepted though is that of 'decoherence' from the work of physicists H Dieter Zeh and Wojciech Zurek. In this interpretation the term 'decoherence' may be used the same as the term 'collapse' of the wave function. Decoherence occurs when particles that are so-called coherent (quantum-like), interact with other particles that are not coherent (classical or already collapsed particles). In other words, decoherence happens due to the classical environment the quantum particle finds itself in. The classical particles are, so to speak, the measuring devices. Another important factor that is now coming to light is that when information is decohered, it is done so into an appropriate and conventional classical environment. This means it fits into the classical world we inhabit with all its determinism and perceived logic.

So, while we cannot experience the quantum world in situ we can and do use it, via electrons, in the various types of modern electronic devices such as cell phones, TVs, and computers. Apart then from the quantum manipulation pervading current 'information technology', there is also research and development into the production of working quantum computers. This R & D is still in its infancy but major breakthroughs are imminent. While digital computers operate by manipulating 'bits' (binary digits) of information, the binary digits being 0 and 1, a quantum computer operates on what are called qubits. Physicist Vlatko Vedral elaborates, "As we know, classical bits, by definition, exist in one of two different states at any given time—a zero or a one. With quantum mechanics, however, we are permitted to have a zero and a one at the same time present in a physical system. In fact we are permitted to have an infinite range of states between zero and one—which we call a qubit." (Vedral V., 2010, p. 137)

Quantum mechanical engineer at MIT, Seth Lloyd, gave further insights into quantum computing when in 1996 he, "showed that conventional quantum computers were themselves universal quantum simulators." (Lloyd, 2010, p. 150) And in his book *Programming the Universe* Lloyd equates the universe itself to a quantum computer. He also refers to decoherence as the creation of information, in that it, "effectively creates new bits of information, bits which previously did not exist. In other words, quantum mechanics, via decoherence, is constantly injecting new bits of information into the world..... Quantum bits program the universe." (Lloyd, 2010, pp. 99-100)

The principle behind a hologram is the interference effect of waves of photons, just like e.g. the interference of the waves of photons in the double-slit measurement experiment. David Bohm, the physicist friend of Einstein explains that quantum mechanics suggests "that phenomenal reality comes about from a deeper order in which it is enfolded. Reality unfolds to produce the visible order and folds back in." (Davies & Brown, 1993, p. 121) Enfolded, he called the 'implicate order', and unfolded, he called the 'explicate order' and he likened this notion to a hologram which he called the 'Holomovement', and extraordinarily he expounded this notion at least a decade before the 'holographic principle' was introduced to the world.

From much of the above detail then we can draw the conclusion that information emanates from the periphery of the quantum computer that is the universe. This information in turn programmes the universe, via decoherence, to form the holographic classical deterministic world including ourselves. So, it appears that we are in fact programmed in everything we do!! Yet, following decisions made in our minds we feel we drive ourselves naturally by way of survival, sex, status, and symbolism for individual growth. For example, we all wish to have sufficient to live on, together with a bit extra for a rainy day. We also wish to be sexually popular and sensually satisfied for procreation and pleasure. We wish to have a status that is well regarded in society. And finally, we wish to belong to the winning team/group etc. But in all of these wishes, we believe, we make the choices to pursue them to varying degrees. Whatever the degree, we believe we make the decisions and then we carry them out. However, this belief scenario of the process of our decision making became problematic in 1985. Psychologist Susan Blackmore tells us that in that year a consciousness scientist, one Benjamin Libet, carried out a specific brain experiment producing, at that time, extraordinary results. The experiment showed that when a person flexes their wrist "the brain processes planning the movement began over one-third of a second before the person had the conscious desire to move. In brain terms this is a very long time." (Blackmore, 2005, p. 87) So, here is a dilemma of major proportions, the least not being legal issues. For example, are we responsible for our decisions and actions if we have no free will? Libet himself offered a sort of solution as he noted that sometimes his experimental participants said they had stopped the movement (flexing the wrist) just before it occurred. So, he carried out a further experiment and following this he argued, that while consciousness did not initiate the action (flexing the wrist), it could stop it from happening. In other words no 'free will' but 'free veto'. This might appear to solve the problem but it is easily argued that the veto itself is part of the deterministic automatism. Further experiments into this dilemma have been carried out, and in this it found unconscious activity up to 10 seconds before the conscious decision to move. Therefore, whether we think we have made a decision to do something and actually do it, or search our memory to weigh up the pros and cons, all this has already happened at an unconscious level. This reality would then appear to give credence to the notion of us being programmed! Well, let us see, by delving a little deeper, if this is really the case?

Just as the physical body evolved, so also in tandem, did its consciousness or mind[143]. Consciousness is partly inherited from our parents and then is refined and expanded, through on-going experience, to evolve into a unique and dynamic conscious self. Its uniqueness comes initially, from genetic inheritance and then, by being constantly adjusted with on-going experience. It is this on-going adjustment of additions, subtractions and manipulative mixtures that also makes it dynamic. Consciousness may be described in one word as 'awareness'. But awareness of what? Awareness, I believe, of information! For example, I am aware that my son is in the adjoining room, my daughter is reading by the window, my wife is out shopping, some tomatoes in the garden are ripe and a beautiful red in colour while others are unripe and green. From experience, I am aware that the ripe tomatoes will smell and taste beautiful, and were I to eat the green ones they would taste bitter. These then are just some instances of conscious information. Information, that we know has found its way into our awareness, from the edge of the universe via decoherence . We have learned that all information, as far as we can tell, whether we are conscious or not, emanates in this way. In fact any and all areas of space, we have learned, operate likewise, down to the smallest subatomic area. This of course also means that some spaces will run into other spaces partly or completely, so e.g. there may be spaces within spaces, within spaces, like layers of an onion. Perhaps they are shaped and packed like Russian matryoshka dolls[144]? Whatever the case they will also be subject to the same information distribution, via decoherence and the 'holographic principle'.

The mind or consciousness means different things to different people. Some people equate it with the soul or religious spirit. To others, the mind is no more than a process within the brain that has yet to be fully understood. It appears then that consciousness has a lot to do with our senses and desires e.g. reactions to particular sensations or just wanting to do something. But, as a conscious being, I can also remember many things and these memories allow me to make certain decisions. When attempts are made to define what consciousness actually is, there is basically two camps, the 'materialists' and the 'dualists'. The materialists,

---

143 Mind and consciousness will mean the same thing throughout.

144 A Russian matryoshka doll, also known as 'nesting doll' fits into a series of larger dolls.

believe that everything can be brought back to the 'matter' in the human being via reductionism. The dualists, on the other hand, look to mind and matter as separate entities, acting in unison in the individual human being. However, philosopher David Chalmers believes there is operating in consciousness what he terms a 'naturalistic dualism' which he claims is a kind of *property* dualism[145] which claims 'that mental phenomena are non-physical properties of physical phenomena, but not properties of non-physical substances'.

Consciousness has also been linked to quantum mechanics, because e.g. the mysteries attached to both, and the role the conscious observer appears to play in collapsing the wave function. There has therefore developed, from eminent scholars, numerous interpretations of consciousness, based on quantum mechanics. But as physicist Stephen Manly advises, "the decoherence time for quantum processes in the brain has been shown by Tegmark to be on the order of $10^{-13}$ to $10^{-20}$seconds.That's vastly shorter than even the most fickle individual can have a flighty thought."[146] (Manly, 2011, p. 88) This then appears to negate the notion of consciousness based on quantum mechanics. I believe however, that quantum mechanics has a definite role-playing part in consciousness, inasmuch as everything else originates from the quantum to the classical so also, for me, does consciousness.

The American physicist Henry Stapp, points out that consciousness cannot be explained by classical physics, "There is nothing in the principles of classical physics that requires, or even hints at, the existence of such things as thoughts, ideas, and feelings,". (Stapp, 2007, p. 10) But he believes quantum physics is well placed for an explanation. Philosopher David Papineau elaborates how Stapp "argues that quantum waves collapse when intelligent brains select one among the alternative quantum possibilities as a basis for future action." (Papineau & Selina, 2012, p. 125) Stapp's proposition I find attractive for the process of our influence on choices for future action.

So, as noted above we believe we make a decision to do something and then do it, or if we even stop and cancel the action in our minds, it matters not! Why? Simply because the action to do, or not to do, is already underway before we think we make the decision. Indeed, we already know there is an automatic part of us in operation, be we conscious or unconscious, e.g. our hearts beating, our intake and

---

[145] Property dualists claim that mental phenomena are non-physical properties of physical phenomena, but not properties of non-physical substances. Property dualists are not committed to the existence of non-physical substances, but are committed to the irreducibility of mental phenomena to physical phenomena. Source: Dualism and Mind: by Scott Calef, *The Internet Encyclopedia of Philosophy*, ISSN 2161-0002, http://www.iep.utm.edu/, 29/1/16.

[146] Tegmark, Max (2000). "The importance of Quantum Decoherence in Brain Processes." *Physical Review* E61 (2000): 4194.

output of air etc. Much of these automatic happenings in our body is inherited. We are born with the heart pumping blood around the body and we instinctively know as babies that we need nourishment and protection to survive as we cry if these needs are not fulfilled. Another example is our almost instantaneous reaction when we are exposed to danger e.g. moving quickly out of the way before a potential accident, or reacting automatically, without prior thought, in a contact sport. But other things we have to learn and then they may well become automatic. Things such as, riding a bicycle, driving a car or learning to play a musical instrument, these things we become capable of doing automatically, as while we are engaged in them our thoughts may be miles away.

So it appears that we are pretty much instant unconscious automatons yet have the classical ability to decide to do something in the longer term to change 'natural automatic' decoherence to 'adjusted automatic' decoherence. 'Natural automatic' decoherence disseminates the information holographically to project e.g. a heartbeat, an inhalation/exhalation of air to the lungs, a tide ebbing and flowing, an electrical storm developing etc. Whereas, 'adjusted automatic' decoherence disseminates the information holographically to project car driving ability, business skills, medical/surgical ability, bicycle riding balance etc. The higher the concentration of 'adjusted automatic' decoherence the greater will be the change to the particular environment. Each time we change from 'natural automatic' to 'adjusted automatic' decoherence, we are changing the environment for our personal desires. It is a branching of the 'many worlds/minds' for our exclusive world/mind. But it also infringes on other classical co-existing worlds/minds to a lesser or greater extent. For example, the greater number of people with the same desires or indeed individuals with a particular desire and greater power, will have the facility for much greater environmental change, and such environmental change will have greater consequences, positive or negative, for many others. Now it seems that we as individuals, classically conditioned and positioned, believe changing our environmental world is of little consequence unless of course we wield massive power. This however, is not the case as individual changes are cumulative and enduring. These changes are not unlike, were it possible, to travel back in time to change some historical event big or small and therefore affect the present significantly. Whereas, with individual environmental change for our behavioural desires we are constantly changing the present to affect the future quite significantly whether we like it or not. But of course such changes may be positive as well as negative.

To reiterate then, our conscious needs and desires are fed-back by the whole body to the brain where they are registered in the strings of our memory banks. 'Natural automatic' decoherence is a constant process taking place. In fact one can say it is a constant flow into our holographic classical world being programmed by the universal quantum computer. This is enabled by continuous entanglement communication between the quantum strings memory banks in the brain and the programming information centre on the periphery of the quantum computer universe. So, while our conscious thoughts cannot penetrate the quantum downloading for choices, of our needs and desires registered in our quantum string memory banks, it can do this unconsciously. This is enacted firstly, via entanglement communication which can be faster than the speed of light, and secondly, because the automatic process may have already begun, we know that 'the delayed choice' mechanism can be initiated to undo the past. Different choices may be selected from the myriad of choices available within the quantum (See the Henry Stapp notion above). Of course our conscious brain is telling us we are doing this at a conscious level, like an on-going play, but in fact we are influencing the process for choices by environmental feedback. That is, our feelings, desires, actions and responses, in pursuit of growth, are fed back into the brain and constantly re-adjust the brain quantum string memory banks. This follows a consciousness process of a 'naturalistic dualism' loop based on a scientific 'positive feedback mechanism'[147] which will result in progressive or regressive entropy having positive or negative consequences for complexity (See Figs: 9-3 and 9-4 main text) illustrating the process.

Learning to do something for more secure living standards (survival), pleasurable and superior procreation (sex), increased positioning (status), and group belonging (symbolism), are natural growth pursuits for our personal, familial and societal environments. These environments, adjusted by 'growth pursuits' loop round, via entangled communication, to select for desired decoherence, from 'natural' to 'adjusted', to continue the loop back into the conventionally classical environments. From this process it can be seen that we, by way of causal desires generate 'Selected Outcomes' rather than use 'free-will' to enact them. In so doing we are both accountable and responsible for all adjusted environmental change. The level of environmental change itself, as noted above, will of course be dependent firstly, on the number of units[148] (people) contributing to the same feedback desire behaviour, and secondly, on each unit's (person's) degree of force for a feedback desire behaviour.

The process of 'Selected Outcomes' itself is what we pursue, as our progressive entropy contribution, for enhanced complexity. We have seen however, that such growth pursuits come at the price of the extraction of low entropy/high information

[147] Example: is when prices are bullish on the stock-market people buy, in the expectation of further price rises, and this in turn pushes the prices up further, so people buy more and this positive feedback continues.

[148] I use the word 'unit' as a generic for a lifeform as, apart from people, other living things have the ability to change environments via the loopback mechanism.

from other environments and even sometimes personal environments, thus initiating regressive entropy/increased disorder. This regressive entropy can readily be seen as individuals/groups/organisations extract excessive progressive entropy that may be greed fuelled and/or wasteful. It is obvious from this to conclude then that a balance is required between the drive for progressive entropy and its potential regressive entropy consequences. Indeed, it is incumbent upon us firstly as individuals to ensure our own pursuits are balanced with greater weight on the progressive side, and secondly, that we ensure that regressive entropy generated by others is neutralised and steered towards the progressive. Such is the environmental accountability and responsibility for ourselves, family, group, planet and universe. This is not an easy task, as our input, based on our growth pursuits, is driven by survival, sex, status, and symbolism, and these in turn we pursue somewhat handicapped as follows:

1) We believe our choices/decisions are made from the neck up (rationally) but are in fact a whole body programme.
2) Our growth pursuits have a tendency to be excessive due to their pleasurable feedback.
3) For most of us, we believe our choices have little or no effects on others or environments but even classically 'chaos theory' dispels this myth.
4) We believe, that with our free will, we enact an 'outside-in' approach to pursue our wants from given environments. This we believe we may do, as an individual right within societal regulations, to achieve growth for ourselves and others without limit. However, the reality is we are all reprogramming environments from the inside-out to facilitate the procurement of our wants. In so doing, environments will be changed not only for ourselves but also for the benefit or detriment of others.

Our pursuit of growth then generates a feedback mechanism of 'adjusted automatic' decoherence into our classical world environments. These environments being, ourselves, our planet, our climate, our culture, our economy etc. It is however, our market economies under capitalism that is the subject of the *Brilliantbranes* proposition and this we will now address.

Firstly, information decohered for the cost saving aspect of businesses has changed the environment to erode the general business customer base. Secondly, information decohered for banking in the pursuit of self-interest has changed the financial environment for the whole economy. And thirdly, information decohered for capital investment has changed the environment of value distribution towards inequality. These three environmental changes are stark examples of regressive entropy and as such are required to be neutralised and adjusted for progressive entropy.

Regarding employment erosion, it is not enough to attempt to generate employment by state initiatives, capital investments, business growth and the likes. To be sure, all these processes are important but the root cause of the erosion environment needs to be tackled. In addition, it is not enough to introduce temporary regulations on banks that are later rescinded or watered down for political expediency or vested interest. Instead, the root cause of self-interest vs public interest has to be addressed. Finally, it is not enough to attempt to achieve a fair distribution of value by taxes that stifle growth. Rather, an environmental progressive change needs to be enacted. These three environmental changes need to be implemented by the feedback process detailed above. Remember it was the weight of the numbers of units (people) involved or the power of a single unit (person) that changes environments.

Generally, economic activity will coincide with the prevailing political views of a state or organization of states. Political views themselves will be influenced by numerous issues such as levels of social services, unemployment, taxes, stem-cell research, and religious versus scientific programmes etc. etc. Political ideologies exist from the extreme left (Communism → Socialism →) to the extreme right (←Conservatism ← Fascism). For our purposes we will refer generically to the left as 'Liberals' and the right as 'Conservatives'. Another prominent ideology that needs mention is that of 'Libertarianism' which can embrace aspects of both the right and the left, however, their focus etc. is on freedom of the individual to act in their own or group's interest. In his book *The Righteous Mind,* social and cultural psychologist, Jonathan Haidt gives excellent details of these ideologies and I present an my abridged version as follows:

**Conservatives:** believe in proportionality (e.g. Payment in proportion to the work done). Conservatives are necessary as they conserve tried and workable methods, policies that help with stability.

**Liberals:** with their views seek overall equality and are essential for innovation, change and experimentation of new methods and approaches.

**Libertarians:** demand freedom to implement their particular policies and pursuits, without interference from state or society in general.

Numerous economic commentators and thinkers over the last 250 years have contributed to our present economic world systems and include the Scottish philosopher Adam Smith, who may be regarded as one of the first who first got people thinking about market economics and capitalism. He set out his views in his best known work published in 1776, *The Wealth of Nations.* In it he introduces the notion of the, "Invisible Hand" as referring to, 'The Law of Supply and Demand'. In other words, if something is required it will be demanded by someone and so it will be produced. This law is, he believed, a 'natural law' and should not be tinkered with in any way by government. As everyone follows their own self-interest, competition will ensure self-interest, and no-one gains the upper hand. The more modern notion of Smith's doctrine is that of 'Laissez faire' i.e. let do or leave alone.

A serious rival to Smith was Karl Marx (1818-1883). Indeed, even today, the mere mention of his name can raise the hackles on the neck of some. In his most famous work *Capital*, which took 18 years to complete, he set out the notion that the capitalist exploited the worker by acquiring the 'surplus value' of their labour as profit. This process led to an accumulation of capital for the capitalist. Thomas Piketty[149], refers to it as, "the 'principle of infinite accumulation,' that is, the inexorable tendency for capital to accumulate and become concentrated in ever fewer hands, with no natural limit to the process." (Piketty, 2014, p. 9) Marx's philosophical notion was of societies going through a series of 'historical developments' ending in 'Communism'. Under Communism, property and 'the means of production' would be held in the hands of the workers, thus eliminating their exploitation. Liberalism/Socialism were not new ideologies but Marx brought them to a whole new level.

John Maynard Keynes (1883-1946) introduced the notion that governments had a duty to help the economy along when it got into depressions. They could do this by spending large amounts (even if it was borrowed) on social or defence goods. Examples are building hospitals, schools, roads and railway systems, navy ships, air-force aircraft, and even weapons. These would all stimulate employment, which he believed was the backbone of the economy, as it would generate spending, which in turn would generate business creation and innovation resulting in a positive feedback loop. Keynesian doctrine was implemented with great success and kept the capitalist economy in line basically up to the 1970s.

Milton Friedman (1912-2006) on the other hand, put 'inflation' as the greatest threat to an economy and not unemployment a la Keynes. He believed that if inflation was kept in check and markets were left free, the economy would always find its natural level of supply and demand. Friedman was completely against government intervention in numerous aspects of economic life. Economist John Cassidy tells us, "Friedman conceded the need for some government activities, such as national defence and law enforcement....though he questioned the government's

[149] Thomas Piketty is Professor at the Paris School of Economics

involvement in public projects, such as highway construction and the provision of public education, which he said the market could supply...he listed fourteen unnecessary government interventions, including tariffs on imported goods, price support programs for farmers, minimum wage rates, Social Security, public housing, the US mail's monopoly, limits on the ownership of radio and television stations, and regulation of the banking system." (Cassidy, 2010, p. 75)

There is no doubt then that Marx was and still is the hate figure of the 'Right', while Friedman, by a long shot, fits the bill as the hate figure of the 'Left'. Indeed, both these men still raise the blood pressure of many.

Economists of all beliefs then, together with Politicians, Entrepreneurs, Religious figures, Union spokespeople, Employed/Unemployed, Charity heads, Health care/ Social welfare bodies spokespeople, and Business associations presidents all give their thoughts and recommendations, coloured by their world view, into the economic debate. Some of the major issues in this debate being, minimum wage rates, unemployment, inflation, government fiscal/monetary policies, regulation/ deregulation, and inequality.

Adam Smith's 'invisible hand' supposedly guiding a 'laissez faire' free market worked for a time and increased the wealth of the capitalist but exploited the poor through a boom time from the beginning of the industrial revolution up to the extraordinary bust in 1929 and the Great Depression. The Great Depression, saw the introduction by government, of greater regulation for banks together with greater transparency of their activities and this cooled world economies down. The depression nonetheless, generated untold unemployment and poverty.

Socialist and Communist movements had taken off in the 19$^{th}$ century fuelled by Marx's ideology and a desire for equality. Left wing parties began to thrive and gave opposition to the Conservative and Libertarian establishments. Communism as an ideology was quite successful in that it has been claimed that by the 1980's one third of the world's population lived in some form of communist state. As a political process however, it was a disaster due in the main to its stifling of entrepreneurial innovation and activity[150].

In most democratic market economies, following World War II, Keynesian policies were implemented, with a view to avert unemployment and increase employment. This resulted in steady growth, with, to be sure some hiccups, up to the 1970s and 1980s. It was then that Milton Friedman's doctrine of little or no regulation in the financial system together with monetary policy to curb inflation, took root. This doctrine was preached, practiced and purveyed by its main acolytes, Ronald

[150] The fact that it was a godless creed also did not help, particularly in God-fearing societies.

Regan and Margaret Thatcher. Indeed, parts of it (de-regulation and mild monetary policy to check inflation) helped the bubble grow until it finally burst in 2008.

Low interest rates and de-regulation do of course boost an economy into a faster gear, but the problem is about managing an economy so it does not burst and also drive the inequality wedge further between the rich and poor. One of the reasons the bursts and inequality occur in neo-classical economics is due to the notion of the 'invisible hand' of rationality guiding 'supply and demand' for best operation and profit. Neuroscientist John Coates believes however, "According to this school of thought, we are walking computers who can calculate the rewards of each course of action open to us at any given moment, and weigh these rewards by the probability of their occurrence...Consequently, neo-classical economics has largely ignored the body. It is economics from the neck up." (Coates, 2012, pp. 29-30)

As noted above three defective structures, within elements of capitalist economies, have generated regressive entropy. These are (a) cost savings in business regarding employees (Employee Erosion), (b) the self-serving role verses economy serving role in banks (Feral Finance), and (c) the distribution of value in capitalist market economies (Indigenous Inequality). Each of these specifics I designate as a, 'systemic cancer rotting enterprising market economies' (SCREMEs), and indeed, those who perpetrate these cancers may be called (SCREMERs). But how are we to change the environment of capitalism so an 'adjusted natural' decoherence flows, which in turn neutralises these self-destruct mechanisms? Well, a procedure needs to be instigated targeting the SCREMEs/SCREMERs which will automatically, not only, knock out the SCREME but more importantly, increase the overall growth within the system. For convenience, I designate these procedures as, 'beneficial economic multiplying entropies' (BEMEs), and indeed, those who initiate/implement them may be called (BEMERs). A BEME is a specific type of meme (cultural replicator) that enables market economies to become more efficient and grow. It is therefore a meme that is **beneficial** with an **economic** specificity, replicating **multiplying** progressive information **entropy.** Information of course being the essence**.**

A BEME therefore, as an economic replicator, may be voluntarily or mandatorily initiated/implemented. The BEMEs' initiation/implementation I propose will herald in an improved capitalism for greater participation in wealth creation, all contributing to greater growth and therefore complexity. In other words, rather than overthrow capitalism as such, an advanced form is required that will encourage greater enterprise, competition, and diversity of markets as never before. I call this 'E-capitalism 1'. So, how will 'E-capitalism 1' work? How will it differ from the existing model? How and where will it be implemented? The basic answers to all these questions will be addressed below, laying out what is envisaged, together with a methodology to set the ball rolling.

'E-Capitalism 1' will neutralise the 'three SCREMEs, namely, (1) Employee Erosion (2) Feral Finance, and (3) Indigenous Inequality. In addition to the SCREMEs' neutralisation, the process will create the structural change for growth. This metamorphosis will arise from the implementation of 'Beneficial Economic Multiplying Entropies' (BEMEs) or economic replicators. No longer will only the existing 'Political', 'Wealth', or 'Self-serving collective' power brokers run the capitalist system, instead, a specific 'Mass collective of BEMERs' power' will influence and instigate change to harmoniously create 'E-Capitalism 1'. These BEMERs will be intelligent, sophisticated, and electronically communicative individuals who will exercise their rights to ensure progressive entropy for themselves, their children, and future generations. In so doing they will neutralise the SCREMEs perpetrated by SCREMERs who extract excessive progressive entropy, under the banner of individual freedom, but at a cost to others.

The formulation of each of these BEMEs will be presented below. However, the BEMERs required to enact their implementation are people like **you** the reader, whom having persevered thus far into this proposition, are no doubt, I believe, a member of the intelligent, sophisticated, and electronically communicative mass. But to become a BEMER, you must put your intelligence into action. This is as simple as e.g. sending a short email, posting a short message on social media, or otherwise communicating or taking action to support a BEME/BEMER or not supporting a SCREME/SCREMER.

I am not trying to reinvent the wheel, as elements of the BEMEs I propose already exist. Rather, what I am proposing will have an architecture that is wider reaching, more formalised, and easily doable for greater diversity and propagation by the electronically communicative masses. The power that may be initiated by this mass of people is in its numbers. For example, Facebook alone has circa 1.5 billion users, and mobilising such numbers to communicate their shared requirements for change, in the business/finance/economic arenas, would itself have revolutionary results. This power has been demonstrated on numerous occasions e.g. President Obama's use of electronic media for campaign funding. Another example of the political power that can be tapped in this regard is that of the 'Arab Spring' which was fuelled in no small way by social media.

Therefore a business-like approach for BEME implementation, such as a marketing/advertising methodology of 'Reach' 'Frequency' and 'Continuity' of the BEME will be required to make the greatest impact. The target audience for all BEMEs should be your social media family and friends followed by media commentators, politicians, and other relevant personnel in groups and businesses.

## BEME (1) Regenerate employment:

This will be voluntarily initiated/implemented and may be termed a 'BEME-Back'. It will take the form of a promotion strategy i.e. a gift back to the customer on the sale of all products or services. It is also a selling promotion that may be used, or not, at a seller's discretion. It is somewhat like the notion of supermarkets' promotions giving coupons/stamps/vouchers for various amounts purchased. The gift will be a percentage of the purchase price, or a percentage of the profit margin if the latter is publically known. The buyer and therefore receiver of the BEME-Back will not immediately have access to its value, rather it will be invested in enterprises to create jobs and therefore prospective customers for business in general. A 'BEME-Back' is a true economic replicator in that, if a sale is likened to a fruit, the 'BEME-Back' is the seed to grow more customers.

The process will be administered in each country by a 'BEME facility' from e.g. 'The International Monetary Fund' (IMF) or some other similar international financial organisation.

Action call: **Support** all politicians and people who, together with organisations, businesses, brands, products and services that, embrace the 'BEME-Back' principle. **Do not support** non-'BEME-Back' people or their organisations, goods and services.

BEMER's Tweet message example: *Job creation via BEME-Back business promotion investment will increase jobs growth & savings. Please support. brilliantbranes.com*

## BEME (2) Regulate banks:

This will be voluntarily initiated and mandatorily implemented and may be termed a 'Bank-BEME'. It will take the form of legislation such as those initiated and implemented by Franklin D Roosevelt in the early 1930's namely, the 'Securities Act' for openness, and 'The Glass-Steagall Act' to deter 'retail banks' from acting like 'Investment banks'. However, in 1999 'The Glass-Steagall Act' was repealed and by then other forms of regulation in the financial system had been extremely diluted or in some cases even ignored, thus reverting the environment. The consequences of course was the Global Financial Crisis (GFC) of 2008. A 'Bank-BEME' is a true economic replicator in that, from within the system, it protects and facilitates for more stable, consistent and widespread economic replication.

Action call: **Support** all politicians and people who, together with financial institutions, organisations, businesses, brands, products and services that, embrace the 'Bank-BEME' principle. **Do not support** non-'Bank-BEME' people or their organisations, goods and services.

BEMER's Tweet message example: *Citizens exploited due to inadequate financial regulation. Please support Bank-BEME to ensure level playing field. brilliantbranes.com*

## BEME (3) Redistribute value:

This will be voluntarily initiated/implemented and may be termed a 'BEME-Aid'. Inequality in the distribution of value results in over- abundance for some and the ultimate destruction of others. This BEME will take the form of a 'collective pressuring' of society to implement a donation process from the wealthy to go directly to overall healthcare and education. "Over a long period of time, the main force in favour or greater equality has been the diffusion of knowledge and skills." (Piketty, 2014, p. 22) Donations from the superrich is not a new or novel phenomenon as Tim Montgomerie, writing in 'The Times' tells us regarding Bill Gates, "Over the past two decades he has given away about $30 billion of his personal fortune..... the new era of billionaire philanthropists who, like Mr Gates, have signed the Giving Pledge: so far, 127 of 1,645 known billionaires have agreed to give away more than half their wealth." (Montgomerie, 2014) A 'BEME-Aid' is a true economic replicator in that it redistributes value for healthier and more knowledgeable participants to pursue economic growth.

What incentive is there for the rich/superrich to make such a donation and what form will this donation take? I propose that the 'BEME facility' referred to above, apart from coordinating 'BEME-Back' processes to regenerate buyers, would also have the power to confer 'degrees' or 'honours' of contribution, somewhat like a university or state. Such level of degree/honour would depend on the amount and/or frequency of the BEME-Aid. To be sure, it can be said that in effect the rich are buying their status degrees! So what? Many of the honours bestowed are political anyway and involve political contributions.

Action call: **Support** all superrich, rich, politicians and people who, together with their businesses, brands, products and services, embrace the 'BEME-Aid' principle. **Do not support** non-'BEME-Aid' people or their organisations, goods and services.

BEMER's Tweet message example*: Escalating inequality is the road to ruin. Please support 'Wealth' BEME-Aid initiative for stabilization & growth. brilliantbranes.com*

## ***Brilliantbranes*** **(the book): The Inception BEME:**

Its formulation is the writing down of its theory. Its launching pad will be its publication for replication (readers). Its theoretical proposition is that capitalism accommodates self-destructive mechanisms within its aspects of business, finance and value distribution. Contemporary science has assisted in the exposure of these negative mechanisms. In addition, physical and biological science has, in its informational processes, assisted in pointing the way to a new form of capitalism, to generate greater growth and societal wealth. By ignoring this science, capitalist market economies will inevitably self-destruct and collapse, to be replaced by, at best, a patch-work of ineffective and uncoordinated markets, or at worst, a dominant hegemony from the extreme left or right.

BEMER's Tweet message example: *Brilliantbranes: a BEME brain-stretching scientificexposéforgrowth,employment&equality,allwithincapitalism.brilliantbranes.com*

Headline in the Business Section of *The Irish Times 3/7/15* "**When an idea appears to be absolutely preposterous**..." *'...that's when we get involved'. Sean O'Sullivan's venture capital firm is as unorthodox as its founder....He pioneered street mapping on computers, is credited with coining the term* 'cloud computing' *(along with George Favaloro of Compaq), and built up a company worth $200 million by the time he was 28."* (Newenham, 2015)

Be a BEMER not a SCREMER

**Change the Hologram**

Only smart people can!

# References

Albert, D. Z., & Galchen, R. (2009, March). A Quantum Threat. *Scientific American*, p. 26.

Aldersey-Williams, H. (2012). *Periodic Tales.* London: Penguin.

Anderson, N. (2014, June 19). Rate of Jobless households is 'far above' the norm in EU. *Irish Independent*, p. 17.

Ayala, F. J. (2012). *The Big Questions Evolution.* London: Quercus.

Ball, P. (2005). *Critical Mass.* London: Arrow books.

Barker, J. (2007). *50 physics ideas you really need to know.* London: Quercus.

Barrow, J. D. (2005). *The Infinity Book.* London: Vintage Books.

Beckenstein, J. D. (2003, August). Information in the Holographic Universe. *Scientific American*, p. 49.

Bizony, P. (2007). *Atom.* London: Icon Books.

Blackmore, S. (2000). *The Meme Machine.* New York: Oxford University Press.

Blackmore, S. (2005). *Consciousness (a very short introduction).* New York: Oxford University Press.

Bodanis, D. (2001). *E=Mc2.* London: Pan Books.

Bohm, D. (1980). *Wholeness and the Implicate Order.* London: Routledge.

Brodie, R. (2009). *Virus of the Mind.* London: Hay House.

BrooksBrooks, M. (2007, June 23). Reality Check. *New Scientist*, pp. 31-32.

Brooks, M. (2010). *The Big Questions Physics (Simon Blackburn Series Editor).* London: Quercus.

Carr, N. (2011). *The Shallows.* New York: W W Norton & Company.

Carter, R. (. (2002). *Mapping the Mind.* London: Phoenix.

Cassidy, J. (2010). *How Markets Fail.* London: Penguin Books.

Chalmers, D. J. (1997). *The Conscious Mind.* New York: Oxford University Press.

Chalmers, D. J. (2010). *The character of Consciousness.* New York: Oxford University Press.

Chatfield, T. (2011). *50 ideas you really need to know Digital @.* London: Quercus.

Chown, M. (2003). *The Universe Next Door.* London: Review.

Clark, S. (. (2010). *The Universe The Big Questions.* London: Quercus.

Clegg, B. (2006). *The God Effect.* New York: St. Martin's Press.

Close, F. (2012). *Neutrino.* Oxford: Oxford University Press.

Coates, J. (2012). *The Hour Between Dog and Wolf.* London: HarperCollins.

Conway, E. (. (2009). *50 economics ideas.* London: Quercus.

Cox, B., & Forshaw, J. (2011). *The Quantum Universe.* London: Allen Lane.

da Costa, P. N. (2012, April 11). Cash At Hand. *Irish Independent*, p. 47.

Damasio, A. (2010). *Self Comes to Mind.* London: William Heinemann.

Darwin, C. (1880). *The Origin of the Species.* London: John Murray.

Davidow, W. H. (2011). *Overconnected.* London: Hedline.

Davies, P. (1995). *About Time.* London: Penguin Books.

Davies, P. (1999). *The 5th Miracle.* New York: Simon & Schuster.

Davies, P. (2002). *How to Build Machine.* London: Penguin Books.

Davies, P. (2007). *The Goldilocks Enigma.* London: Penguin Books.

Davies, P., & Brown, J. (1993). *The Ghost in the Atom.* New York: Cambridge University Press.

Dawkins, R. (2006). *The Selfish Gene.* New York: Oxford University Press.

Dawkins, R. (2007). *The God Delusion.* London: Black Swan.

Dawkins, R. (2009). *The Greatest Show on Earth.* London: Bantham Books.

Dennett, D. C. (1993). *Consciousness Explained.* London: Penguin books.

Deutsch, D. (1998). *The Fabric of Reality.* London: Penguin Books.

Deutsch, D. (2011). *The Beginning of Infinity.* London: Viking.

Diamond, J. (2005). *Guns, Germs and Steel.* London: Vintage Books.

Doidge, N. (2007). *The Brain That Changes Itself.* London: Penguin Books.

Donald, M. (2001). *A Mind So Rare.* London: W.W. Norton & Company.

Douglas, k. (2010, April 3). Nine Big Brain Questions (8 How powerful is the subconscious?). *New Scientist*, p. 32.

Economist, T. (2013, December 7). The Lobor scandal. *The Economist*, p. 72.

Ellis, G. (2013, August 17). View from the top. *New Scientist*, pp. 28-29.

Feynman, R. (1985). *QED.* Princeton: Princeton University Press.

Feynman, R. P. (1998). *Six Easy Pieces.* London: Penguin Books.

Ford, K. W. (2011). *101 Quantum Questions.* London: Harvard University Press.

Galbraith, J. K. (1977). *The Age of Uncertainity.* Sydney: Hutchinson.

Gardner, M. (1997). *Relativity Simply Explained.* New York: Dover Publications.

Gell-Mann, M. (1995). *The Quark and the Jaguar.* London: Abacus.

## REFERENCES


Gleick, J. (2011). *The Information.* New York: Pantheon.

Goggan, P. (2009). *The Money Machine.* London: Penguin Books.

Greene, B. (2000). *The Elegant Universe.* London: Vintage.

Greene, B. (2005). *The Fabric of the Cosmos.* London: 2005.

Greene, B. (2011). *The Hidden Reality.* London: Allen Lane.

Greenfield, S. (2007, October). How Does Consciousness happen? *Scientific American*, pp. 50-57.

Gribbin, J. (1991). *In Search of Schrodinger's Cat.* London: Blackswan.

Gribbin, J. (1996). *Schrodinger's Kittens.* London: Phoenix.

Gribbin, J. (2007). *In Search of Superstrings.* Cambridge: Icon Books.

Gribbin, J. (2009). *In Search of the Multiverse.* New Jersey: John Wiley & Sons, Inc.

Haidt, J. (2012). *The Righteous Mind.* London: Allen Lane.

Hawking, S. (1995). *A Brief History of Time.* London: Bantam.

Hawking, S., & Mlodinow, L. (2010). *The Grand Design.* London: Bantam Press.

Hawking, S., & Mlodinow, L. (2010). *The Grand Design.* London: Bantam Press.

Heffernan, M. (2012). *Wilful Blindness.* London: Simon & Schuster UK Ltd.

Henderson, M. (2008). *50 Genetic Ideas* . London: Quercus.

Henig, R. M. (2001). *A Monk and Two Peas.* London: Phoenix.

Hey, T., & Walters, P. (2003). *The New Quantum Universe.* Cambridge: Cambridge University Press.

Holand, J. (2012, 10 25). Quantum leaps for mankind (Science Today). *The Irish Times,* p. 12.

Hood, B. (2009). *Supersense.* London: Constable.

Hood, B. (2011). *The Self Illusion.* London: Constable.

Ion, S. D. (2014, January 19). The Lights will go out if we don't go Nuclear (Interview by Jeremy Taylor). *The Sunday Times Magazine*, p. 66.

Jibu, M., & Yasue, K. (1995). *Quantum brain dynamics and consciousness.* Philadelphia: John Benjamins Publishing Company.

Kaku, M. (1995). *Hyperspace.* New York: Oxford University Press.

Kaku, M. (2005). *Parallel Worlds.* London: Penguin Books.

Kasper, J. E., & Feller, S. A. (2001). *The complete book of Holograms.* New York: Dover Publications, Inc.

King, A. (2013, June 6). Alfred Russel Wallace: evolution's forgotten man. *The Irish Times*, p. 12.

King, S. D. (2013). *When The Money Runs Out.* London: Yale University Press.

Koch, C. (2007, October). How Does Consciousness Happen? *Scientific American*, pp. 50-57.

Koch, C. (2012). *Consciousness.* London: The MIT Press.

Kotler, P. (1986). *Principles of Marketing.* New Jersey: Prentice---Hall International.

Kuhn, T. S. (1970). *The Structure of Scientific Revolutions.* London: University of Chicago Press.

Lawrence Krauss, NASA. (2012, May 5). *Statistics Brain*. Retrieved May 17, 2013, from 2012 Statistic Brain Research Institute publishing as Statistics Brain: http://www.statisticsbrain.com/universe-statistics/

Lawton, G. (2010, August 7). We have ways of making you buy. *New Scientist*, p. 33.

Lindstrom, M. (2012). *Brainwashed.* London: Kogan Page.

Lloyd, S. (2007). *Programming the Universe.* London: Vintage Books.

Lloyd, S. (2010). The Computational Universe. In P. Davies, & N. H. Gregersen, *Information and the Nature of Reality* (pp. 99-100). New York: Cambridge University Press.

Lynch, Z., & Laursen, B. (2010). *The Neuro Revolution.* New York: St. Martin's Griffin.

Manly, S. (2011). *Visions of the Multiverse.* New Jersey: The Career Press.

Marshall, M. (2011, August 13). Dawn of the Living. *New Scientist*, p. 33.

Marshall, M. (2012, February 18). Moral Choices Show we are deeply split. *New Scientist*, p. 10.

Mc Fadden, J. (2000). *Quantum Evolution.* London: Flamingo.

McCrone, J. (2000). *Going Inside.* London: Faber & Faber.

McEvoy, J. P., & Oscar, Z. (2004). *Introducing Quantum Theory.* Cambridge: Icon Books.

Mlodinow, L. (2008). *The Drunkard's Walk (E-book).* London: Allen Lane.

Moyer, M. (2012, February). Is Space Digital? *Scientific American*, p. 25.

Nahin, P. J. (2012). *The Logician & The Engineer.* New Jersey: Princeton University Press.

Naughton, J. (2012). *From Gutenberg To Zuckenberg.* London: Quercus.

Ne'eman, Y., & Kirsh, Y. (1986). *The Particle Hunters.* Melbourne: Cambridge University Press.

Nettle, D. (2009). *Personality.* New York: Oxford University Press.

Papineau, D., & Selina, H. (2012). *Introducing Consciousness A graphic Guide:.* London: Icon Books Ltd.

Pearce, F. (2013, November 9). A New Course in Global Emissions. *New Scientist*, pp. 6-7.

Penrose, R. (1999). *The Emperor's New Mind.* Oxford: Oxford University Press.

Penrose, R. (2005). *shadows of the mind.* London: Vintage.

Penrose, R. (2010). *Cycles Of Time.* London: The Bodley Head.

Pidwirny, M. (2006). *"The Nature of Radiation'. Fundamentals of Physical Geography, 2nd Edition.* Retrieved November 4, 2012, from http://www.physicalgeography.net/fundamentals/6f.html.

Piketty, T. (2014). *Capital In The Twenrt-First Century (Translated by Arthur Goldhammer).* London: The Belnap Press of Harvard University Press.

Pinker, S. (2008). *The Stuff of Thought.* London: Penguin.
Pirani, F., & Roche, C. (2006). *Introducing The Universe.* Cambridge: Icon Books.
Prigogine, I., & Stengers, I. (1990). *Order out of Chaos.* London: Flamingo.
Rae, A. (2004). *Quantum Physics.* New York: Cambridge University Press.
Randall, L. (2006). *Warped Pasages .* London: Penguin Books.
Randall, L. (2011). *Knocking on Heaven's Door.* London: The Bodley Head.
Rankin, W. (. (2007). *Introducing Newton.* Cambridge: Icon Books UK.
Regis, E. (2008). *What is Life?* New York: Farrar, Straus and Giroux.
Reich, E. S. (2009, February 28). Camels, Heisenberg and quantum uncertainity. *New Scientist*, p. 12.
Reuters. (2013, June 10). US data spying leaker identified. *The Irish Times*, p. 10.
Robins, D. (2010, August 4). *The Higgs Boson.* Retrieved November 19, 2012, from http://www.physics.buffalo.edu/pasi/HiggsbosonLecture1.pdf: http://www.physics.buffalo.edu
Rosenblum, B., & Kuttner, F. (2007). *Quantum Enigma.* London: Gerald Duckworth & Co. Ltd.
Rowe, D. (2010, June 19). Tell me lies, tell me sweet little lies... *New Scientist*, p. 28.
Sample, I. (2014, January 14). Canadian Arctic fossils reveal how fish evolved into four-legged land animals . *The Irish Times- (Guardian service)*, p. 10.
Scalzi, J. (2008). *The Rough Guide to the Universe.* London: Rough Guides Ltd.
Schrodinger, E. (1967). *What is Life? 'The Physical of the Living Cell' with Mind And Matter & Autobiographical Sketches.* New York: Cambridge University Press.
Searle, J. R. (2004). *Mind: a brief introduction.* New York: Oxford University Press.
Sheldrake, R. (2011). *The Presence of the Past.* Sydney: Icon Books.
Shermer, M. (2014, August). ClimateApocalypse (Skeptic). *Scientific American*, p. 69.
Shermer, M. (2014, July). The Myth of Income Inequality. *Scientific American*, p. 71.
Singh, S. (2005). *The Big Bang.* London: Harper Perennial.
Smith, J. M., & Swathmary, E. (2009). *The origins of Life.* New York: Oxford University Press.
Smithers, A. (2013). *The Road To Recovery.* Chichester: Wiley.
Smolin, L. (2008). *The Trouble with Physics.* London: Penguin books.
Smolin, L. (2013). *Time Reborn.* New York: Houghton Mifflin Harcourt.
Squires, N. (2013, 11 27). Pope sets out his radical blueprint for a 'bruised, hurting and dirty' church. *Irish Independent*, p. 32.
Stapp, H. P. (2007). *Mindful Universe.* New York: Springer.
Stenger, V. J. (2012, March 17). The God hypothesis. *New Scientist, 'the god issue'*, p. 46.
Stiglitz, J. (2010). *Freefall.* London: Penguin Books.
Susskind, L. (2009). *The Black Hole War.* New York: Back Bay Books.

Susskind, L., & Lindesay, J. (2005). *An Introduction to Black Holes, Information and the String Theory Revolution. The Holographic Universe.* London: World Scientific Publishing Co. Pte. Ltd.

Talbot, M. (1996). *The Holographic Universe.* London: HarperCollins.

Taleb, N. N. (2008). *The Black Swan.* London: Penguin Books.

Tegmark, M. (2014). *Our Mathematical Universe.* London: Allen Lane.

Teilhard de Chardin, P. (2008). *The Phenomenon of Man.* New York: harperperennial modernthought.

Toffler, A. (1990). Forward: Science and Change. In I. Prigogine, & I. Stengers, *Order out of Chaos* (p. xiv). London: Flamingo.

Tononi, G. (2012). *PHI.* New York: Pantheon Books.

Turner, M. S. (2009, September). The Universe. *Scientific American*, pp. 22-28.

Vedral, V. (2010). *Decoding Reality 'the universe as quantum information'.* New York: Oxford University Press.

Vedral, V. (2011). Living in a quantum World. *Scientific American*, 20-25.

Verma, S. (2005). *The Little Book of Scientific principles, Theories & Things.* Sydney: Reed New Holland.

Watson, S. (2008). Going Digital. A mathematical Theory of Communication. In M. Sreer, H. Birch, & A. Impney, *Defining Moments in Science* (p. 333). London: Cassell.

Webb, T. (2014, July 1). Power shortage could dim lights. *The Times*, p. 4.

Wheeler, J. A., & Ford, K. (2000). *Geons, Black Holes, and Quantum Foam (Ebook).* New York: Norton & company Ltd.

Wiggins, A. W., & Wynn, C. M. (2003). *The Five Biggest Unsolves Problems in Science.* New Jersey: John Wiley & Sons.

Zohar, D. (1990). *The Quantum Self.* New York: Quill/William Marrow.

# Measurements

Some of the measurements in this book are either extremely large or extremely small. So, I will be using powers-of-ten notation so not to have to write such large numbers. For those who have not used such notation since school or college, the following will give explanation:

10 multiplied by itself may be stated as 10 to the power of 2 and written as $10^2$ equals 100. Along with this other examples are listed below:

## For large numbers:

| | | | |
|---|---|---|---|
| One hundred | 100 | $10^2$ | Hector (h) |
| One thousand | 1,000 | $10^3$ | Kilo (k) |
| One million | 1,000,000 | $10^6$ | Mega (M) |
| One billion | 1,000,000,000 | $10^9$ | **Giga (G)** |
| One trillion | 1,000,000,000,000 | $10^{12}$ | Tera (T) |

## For small numbers:

| | | | |
|---|---|---|---|
| One hundredth | .01 | $10^{-2}$ | centi (c) |
| One thousandth | .001 | $10^{-3}$ | Milli (m) |
| One millionth | .000,001 | $10^{-6}$ | Micro (μ) |
| One billionth | .000,000,001 | $10^{-9}$ | Nano (n) |
| One trillionth | .000,000,000,001 | $10^{-12}$ | Pico (p) |

## Atomic Particles:

Atom: The atom consists of an atomic nucleus surrounded by a cloud of electrons
Protons and neutrons = atomic nucleus
Each Proton and Neutron contains 3 Quarks
Electrons surround the autonomic nucleus in a cloud
**See Fig: 2-4 main text for approximate sizes**

| Common base 10 numbers | Binary base 2 numbers |
|---|---|
| 1 | 1 |
| 2 | 10 |
| 3 | 11 |
| 4 | 100 |
| 5 | 101 |
| 6 | 110 |
| 7 | 111 |
| 8 | 1000 |
| 9 | 100 |
| 10 | 1010 |

A joule is a unit of energy
1 electron volt = $1.60217646 \times 10^{-19}$ joules
Energy and Mass are often measured in electron volts, abbreviated as eV:

| Gigaelectronvolt | GeV | = 1 billion eV | |
|---|---|---|---|
| Teraelectron volt | TeV | = 1 trillion eV | (or 1,000 GeV) |

Mass: (1GeV of mass energy = $1.78 \times 10^{-27}$ Kg)

Photons: (electromagnetic force) massless
Weak gage bosons: (Weak force) w± = 80GeV Z=91GeV
Gluons: (Strong force) Massless

## Temperature:

| Temperatures | Notation | Water boils | Water Freezes | Absolute freezing |
|---|---|---|---|---|
| Celsius | C° | 100. | 0. | -273.15 |
| Fahrenheit | F° | 212. | 32. | -459.67 |
| Kelvin | K | 373.15 | 273.15 | 0. |

## Speed of light:

| Exact | 299,792,458 | Metres/second |
|---|---|---|
| Approximately | 186,000 | Miles/second |
| Approximately | 300,000 | Kilometres/second |

Data:

| Binary digit | 1 or 0 |
|---|---|
| Byte | 8 bits |
| KB (Kilobyte) | 1024 Bytes |
| MB (Megabyte | 1024 Kilobytes |
| GB (Gigabyte) | 1024 Megabytes |
| TB ( Terabytes) | 1024 Gigabytes |

# Index


**A**

abortions 146
absolute freezing 74, 85, 90
accountability 51, 145, 146, 198, 213
accumulation 144, 165, 185, 193, 211, 213, 241
Adam Smith 185, 188, 218, 241, 242
adrenal 105, 179
algebra 54, 90
Alpha 41, 218
altruism 101, 151
Amphibians 40
androgenic 139
Angelina Jolie 211
animal 40, 44, 45, 50, 77, 110, 115, 139
animals 40, 44, 45, 48, 51, 58, 77, 99, 101, 102, 109, 153, 161, 253
Animals 45, 48
Anthropic Principle 47, 53
anti-particle 32
antiparticles 66, 73, 77
antitrust 24
apes 101
Aristarchus 26
Aristotle 26, 115, 185
assets 191, 192, 209, 210
astronomical 25, 26
atom 30, 43, 61, 65, 66, 75, 76, 156, 256
Atom 249, 250, 256
atomic 16, 31, 38, 66, 69, 74, 153, 256
atoms 19, 32, 35, 36, 43, 58, 59, 66, 68, 70, 76, 85, 88, 97, 102, 115, 116, 119, 127, 231
Australia 83, 95, 189, 192
automatic 56, 113, 124, 197
automatically 23, 56, 100, 105, 112, 113, 128, 138, 189, 194, 218
awareness 111, 112, 113, 119, 235
axon' 108
Ayala 42, 45, 48, 49, 101, 249

**B**

Bacterium 45
bailing out 173
banks 19, 124, 128, 171, 172, 173, 174, 175, 178, 179, 180, 181, 193, 197, 198, 201, 202, 206, 207, 213, 218, 245
Banks 172, 173, 176, 180
behaviour 19, 49, 58, 81, 93, 116, 136, 137, 139, 140, 141, 142, 143, 144, 145, 147,

148, 151, 170, 179, 180, 181, 189, 197, 198, 199, 217, 243
BEME 19, 20, 201, 202, 203, 204, 205, 206, 207, 208, 209, 210, 214, 218, 219, 221, 245, 246, 247
BEMEs 201, 202, 203, 214, 244
benefit income 163
Bernanke 174
Big Bang 30, 31, 37, 38, 40, 75, 79, 87, 230, 253
Bill Gates 50, 211, 246
binary' 55, 90
binary digits 16, 74
biological 23, 40, 45, 47, 51, 53, 92, 96, 101, 137, 140, 143, 152, 153, 155, 198, 201, 204, 229
bipedal 101
bits 16, 74, 85, 86, 88, 90, 91, 98, 102, 233
Bizony 66, 75, 249
blackbody radiation 29, 30
Black Hole 36
black holes 19, 37, 62, 98, 99, 124, 230
Blackmore 57, 113, 234, 249
Bob Geldof 211
Bohm 80, 81, 86, 97, 98, 118, 123, 129, 233, 234, 249
Bohr 65, 72, 79, 232
Boltzmann 29, 59, 88, 91
Bono 211
bonuses 179
Boole 90
Boolean logic 90
brain 21, 23, 49, 51, 57, 77, 96, 105, 106, 107, 108, 109, 112, 113, 114, 115, 116, 117, 118, 119, 122, 123, 124, 127, 128, 129, 130, 138, 139, 156, 218, 234, 236, 238, 251
brains 45, 51, 101, 110, 113, 116, 119, 120, 140, 144, 236
brane 76, 216
branes 14, 76
breeding selection 45
Brodie 50, 249
Brokers 175
Brooks 249
bull market 172, 179
business 13, 14, 18, 19, 20, 22, 83, 91, 105, 106, 156, 157, 158, 161, 162, 163, 164, 165, 166, 167, 168, 169, 170, 171, 172, 173, 174, 180, 183, 184, 185, 195, 199, 200, 201, 204, 205, 206, 207, 211, 218, 221, 241, 245
businesses 136, 151, 161, 162, 163, 164, 166, 167, 168, 169, 170, 171, 172, 173, 187, 199, 203, 205, 211, 213, 214
Businesses 158, 162, 166, 171, 184
Buyers 163, 164, 205, 206
buying 158, 161, 211, 246

## C

Calculus 54, 55, 89
Cambridge 44, 46, 54, 250, 251, 252, 253
Canada 95, 192
capital 163, 172, 174, 175, 185, 191, 192, 193, 194, 195, 196, 199, 209, 241
Carbon 44
carbon capture 154, 155
cardiovascular 105
Carter 108, 122, 249
Cassidy 176, 186, 241, 249
Catholic 27, 54
Catholic Church 27, 54
Celestial 21, 27
cells 40, 42, 45, 48, 97, 99, 102, 107, 108, 115, 117, 142, 156
Cern' 157
Chalmers 82, 116, 117, 120, 236, 249

Chaos Theory 83
Charity 186, 242
chimpanzee 101
China 146, 158, 187
choices 83, 88, 111, 124, 129, 141, 182, 203, 217, 238
Christianity 115, 149
Chromodynamics 74
Citizenry exploitation 202
Clark 27, 31, 42, 57, 89, 99, 124, 230, 250
classical 19, 22, 23, 53, 54, 55, 57, 59, 62, 64, 65, 72, 73, 74, 75, 80, 84, 85, 86, 112, 117, 119, 124, 162, 165, 189, 197, 198, 216, 217, 218, 231, 233, 236, 243
Clausius 58
climate 53, 140, 152, 154, 155, 213
Coates 128, 139, 178, 179, 189, 243, 250
Cognitive 142
collapse 75, 81, 84, 86, 96, 119, 173, 181, 233, 236
Collective 183
communists 81
competition 72, 139, 168, 174, 185, 241
complexity 23, 38, 40, 41, 51, 89, 92, 100, 103, 104, 109, 144, 151, 159, 165, 203, 228, 229
computers 19, 55, 65, 74, 75, 155, 156, 157, 169, 189, 233, 243
computer virus 159
consciousness 17, 18, 19, 41, 47, 48, 49, 51, 57, 79, 81, 86, 101, 109, 110, 111, 112, 113, 114, 115, 116, 117, 118, 119, 123, 127, 216, 234, 235, 236, 251
Conservatism 183, 184, 240
Conservatives 183, 184, 240
continuity 48, 203
conventional states 85
Copenhagen 79, 80, 81, 86, 213, 232
Copernicus 21, 27, 54, 185
correspondence principle 65
corruptions 20, 215
cortex 107, 108, 123, 124
cortisol 139
cosmological 25, 30
Costa 250
Cost-Push 187
Crick 46, 114
Cultural' 137
Culture 49, 141
currency 179, 180
customer 18, 162, 170
Customer 13
cytoplasm 102

**D**

Damasio 114, 127, 138, 250
Dark Energy 35
Dark Matter 35
Darwin 42, 44, 45, 47, 48, 51, 185, 250
Davies 31, 66, 75, 80, 81, 82, 92, 118, 250, 252
Dawkins 18, 20, 26, 46, 49, 51, 151, 159, 204, 250
deceive 178
deception 178
decision 23, 57, 71, 83, 111, 113, 124, 138, 145, 197, 217, 229, 235
decisions 21, 57, 83, 103, 113, 124, 138, 141, 176, 189, 218, 235
decohered 102, 124, 198
decoherence 84, 85, 86, 88, 100, 102, 111, 112, 117, 118, 119, 124, 128, 130, 197, 202, 233, 235, 236
decoherence' 84, 233
Decoherence 84, 117, 233, 236
decoherent 84
delayed choice 71, 197

Delayed choice experiment 71
Demand-Pull 187
democratic 173, 183, 188, 194, 242
democratically 182
Democrats 183
dendrite' 108
dendrites 118
Denis O'Brien 211
Dennett 142, 250
deposits 172, 176, 178, 180
deregulation 18, 166, 186, 188, 242
Descartes 54, 105, 115, 116
desires 38, 93, 95, 113, 137, 141, 170, 171, 235
detector 69, 70, 71
determinism 56, 62, 197
deterministic 23, 56, 57, 80, 117, 124, 197, 234
Deutsch 50, 75, 82, 83, 84, 95, 110, 250
devalue 180
digital 90, 157, 158, 159, 161
disasters 18, 213
disintegrate 23, 58, 63, 89
disorder 18, 51, 58, 87, 88, 89, 91, 216, 227
distribution 23, 24, 45, 59, 68, 69, 70, 88, 112, 168, 171, 180, 182, 183, 191, 208, 235, 246
dividends 163, 192
DNA 45, 46, 47, 48, 102, 104, 110
dogma 26
dopamine 139, 179
double slit 27, 67, 68, 73
dualists 114, 115, 235

**E**

E-capitalism 1 13, 16, 213
E-Capitalism 1 197, 200, 201, 219, 243, 244
economic 13, 19, 20, 23, 24, 53, 83, 142, 148, 153, 155, 156, 165, 169, 174, 176, 180, 183, 185, 186, 188, 190, 193, 195, 198, 199, 200, 201, 214, 215, 218, 225, 240, 241, 242, 243, 244
Economic 13, 168, 191, 201, 244
economics 13, 19, 22, 23, 148, 182, 183, 185, 186, 189, 194, 199, 218, 241, 243, 250
Economics 20, 24, 182, 194, 218, 241
economies 24, 52, 162, 163, 165, 168, 169, 170, 171, 173, 180, 181, 183, 186, 188, 192, 194, 195, 199, 200, 201, 206, 218, 225, 242, 243
economy 166, 167, 182, 195
education 23, 42, 49, 52, 95, 103, 140, 146, 151, 152, 153, 156, 186, 199, 200, 209, 211, 213, 214, 242, 246
Einstein 15, 16, 19, 21, 29, 30, 31, 35, 54, 60, 61, 62, 64, 67, 68, 73, 80, 81, 141, 185, 217, 232
election 180
electrodynamics 74
electromagnetic 28, 55, 57, 74, 119, 256
electromagnetism 28, 31, 54, 57, 62, 74
electrons 29, 32, 43, 60, 65, 66, 68, 70, 72, 78, 85, 156, 231, 256
Electrons 66, 256
E=MC2 29
emotions 113, 138, 218
Emotions 138, 218
empiricism 189
employee 147, 157, 164, 170, 176, 199
Employee 13, 165, 199, 201, 202, 218, 244
employer 147, 164
Employer 13
employment 18, 19, 140, 148, 169, 170, 185, 187, 188, 204, 205, 241, 242

energy 16, 22, 23, 29, 30, 31, 37, 44, 58, 59, 61, 64, 66, 72, 75, 88, 92, 93, 95, 96, 97, 108, 136, 152, 153, 154, 155, 156, 159, 217, 218, 227, 229, 232, 256
enfolded 81, 97, 118, 123, 234
entangled 73, 85, 96
entanglement 73, 77, 85, 96, 97, 119
entertainment 156, 157, 171, 211, 213
Entrepreneurs 163, 184, 186, 242
entropy 17, 18, 19, 23, 40, 41, 51, 54, 58, 59, 62, 87, 88, 89, 91, 92, 93, 95, 96, 97, 98, 99, 103, 104, 137, 144, 145, 146, 148, 151, 159, 165, 181, 185, 195, 197, 198, 199, 201, 202, 210, 216, 227, 228, 229, 243
environment 14, 18, 23, 24, 47, 49, 51, 53, 63, 84, 85, 86, 87, 92, 93, 101, 102, 104, 110, 112, 113, 124, 128, 130, 136, 137, 140, 141, 144, 145, 148, 152, 159, 170, 177, 189, 197, 198, 202, 206, 217, 218, 228, 229, 233, 238
environmental 18, 49, 53, 112, 129, 143, 145, 146, 154, 159, 198, 216, 238
Environmental 137, 140
equilibrium 58, 59, 88, 92, 93, 159, 216, 227, 228
equivalence 29, 61
Euclidean 112
eukaryotic 102
Euro 180
European Commission 179, 180, 216
event horizon 36, 37, 98, 99, 229, 230
Everett 82
evolution 18, 20, 25, 40, 42, 44, 46, 47, 48, 49, 54, 63, 87, 92, 110, 215, 229, 251
Evolution 18, 40, 48, 51, 89, 198, 249, 252
experience' 124
explicate 81, 97, 118, 234
extraordinarily differentiated 114
eyes 49, 109, 214

**F**

Facebook 158, 219
Fascism 183, 240
FATCA 193
Feller 37, 97, 251
Feral Finance 201, 202, 244
Feynman 19, 74, 75, 84, 250
financial 13, 18, 19, 24, 49, 158, 159, 163, 166, 168, 171, 172, 173, 174, 176, 177, 178, 179, 180, 181, 186, 188, 191, 193, 199, 200, 207, 221, 242, 246
fish 40, 51, 170, 203, 253
fluctuations 67, 73, 74, 112, 117
Forbes 211
Ford 36, 54, 60, 65, 82, 231, 250, 254
fractal 100, 112
Fractal 112
fractional 100
France 95, 158, 192
freedom 181, 184, 195, 240
free will 23, 57, 62
free-will' 57, 113, 234
frequency 28, 29, 59, 64, 72, 159, 203
Friedman 186, 188, 241, 242
future 14, 21, 23, 25, 36, 38, 45, 51, 56, 64, 71, 83, 86, 116, 119, 120, 144, 151, 154, 162, 173, 193, 199, 200, 205, 214, 219, 236
fuzz ball 99, 124, 230

**G**

galaxies 16, 32, 36, 55, 58, 82, 99
Galbraith 183, 193, 200, 250
Galileo 27, 54

Gamma 28
Gamow 30
Gardner 61, 62, 250
Gastrointestinal 104
GDP 95, 186, 191
Gell-Mann 74, 250
gene 18, 45, 46, 47, 48, 49, 137, 145, 148, 218
General relativity 30
genes 18, 45, 46, 48, 49, 50, 51, 96, 103, 104, 137, 151, 198, 204
genesis 32, 98
Genesis' 25, 44
genetics 45, 51, 96
genotype' 48
Gentleman 210
Germany 57, 95, 149, 158, 187, 192, 218
GFC 18, 163, 168, 179, 206, 213
Gleick 96, 250
global 13, 18, 155, 159, 166, 173, 178, 186, 187, 192, 193, 214
global financial crises 18, 173
God 25, 26, 44, 250, 253
Godel 15, 118
Goggan 178, 250
Golden Rule 142
goldfish 38, 100, 218
governments 24, 155, 180, 185, 187, 188, 198, 207, 209, 241, 246
gravitation 27, 55
Graviton' 76
gravity 27, 29, 30, 31, 53, 55, 56, 57, 61, 62, 67, 76, 85, 118
greed 18, 145, 148, 149, 173, 179, 188, 200, 242
Greene 62, 71, 98, 99, 129, 226, 251
Gribbin 14, 76, 80, 91, 251
growth 38, 104, 136, 144, 146, 151, 155, 157, 165, 179, 187, 188, 192, 194, 195, 199, 200, 203, 205, 214, 221, 242, 245, 246
Growth 136, 144
growth of the economy 192, 195

**H**

Haidt 111, 138, 141, 142, 184, 206, 240, 251
Hawking 11, 26, 36, 38, 71, 79, 98, 100, 229, 230, 251
healthcare 141, 146, 152, 153, 155, 209, 211, 246
Hegel 185
Hegelian 185
Heisenberg's 72, 96
Heliocentric' 26, 27
helium 32
heresy 26
Hertz 28
hidden variables 80, 86, 97, 117, 118
Higgs 31, 217, 253
Higgs' 31, 217
highly integrated 114
hologram 22, 38, 81, 97, 98, 112, 123, 217, 234
holographic principle 37, 38, 81, 98, 99, 112, 235
Holographic Principle 37, 97, 123
Holomovement 81, 234
Holonomic' 123
Homo sapiens 40
Hood 141, 251
hormones 105, 139
House of Un-American Activities 81
Hubble 30
Human beings 87, 93, 101, 102, 109
hunger 18, 213
hydroelectric 153
hydrogen 32, 46, 61, 102

Hydrogen 43, 44
hyperpersonal' 41
hypothalamus' 107

**I**

ideological 140, 148, 149, 173
ideologies 53, 142, 183, 184, 185, 240, 241
ideology 19, 103, 183, 188, 213, 218, 242
ignorance 92, 148, 154, 216, 228
Immune 104
implicate 81, 97, 118, 234
incubator 38, 100, 218
India 146, 158
indigenous 173, 195
industrialization 155
inefficiencies 20, 215
inegalitarian 191
inequality 142, 177, 186, 189, 192, 193, 194, 195, 199, 201, 202, 208, 209, 211, 214, 218, 221, 242, 243, 244, 246
inertia 61
infants 111
inflation 186, 187, 188, 241, 242
Inflation 187
information 15, 16, 18, 19, 21, 22, 23, 31, 32, 37, 38, 41, 46, 51, 52, 53, 56, 64, 71, 72, 73, 74, 75, 77, 80, 81, 85, 87, 88, 89, 90, 91, 92, 93, 95, 96, 97, 98, 99, 100, 103, 105, 108, 109, 110, 111, 112, 115, 116, 119, 123, 124, 128, 137, 138, 139, 146, 152, 156, 157, 158, 160, 175, 176, 178, 183, 197, 198, 201, 218, 228, 229, 230, 232, 233, 235, 243, 254
Infrared 28
infringe 103, 136, 206
inheritance 45, 110, 111, 137, 144, 163, 171, 235
Integumentary 104
intelligence quotient 49
interference 27, 37, 67, 69, 70, 71, 72, 78, 84, 97, 112, 119, 184, 231, 234, 240
interference pattern 37, 67, 69, 70, 71, 231
internet 50, 157, 177
intrinsic spin 65
invest 146, 151, 199, 205
investment 24, 155, 161, 162, 163, 168, 171, 172, 173, 180, 184, 206, 207, 213, 221, 245
Investor 13
Irish 40, 73, 154, 156, 158, 159, 167, 168, 174, 203, 204, 211, 212, 232, 249, 250, 251, 253
Italy 158, 180, 192

**J**

Jibu 77, 118, 123, 251
John Bell 73, 81, 232
John von Neumann 72, 80, 91
joule 256
Joule 58
Judeo 185

**K**

Kaku 30, 58, 84, 251
Kaluza 62
Kasper 37, 97, 251
Kepler 27
Keynes 185, 186, 187, 241
knowledge 15, 26, 27, 41, 42, 51, 55, 88, 96, 103, 110, 111, 166, 191, 193, 195, 209, 246
Koch 114, 117, 118, 251
Koran 26
Kuttner 78, 253

**L**

Lamarck 42
Landauer limit 96
Laplace 56
Laursen 107, 252
Left 183, 186, 188, 242
Leibniz 54, 55, 89, 90
Lemaitre 30
Liberalism 184, 185, 241
Liberals' 183, 240
Libertarianism 183, 184
Libertarians' 183
Libet 57, 124, 234
LIBOR 178
light 26, 27, 28, 29, 37, 38, 54, 57, 59, 60, 61, 62, 66, 67, 68, 69, 71, 72, 73, 74, 75, 81, 90, 95, 98, 123, 142, 169, 217, 229, 231
Lindstrom 252
lithium 32
Lloyd 75, 85, 90, 177, 233, 252
locality 56, 63, 123
love 101, 104, 147
luck penny 204
Lynch 107, 177, 252

**M**

malaria 213
Maldacena 99, 129
Malthus 44, 146
Mammals 40
management 23, 51, 92, 93, 95, 142, 146, 159, 165, 173, 193, 204, 216, 229
Mandelbrot 100
manipulation 65, 74, 101, 119, 156, 167, 168, 178, 179, 217, 219, 233
Manly 28, 71, 82, 117, 236, 252
many histories 84, 86
many worlds 81, 82, 83, 84, 85
Margin 165
market 20, 24, 52, 130, 158, 159, 162, 163, 164, 165, 166, 168, 169, 170, 171, 173, 174, 180, 181, 185, 186, 188, 189, 192, 194, 195, 199, 200, 201, 205, 206, 215, 218, 238, 241, 242, 243
Mark Zuckerberg 211
Marx 185, 186, 188, 241, 242
Mass 29, 201, 244, 249, 256
materialists 114, 116, 235
mathematician 15, 27, 56, 57, 62, 75, 89, 91, 105, 189
matryoshka 112, 235
Maxwell 27, 28, 57, 58, 59, 62, 68, 89, 96
Maxwell's demon 89, 96
McFadden 70, 72, 85, 107, 118, 119
measurement problem 68, 80, 84, 96
meme 47, 49, 50, 51, 52, 159, 198, 201, 202, 243
MEME 20, 51
memes 49, 50, 52, 142, 143, 159, 198, 199, 204
Memes' 49, 142
memory 64, 97, 108, 121, 122, 123, 124, 128, 156, 197, 198, 235
Mendel 45
metaphysics 41
microscopic 37, 58, 98, 99
Microwaves 28
Missing Link 42
Mlodinow 38, 71, 138, 251, 252
molecule 43, 44, 46, 96
molecules 45, 48, 58, 68, 69, 70, 88, 89, 110, 116, 117, 119, 138, 231
Monetary 180, 186
monetary policy 188, 242

money 139, 161, 164, 166, 169, 172, 173, 178, 184, 187, 211, 214, 219
monopoly 186, 242
Moral 137, 142, 148, 176, 252
Moral Hazard 176
Morals 142
Mormon 26
mortgage 175
Moses 26
Motivation 20, 215
M-theory 77, 88
multicellular 40, 48
multiverse 47, 81
Muscular 104
mysteries 25, 40

**N**

Natural Dualism 115
Natural Selection 42, 45
needs 24, 51, 61, 93, 111, 137, 141, 144, 145, 146, 153, 154, 156, 161, 162, 165, 169, 170, 171, 195, 198, 200, 201, 202, 203, 205, 211, 214, 216
Netflix 157
Nettle 143, 252
neuron 108, 115, 117, 156
neurons 96, 107, 108, 115, 118, 122
neutrino 66
neutrinos 66
Neutron 256
neutrons 32, 43, 65, 66, 76, 256
Newton 27, 54, 55, 56, 61, 62, 67, 89, 111, 115, 185, 253
Nitrogen 44
nonlocality 123
Nuclear 153, 251
nuclear reactors 153, 154
nucleus 31, 43, 45, 46, 61, 65, 66, 76, 102, 156, 256

**O**

observation 36, 70, 71, 77, 79, 80, 81, 84, 85, 86, 189, 232
Occupational status 147
OECD 214
OkCupid 219
Omega 41, 218
Oprah Winfrey 211
ordered 18, 23, 41, 88, 92, 197, 228
orderliness 18, 41, 228
orderliness' 18
Oxygen 43, 44

**P**

Paley 44
Papineau 118, 119, 236, 252
parallel universes 81, 82
particle 32, 60, 65, 66, 70, 72, 73, 75, 80, 84, 96, 232, 233
particles 16, 19, 31, 32, 38, 66, 67, 68, 69, 70, 71, 72, 73, 74, 77, 82, 84, 85, 96, 97, 118, 217, 231, 232, 233
penalty 178
Penrose 118, 252
Penzias 30
periodic table 43
periphery 99, 112, 119, 197, 217
peristalsis' 105
personality 137, 143
phenotype' 49
PHI 114, 115, 254
philanthropic 170, 201
philantrocapitalism 211
Photons 70, 256

physicists 19, 31, 34, 37, 38, 59, 63, 70, 81, 96, 99, 117, 119
Piketty 12, 177, 180, 185, 190, 191, 193, 194, 196, 209, 241, 252
pilot wave 80, 86
pineal 105, 115
Pirani 29, 56, 252
pituitary' 107
Planck 29, 31, 59, 60, 64, 65, 68, 95, 98
Planck Constant' 64
planets 17, 21, 27, 32, 35, 38, 54, 55, 58, 61, 82, 99
plant 40, 45, 50
Plants 45
Plato 21, 103
political 21, 24, 53, 81, 102, 140, 142, 157, 158, 161, 173, 174, 179, 180, 182, 183, 184, 185, 186, 188, 192, 206, 211, 218, 240, 242, 244, 246
politics 148, 157, 185, 216
pollution 18, 23, 142, 145, 159
Popper 189
positive feedback 130, 166, 177, 179, 186, 241
poverty 18, 142, 168, 182, 184, 187, 188, 194, 211, 242
power 24, 50, 75, 89, 90, 102, 109, 141, 148, 154, 157, 158, 178, 183, 184, 201, 209, 219, 225, 244, 246, 255
pregnancy 145
President Obama 157, 219, 244
Prigogine 216, 253, 254
primates 101
Primates 40
primitive 40, 107, 138, 141, 144, 145
Princeton 16, 81, 250, 252
Products 163
profit 145, 161, 162, 163, 164, 165, 166, 169, 171, 172, 185, 204, 205, 206, 241, 245
Profit 164
profit margin 204, 245
program 85, 195, 234
programme 18, 81, 82, 100, 112, 119, 219
Programming 75, 233, 252
progressive 20, 23, 25, 92, 93, 95, 100, 103, 104, 137, 144, 145, 148, 151, 157, 165, 184, 185, 193, 198, 199, 201, 202, 203, 206, 209, 210, 213, 214, 215, 216, 219, 229, 243
Progressive' 92
prokaryotic 102
property 72, 110, 115, 185, 191, 241
Proportionality 195
proteins 46, 117
Proton 256
protons 32, 43, 65, 66, 68, 76, 231
psyche 62, 115
Ptolomy 26
purchase 138, 163, 164, 168, 175, 204, 206, 245
purification 173, 180, 181, 200, 219
Putin 140

**Q**

quantum 17, 19, 22, 27, 29, 30, 31, 44, 54, 59, 60, 62, 63, 64, 65, 67, 68, 71, 72, 73, 74, 75, 77, 78, 79, 80, 81, 82, 84, 85, 88, 95, 96, 97, 99, 102, 112, 117, 118, 119, 123, 124, 128, 156, 197, 216, 217, 230, 231, 232, 233, 234, 235, 236, 253, 254
quantum computer 74, 75, 88, 112, 119, 197, 233
quantum simulators 75, 233
quantum Zeno effect 119
Quarks 256
quasars 71, 84

qubit 74, 233
qubits 74, 233

**R**

radiation 28, 29, 30, 31, 36, 37, 44, 57, 59, 62, 64, 70, 98, 229
radical 27, 82, 195, 253
Radio 28
Randall 65, 73, 76, 253
Rankin 55, 253
reach 31, 41, 58, 60, 71, 74, 87, 88, 90, 109, 203, 227
Recession 187
recompensed Income 163
recreate 19, 209, 246
Recreate 202, 203, 218, 245
redistribute 19, 209
Redistribute 202, 207, 218, 246
reductionism 114, 236
Regan 188, 243
Regressive' 92
regulate 19, 142, 174
Regulate 202, 206, 218, 245
regulation 168, 172, 174, 178, 179, 180, 186, 188, 207, 221, 242, 243, 246
Relative State 82
relativity 29, 31, 54, 62, 67, 80, 90
religions 41, 42, 50, 142, 161, 184
religious 26, 53, 112, 115, 140, 145, 146, 147, 148, 149, 183, 186, 200, 203, 235, 240
remuneration 164, 165, 177, 191, 192, 199, 213
renewable energy 152, 155
replicating 41, 46, 50, 199, 201, 228, 243
replicator 20, 44, 52, 142, 159, 201
reproductive 104
reserves 174
resources 23, 140, 153, 155, 182, 187, 198
Respiratory 105
responsibility 51, 140, 144, 145, 146, 198, 213
return on capital 195
revolution 20, 21, 27, 155, 185, 188, 194, 200, 214, 215, 219, 242
revolutionary 15, 20, 21, 22, 27, 200, 215
Revolutions 21, 27, 185, 251
Right 186, 242
RNA 46, 48
robotics 18
Roche 252
Rosalind Franklin 46
Rosenblum 78, 253
Ryanair 183

**S**

Schrodinger's cat 79
SCREME 170, 180, 181, 195, 199, 202, 218, 243
SCREME's 170, 218
SCREMEs 198, 199, 200, 201, 202, 244
Second Law 58, 88, 89, 92, 216, 227
Securitization 175
selfish 18, 145, 148, 151, 204, 218
selfishness 18, 92, 200, 228
selflessness 101
Selina 252
selling 158, 161, 165, 204, 245
sex 63, 101, 103, 104, 137, 139, 140, 145, 146, 148, 179, 183, 184, 198
Sex 23, 103, 137, 144, 145, 146, 180, 201
Sex' 23, 103, 137, 144, 180
Shannon 90, 91
Shannon limit 90
Silicon 156
singularity' 30, 37, 229

SINS' 204
Sir' 210
skills 87, 88, 95, 161, 163, 191, 193, 195, 205, 208, 209, 213, 246
Smith 47, 48, 185, 209, 241, 253
Smithers 172, 174, 181, 253
Socialism 183, 185, 240, 241
Socialist 188, 242
social mobility 194
space 16, 27, 30, 31, 37, 38, 56, 60, 61, 62, 66, 70, 73, 74, 76, 77, 82, 98, 99, 100, 102, 108, 111, 112, 123, 124, 155, 216, 217, 230, 235
space-time 16, 38, 61, 62
Space-time 62
Special Relatively 29
spectrum 28, 50, 198
speed 23, 29, 56, 57, 60, 61, 62, 66, 72, 73, 74, 89, 90, 97, 142, 156, 177, 179, 232
speed of light 29, 57, 60
Speed of light 257
spins' 77
spooky action at a distance 73, 77, 232
Standard Model 67
Stapp 118, 119, 120, 129, 236, 238, 253
stars 16, 17, 30, 32, 35, 38, 54, 55, 58, 61, 66, 82, 99
Statistical mechanics 88
Status 23, 103, 137, 144, 147, 148, 180
Status' 23, 103, 137, 144, 180
stem cell 157, 159
Stengers 216, 253, 254
Steroid 139
Stiglitz 175, 187, 253
St. Patrick 203
strings 75, 76, 77, 91, 99, 124, 128, 139, 230
string theory 75, 76, 77, 99, 129, 230, 232
String Theory 67, 75, 98, 254
subatomic 38, 66, 69, 100, 111, 124, 235
Subprime 175
Sun 32, 153
supergravity 76
supernatural 26
superposition 71, 72, 75, 102
superpositions 72, 77, 79, 86, 119, 232
superstring' 77
supersymmetrical 77, 100
supersymmetry' 77
Supply and Demand 185, 241
Survival 23, 42, 103, 137, 144, 180
Survival' 23, 103, 137, 144, 180
Survival of the Fittest 42
Susskind 98, 99, 253, 254
swastika 103, 149
symbol 103, 115, 149
Symbolism 23, 103, 137, 144, 149
Symbolism' 23, 103, 137
symmetries 34
Symmetry 33
synapse' 108
Szathmary 47, 48

**T**

Taleb 189, 254
tax 166, 167, 168, 169, 192, 193, 194, 196, 204, 209, 211
Tax 167, 193
technology 18, 19, 20, 31, 50, 54, 63, 71, 74, 87, 102, 152, 153, 154, 155, 156, 157, 158, 159, 168, 173, 177, 200, 205, 215, 219, 233
Tegmark 85, 117, 118, 128, 236, 254
telescope 31, 54
temperature 29, 31, 35, 59, 73, 74, 111, 119, 166

Temperature 257
testosterone 139, 179
Thatcher 188, 243
the 'hard' problem 116
Theory of Everything 67, 76
thermodynamics 54, 88, 92, 216, 229
thermonuclear fusion 153, 155
Toffler 216, 254
Tononi 114, 127, 254
Traders 178, 179
transistor 156
Transistors 156
transparency 140, 160, 168, 178, 188, 193, 206, 207, 219, 242
transparent 20, 207, 215
tubules 118
Twitter' 50

**U**

UK 81, 95, 154, 158, 169, 179, 183, 204, 219, 251, 253
ultraviolet 28, 29, 59
uncertainty principle 73, 74
Uncertainty Principle 72, 96
undemocratically 182
underprivileged 214
unemployment 18, 140, 152, 163, 168, 176, 180, 186, 187, 188, 241, 242
Unemployment 187, 202
unfolded 81, 97, 118, 123, 234
United States 177, 192, 193, 195, 207
universal quantum simulator 75
universe 15, 16, 17, 22, 23, 25, 26, 30, 31, 33, 35, 36, 37, 38, 41, 51, 58, 59, 61, 62, 65, 66, 67, 73, 75, 77, 79, 82, 84, 85, 87, 88, 96, 97, 99, 100, 110, 111, 112, 115, 118, 119, 123, 127, 137, 197, 217, 230, 231, 232, 233, 234, 235, 252, 254
Urinary 105

**V**

value 19, 24, 74, 90, 139, 163, 165, 168, 172, 182, 183, 185, 187, 202, 204, 207, 208, 209, 210, 211, 214, 218, 241, 246
Vatican 27, 41
Vedral 21, 74, 95, 104, 119, 233, 254
vertebrates 40
viruses 105, 159, 174, 180
Von Neumann 15

**W**

Wallace 42, 44, 251
Wars 149
Watson 12, 46, 90, 91, 254
wave 27, 37, 60, 62, 69, 70, 71, 72, 73, 79, 80, 81, 84, 86, 96, 102, 112, 117, 119, 232, 233, 236
wave function 70, 71, 79, 80, 81, 84, 86, 96, 117, 232, 233, 236
waves 28, 57, 59, 63, 67, 68, 69, 70, 71, 77, 78, 80, 97, 119, 231, 234, 236
wealth 19, 147, 178, 183, 184, 188, 190, 191, 192, 194, 208, 211, 212, 213, 242, 246
wealthy 140, 192, 201, 211, 212, 213
Webb 154, 254
welfare 163, 168, 169, 170, 182, 186, 211, 212, 242
Wheeler 16, 19, 71, 75, 79, 82, 87, 98, 224, 232, 254
wilful blindness 148, 162
Wilson 30
windmills 153

**X**

X-rays 28, 57

**Y**

Yasue 77, 118, 123, 251
Young 27, 67

**Z**

Zohar 118, 254

www.ingramcontent.com/pod-product-compliance
Lightning Source LLC
Chambersburg PA
CBHW062131280526
45788CB00001B/129

* 9 7 8 1 5 3 0 5 7 1 8 8 8 *